SCHOLARS, DOLLARS, AND BUREAUCRATS

STUDIES IN HIGHER EDUCATION POLICY

SCHOLARS, DOLLARS, AND BUREAUCRATS

Chester E. Finn, Jr.

THE BROOKINGS INSTITUTION
Washington, D.C.

Copyright © 1978 by

THE BROOKINGS INSTITUTION

1775 Massachusetts Avenue, N.W., Washington, D.C. 20036

Library of Congress Cataloging in Publication Data:

Finn, Chester E 1944–
  Scholars, dollars, and bureaucrats.

  (Studies in higher education policy)
  Includes bibliographical references and index.
  1. Federal aid to higher education—United States.
2. Higher education and state—United States. I. Title. II. Series.
LB2342.F55   379′.1214′0973   78-13363
ISBN 0-8157-2828-x
ISBN 0-8157-2827-1 pbk.

9 8 7 6 5 4 3 2 1

For
RENU, ARTI, AND ALOKE
with love

THE BROOKINGS INSTITUTION is an independent organization devoted to nonpartisan research, education, and publication in economics, government, foreign policy, and the social sciences generally. Its principal purposes are to aid in the development of sound public policies and to promote public understanding of issues of national importance.

The Institution was founded on December 8, 1927, to merge the activities of the Institute for Government Research, founded in 1916, the Institute of Economics, founded in 1922, and the Robert Brookings Graduate School of Economics and Government, founded in 1924.

The Board of Trustees is responsible for the general administration of the Institution, while the immediate direction of the policies, program, and staff is vested in the President, assisted by an advisory committee of the officers and staff. The by-laws of the Institution state: "It is the function of the Trustees to make possible the conduct of scientific research, and publication, under the most favorable conditions, and to safeguard the independence of the research staff in the pursuit of their studies and in the publication of the results of such studies. It is not a part of their function to determine, control, or influence the conduct of particular investigations or the conclusions reached."

The President bears final responsibility for the decision to publish a manuscript as a Brookings book. In reaching his judgment on the competence, accuracy, and objectivity of each study, the President is advised by the director of the appropriate research program and weighs the views of a panel of expert outside readers who report to him in confidence on the quality of the work. Publication of a work signifies that it is deemed a competent treatment worthy of public consideration but does not imply endorsement of conclusions or recommendations.

The Institution maintains its position of neutrality on issues of public policy in order to safeguard the intellectual freedom of the staff. Hence interpretations or conclusions in Brookings publications should be understood to be solely those of the authors and should not be attributed to the Institution, to its trustees, officers, or other staff members, or to the organizations that support its research.

Foreword

DIRECTLY AND INDIRECTLY, the federal government channels nearly $14 billion a year into higher education. Millions of students pay for their college educations with help from Washington. Nearly every campus in the land is involved with the national government, both financially and through diverse regulatory and reporting requirements.

Yet these activities reflect no comprehensive or purposeful policy. From Washington's standpoint, higher education is a means to numerous ends rather than an end in itself. One of the few types of assistance missing from the catalog of federal aid to higher education is direct institutional support for teaching and learning.

As higher education emerges from a prolonged period of expansion into a decade or more of probable retrenchment, the absence of coherent policies to guide the federal government's manifold relations with it is likely to cause difficulty. As a growing proportion of students and colleges comes to regard Washington as the source of the money that makes the difference between vitality and decay, federal officials will have more and more need for well-defined objectives and principles. And federal regulations, even when imposed for sound purposes, are themselves a growing source of anxiety on college campuses.

In this book, the second in the Brookings series of Studies in Higher Education Policy, Chester E. Finn, Jr., maps the present terrain of federal spending and regulatory activities that bear on higher education, examines the policymaking structures, accounts for the absence of a comprehensive national policy, and explains some of the difficulties inherent in any effort to formulate one.

Finn holds out scant hope for fundamental changes. But his is not a counsel of despair or even disappointment, for he concludes that the present arrangements, although jumbled and sometimes confusing, are also reasonably well suited to a diversely constituted higher education system and to multiple yet limited federal objectives. His suggestions for reform reflect his belief that adaptation, rather than reconstruction, is what the system needs.

ix

The present volume is a companion to the first in the series, *Public Policy and Higher Education*, which Finn coedited with David W. Breneman. It is also a late sequel to Alice M. Rivlin's 1961 Brookings study, *The Role of the Federal Government in Financing Higher Education.*

The author has drawn on his experience in the executive and legislative branches of the government as well as on fresh scholarship. In its early stages, this work benefited from the research assistance of Steven Jones. Successive versions were improved in consequence of thoughtful criticism by Gilbert Y. Steiner, James L. Sundquist, Martha Derthick, Stephen Hess, Lawrence D. Brown, David W. Breneman, Susan C. Nelson, Noel Epstein, Charles B. Saunders, Jr., Charles F. Adams, Jr., Terry W. Hartle, David S. Mundel, Marc F. Plattner, and Alan Wagner. The author acknowledges with particular gratitude the contribution of Dr. Wagner, then with the Washington office of the College Entrance Examination Board, in developing specifications for the revised basic grants program recommended in chapter 4.

The manuscript was edited by Caroline Lalire; its factual content was verified by Penelope Harpold and Mara O'Neill. It was typed by Radmila Nikolić and Celia Rich. The index was prepared by Brian Svikhart. The aid of Donna Daniels Verdier, administrative assistant to the director of the Government Studies program, was of singular value to the author throughout the project.

The views expressed in this book are those of the author and should not be ascribed to any of the persons consulted during its preparation, or to the officers, trustees, or other staff members of the Brookings Institution.

BRUCE K. MACLAURY
President

August 1978
Washington, D.C.

Contents

Tables

Time for Another Look

Is the well-being of American higher education a proper concern of the federal government? The Constitution makes no mention of education, and the Tenth Amendment appears to reserve it to the states and to private citizens. The basic responsibility for building, supporting, and governing colleges and universities remains in state and private hands. With rare exceptions, the federal government has shunned any obligation to ensure the welfare of individual campuses or the health of the nation's higher education system.[1] In no other major industrial country does the central government enjoy that freedom.

Yet the federal government has played a role in the American higher education drama for more than a century, gradually shifting from bit player to supporting actor. Today, the academic enterprise can trace about $14 billion of its annual revenues to Washington, and every campus in the land is entangled in the rules and regulations of numerous federal agencies. The national government's investment in higher education is large and its influence profound. What is remarkable is the amorphous and seemingly heedless character of its involvement. Social objectives but distantly related to higher education have elicited hundreds of policies and programs that leave a deep imprint on the shape and character of the higher education system. Yet they remain haphazard. "With respect to higher education," James Perkins concludes, "the fed-

1. Throughout the book, "higher education" is used to refer to the set of approximately three thousand nonprofit, degree-granting institutions commonly thought of as colleges and universities. Although I occasionally employ the word "postsecondary" for variety, I do not mean to include the vocational, proprietary, and non-degree granting institutions that are frequently subsumed (along with the more traditional campuses) under the "postsecondary education" heading. I share John Silber's suspicion that "the term 'postsecondary education' [was] devised by those who had no answer to the question 'Higher than what?'" See John R. Silber, "The Rest Was History," in *The Third Century: Twenty-six Prominent Americans Speculate on the Educational Future* (Change Magazine Press, 1977), p. 196.

eral government has made no decision. It has made bits and pieces of decisions about specific and limited issues."[2]

Of course, this situation is not unique to higher education. Federal policy in many other areas is a matter of "bits and pieces." Nor is that always a bad state of affairs, for in confining its actions to "specific and limited issues," Washington respects the primacy of the states and the private sector, buttresses the federal system, and obtains what it wants without shouldering the burdens of others.

Why, then, reopen the question of federal responsibility for higher education? The world's largest and generally strongest group of colleges and universities got that way without a comprehensive national policy. Indeed, many feel that the freedom of these institutions from a federal straitjacket has enhanced their diversity and quality. Still, several developments do justify this fresh look at the relation between higher education and the federal government.

First, higher education sees itself nearing another in its long series of self-proclaimed crises. This time there appears to be some cause for public concern with its welfare, at least for asking whether present federal policy provides more help or hindrance and what, if anything, Washington might reasonably be expected to do differently.

Second, many higher education leaders believe that the federal government does have an obligation, even if it has not yet been fully acknowledged, to ensure the well-being of the postsecondary enterprise itself. Their willingness to act on that belief, and their success in winning some converts to it, confront federal officials with a political challenge quite apart from the merits of the substantive arguments. "Federal policy should be altered," Clifton Conrad and Joseph Cosand assert, "to reflect a major commitment to the health and diversity of public and private higher education in America."[3]

Third, the federal government has been edging up to a limited acknowledgment of responsibility for the well-being of higher education, though without mounting the programs to honor such a commitment one would expect. In explaining a program of emergency assistance for

2. James A. Perkins, "Coordinating Federal, State, and Institutional Decisions," in John F. Hughes, ed., *Education and the State* (American Council on Education, 1975), p. 189.

3. *The Implications of Federal Education Policy*, ERIC/Higher Education Research Report no. 1, 1976 (American Association for Higher Education, 1976), pp. 60–61.

colleges and universities authorized in 1972 but never funded, for example, Congress declared that "the Nation's institutions of higher education constitute a national resource which significantly contributes to the security, general welfare, and economy of the United States," thereby hinting that the Tenth Amendment did not exhaust the constitutional provisions bearing on higher education.[4]

Fourth, the question of government regulation and of the links between money and control has lately emerged as an important issue. "In recent years," President Derek Bok of Harvard University wrote, "the government has shown increasing signs of acting in questionable ways to regulate the principal academic functions of higher education."[5] The extent to which this is true, and the remedies that may be appropriate for Washington and for the campuses, invite the attention of both government officials and academic leaders.

Fifth, in a time of growing concern about the effectiveness of government generally, and about the costs and benefits of federal programs particularly, there is reason to ask what the taxpayer is getting for his $14 billion. Would a more self-conscious "higher education policy" serve public purposes any better? And if, as is widely alleged, the federal government lacks the organizational ability to develop and effect such a policy, what changes might reasonably be contemplated?

This book traces the principal channels through which funds flow from Washington to the nation's colleges and universities and to the students who attend them. It describes and appraises a number of the major programs, the increasingly perplexing issue of federal regulation, and the means by which federal higher education policy is made.

Underlying the discussion is a subtle but fundamental question: is the national interest in higher education adequately served by the present arrangements, manifold but messy, that entwine the federal government with colleges and students? Insofar as it may not be, do the apparent shortcomings in these arrangements lend themselves to modest adjust-

---

4. Education Amendments of 1972, 86 Stat. 245. Five years later, presumably mirroring what it took to be the intent of Congress, the Congressional Budget Office proclaimed that one goal of federal higher education policy "is to *help keep institutions financially alive and productive.*" "Postsecondary Education: The Current Federal Role and Alternative Approaches" (Congressional Budget Office, February 1977; processed), p. xv.

5. Derek C. Bok, "The President's Report, 1974–1975," *Harvard Today*, vol. 18 (Winter 1976), p. 10.

ments or do they call for a sweeping overhaul of policy, program, and structure? What are the political prospects for changing established practices in this domain of domestic social policy, and are the benefits of change apt to outweigh the costs of making the attempt?

The Evolving Federal Role

The debate over federal aid to higher education first arose in the early days of the Republic, when George Washington and several of his successors urged the establishment of a national university. "A well constituted seminary in the center of the nation," President Madison insisted in 1810, "would be universal in its beneficial effects" and the "additional instruction emanating from it would contribute not less to strengthen the foundations than to adorn the structure of our free and happy system of government."[6] A committee of the House of Representatives endorsed the idea, but neither then nor later did a national university find favor with the full Congress. Higher education was no concern of the federal government, insisted those who construed the Constitution strictly, and they drew support from sectional interests, from people who wanted as little government in Washington as possible, and from educators who feared federally subsidized competition if not federal control. Arguing against another proposal for a national university in 1873, President Charles W. Eliot of Harvard explained that "our ancestors well understood the principle that to make a people free and self-reliant, it is necessary to let them take care of themselves, even if they do not take quite as good care of themselves as some superior power might."[7]

In the meantime, though nothing so overt as a national university was established, the federal government had begun to intrude itself into higher education in numerous ways. West Point was founded in 1802; few could object to government's providing for the training of its own military officers, a worthy end for which higher education supplied an obvious means. The ordinance authorizing the sale in 1787 of two mil-

6. Quoted in Richard Hofstadter and Wilson Smith, eds., *American Higher Education: A Documentary History*, vol. 1 (University of Chicago Press, 1961), p. 177.

7. Quoted in Frederick Rudolph, *The American College and University* (Vintage Books, 1962), p. 185.

lion acres of the Northwest Territory to the Ohio Company set aside two townships "for the support of a literary institution" that was to become Ohio University at Athens. One by one, most of the new states of the early nineteenth century obtained similar land grants for the purpose of creating or sustaining universities. Congress systematized that practice in the celebrated Morrill Act of 1862, which is generally regarded as the first large federal step into the financing of higher education. Its passage, too, was marked by controversy, with President Buchanan vetoing an early version. Once the South had seceded and the Republicans had won the White House it became possible to enact such a measure, but even then it was necessary to cloak the federal interest in higher education under less contentious objectives: the orderly disposition of public lands, the betterment of agriculture, and the furtherance of the "mechanic arts."

The Morrill Act set other precedents as well. Instead of giving money directly to individual colleges and universities, Congress devised a population-based formula for apportioning resources among the states. Instead of allowing the recipients to use the proceeds as they saw fit, Congress attached a number of regulations, including a requirement that the resulting funds be treated as a permanent endowment. Instead of permitting the payment of administrative expenses from the federal funds, Congress insisted that the states cover all such costs with other resources, "so that the entire proceeds of the sale of said lands shall be applied, without any diminution whatever, to the purposes hereinafter mentioned." And instead of trusting the recipients to make good use of the money, Congress required an annual report "regarding the progress of each college, recording any improvements and experiments made, with their cost and results."[8]

In subsequent decades the laws and programs multiplied. Agricultural research and extension services pumped more federal money into the land-grant colleges. The Smith-Lever Act (1914) provided additional support for agriculture and for home economics. Three years later the Smith-Hughes Act provided for college-level training of teachers for vocational education. The National Defense Act of 1916 created the Reserve Officers Training Corps on college and university campuses. The Public Works Administration provided states and localities with

8. 12 Stat. 504.

millions of dollars during the depression for the construction of school and college buildings. Creation of the National Cancer Institute in 1937 marked the beginning of substantial federal support for the training of health professionals and the conduct of biomedical research.

World War II brought several sizable initiatives, notably a vast increase in federal support for university-based research and development. Established by President Roosevelt in 1940, the National Defense Research Committee made an important decision at its first meeting: to use existing institutional resources, including colleges and universities, wherever possible, instead of building new federal research facilities. Inaugurated the same year, the Engineering, Science, and Management War Training Program, and its successors, provided for the training of skilled technical personnel on the nation's campuses. And the Servicemen's Readjustment Act of 1944, better known as the GI bill, launched a huge program of college-level education benefits for veterans.

By 1947 the Bureau of the Budget could tabulate federal education expenditures at the "post-high school level" totaling $1,772 million a year, and being funneled through fifteen separate agencies.[9] But much more was to come: the National Science Foundation in 1950; the College Housing Loan Program the same year; the Korean War GI bill in 1952; the enormous growth of the National Institutes of Health in the late 1950s; and, of course, the National Defense Education Act of 1958, which provided, among other things, for graduate student fellowships and for subsidized loans to needy undergraduates.

In every instance, higher education provided a means to some other end. The colleges and universities themselves were ancillary to the federal missions in which they were enlisted. This condition suited many of their leaders—some because of a principled opposition to federal funds unless carefully delimited in scope and purpose, others because they feared the controls that would follow if Washington considered higher education as an end in itself. Thus in 1952 the Commission on Financing Higher Education, composed in large part of distinguished university presidents, reported its "unanimous conclusion that we as a nation should call a halt at this time to the introduction of new programs

9. *Higher Education for American Democracy*, A Report of the President's Commission on Higher Education, vol. 3, *Organizing Higher Education* (Government Printing Office, 1947), pp. 38–39.

of direct federal aid to colleges and universities."[10] President Eisenhower's Committee on Education Beyond the High School echoed that
sentiment five years later with its insistence that Washington should
attend to higher education "only by methods which strengthen State
and local effort and responsibility."[11]

Yet the list of programs continued to lengthen and appropriations
soared as one after another objective was embraced by Congress and
as the cognizant federal agencies turned to colleges and universities to
help accomplish them. It is not surprising that when careful observers
like Homer Babbidge and Robert Rosenzweig looked about them in
1962, they discerned an "enlargement of the Federal interest to coincide
more nearly with the national interest"[12] in higher education. They regarded this as a hopeful sign that Washington was on the verge of pro-
claiming an interest in higher education per se, which they recognized
would mark a historic change in the government's stance toward colleges
and universities. Without assuming that vast, unrestricted sums would
begin to flow from the Treasury to thousands of campuses, they anticipated a further broadening of the categories of university activities that
the government would willingly underwrite.

"It seems clear," Alice Rivlin wrote in 1961, "that the federal government should plan to increase substantially its support of higher education
in the near future." In her view, however, it would not suffice simply to
put more resources into familiar programs of scientific research and
manpower training. "If the increased federal money is to do any real
good," Rivlin insisted, "it must be directed toward support of the instructional functions of institutions of higher education."[13]

Seventeen years later it appears these prescriptions and forecasts have
come true only in part. Although there has been an avalanche of new
programs that furnish federal funds to colleges and universities, not more
than a few small programs offer anything close to unrestricted income

10. *Nature and Needs of Higher Education* (Columbia University Press, 1952),
pp. 157–58.

11. Quoted in Charles A. Quattlebaum, *Federal Educational Policies Programs
and Proposals*, pt. 1, prepared by the Legislative Reference Service for the House
Education and Labor Committee, 90:2 (GPO, 1968), p. 81.

12. Homer D. Babbidge, Jr., and Robert M. Rosenzweig, *The Federal Interest in
Higher Education* (McGraw-Hill, 1962), p. 186.

13. Alice M. Rivlin, *The Role of the Federal Government in Financing Higher
Education* (Brookings Institution, 1961), pp. 172–73.

for institutions of higher education; nor is there much support for the "instructional functions" that Rivlin had urged in 1961. For the most part, the federal government treats higher education today as it did when the Morrill Act was passed: as a means to other ends.

Federal Programs Today

The federal government's expenditure of $14 billion on higher education can usefully be examined in two ways: by looking at the financing mechanisms through which the funds are allotted, and by determining the principal objectives of the hundreds of discrete government programs. It is hard to improve upon the five general purposes set forth in 1973 by the National Commission on the Financing of Postsecondary Education:

support for research in areas of national interest; equal access to postsecondary education for low-income and other educationally disadvantaged students; strengthening collegiate institutions of certain types and strengthening all collegiate institutions in certain functions; work-force training to increase the supply of skilled persons in critical occupations and to expand employment opportunities for unskilled persons; and special benefits to certain classes of persons, such as veterans, survivors of Social Security beneficiaries, and handicapped and disabled persons.[14]

Of the 400-odd separate programs through which Washington channels funds into higher education almost all can reasonably be located under one or more of those headings,[15] although the general categories do not begin to suggest the rich and sometimes bizarre array of specialized undertakings for which colleges and universities obtain federal support.

The main omission from this bulky catalog of programs delivering financial support to institutions of higher education is money intended to help sustain their primary educational missions. But the tangled history

14. *Financing Postsecondary Education in the United States* (GPO, 1974), p. 106. For a more activist statement of (three) federal higher education goals, see Congressional Budget Office, "Postsecondary Education."

15. Pamela Christoffel and Nancy Greenberg, "A Compilation of Federal Programs Financing Postsecondary Education: An Update, Fall 1974," 2 vols. (College Entrance Examination Board, September 1974; processed).

of federal involvement with higher education made that gap all but inevitable.

From the outset, funds making their way from Washington into campus bursaries have traveled circuitous routes. There are two ways to think about this outcome, neither of them wrong: one can conclude that those favoring federal aid to higher education have resorted to subterfuge in order to elude the opposition of persons hostile to such aid but willing to see the government make use of collegiate resources for more limited public purposes. Or one can judge that, the Tenth Amendment having left institutional maintenance to others, the federal government has simply enlisted universities in a broad range of worthy —but individually narrow—undertakings in which they were able and willing to participate in return for reimbursement of their costs. Although these programs add up to a sizable sum of money for Washington, and now make up a vital portion of the revenues of many educational institutions, the statutes did not intend them as general support, nor, in most cases, can the funds be used that way.[16]

The present financing mechanisms of the federal government fall into three categories: programs that assist individuals to pay the costs of their own higher education; programs that channel funds from government agencies directly into colleges and universities to compensate them for services rendered; and provisions in the tax laws that reduce federal revenues by affording private outlays for higher education favorable tax treatment.[17] Table 1-1 shows the approximate sums that flowed through each of those major channels in fiscal 1977, as well as some of their larger tributaries.

16. As with most recipients of federal categorical programs, a controversy surrounds the actual effects of "restricted" income on the financial condition of colleges and universities. It stands to reason that if a campus is being paid to do something that it wanted to do, and *would have done anyway* using resources obtained elsewhere, the federal money serves to release institutional funds for other purposes of the college's own devising. If, on the other hand, the campus would not have used its own resources for that purpose, it does not gain any disposable income. And if Washington induces it to undertake such a project but does not fully compensate it for the costs associated with the project, cooperation with the government may actually eat into the college's unrestricted funds.

17. Tax expenditures are treated only cursorily in this study. For more extended analysis, see Emil M. Sunley, Jr., "Federal and State Tax Policies," in David W. Breneman and Chester E. Finn, Jr., eds., *Public Policy and Private Higher Education* (Brookings Institution, 1978). Frequent references will be made to that volume, which is a companion to this book.

Table 1-1. *Federal Expenditures for Higher Education,
Fiscal Year 1977*[a]

Millions of dollars

Category	Amount
Assistance to students	
Department of Health, Education, and Welfare	
Office of Education	
Basic educational opportunity grants[b]	1,387
"Campus-based" aid and state student incentive grants[c]	865
Guaranteed loans[d]	344
Other[e]	88
Social security—dependents' and survivors' education benefits[f]	1,181
Health training and other HEW[g]	215
Veterans' education benefits[h]	2,802
Department of Defense[i]	330
Other[j]	109
Subtotal	7,321
Payments to institutions	
Research and development conducted in colleges and universities[k]	2,724
Programs for disadvantaged students and developing institutions[l]	130
Vocational education[m]	166
Other Office of Education programs[n]	118
Special institutions[o]	99
Health resources[p]	769
Department of Defense[q]	326
Other[r]	111
Subtotal	4,443
Tax expenditures[s]	
Exclusion of scholarships and fellowships	245
Parental personal exemptions for students 19 and over	750
Deductibility of individual contributions	525
Deductibility of corporate contributions	235
Exclusion of veterans' education benefits	260
Exclusion of social security student benefits[t]	73
Subtotal[u]	2,088
Total,[v] all expenditures	13,852

Sources. Figures for 1977–79 are derived from *Special Analyses, Budget of the United States Government, Fiscal Year 1979*, called *Budget 1979* in the notes, where specific references are given. Figures for 1976 are from *Special Analyses, Budget of the United States Government, Fiscal Year 1978*, indicated as *Budget 1978*.

a. The figures in this table represent actual expenditures in fiscal year 1977, which corresponds to school year 1976–77. Since several student aid programs are "forward-funded," some of these outlays represent appropriations made for fiscal 1976, but not available to students until 1976–77.

b. *Budget 1979*, table J-2. This is a forward-funded program. Hence the figure corresponds to appropriations for fiscal year 1976. The program has been growing rapidly: outlays in fiscal 1976 came to $905 million; President Carter's initial budget request for 1979 was $1,936 million, later enlarged so as to assist middle-income students as well.

c. *Budget 1979*, table J-2.

d. *Budget 1979*, table J-2. The true cost of this program tends to be considerably understated, since the

Assistance for Students[18]

The largest and still the fastest growing mode of federal expenditure for higher education is assistance to individuals. Increased support for students accounts for almost $6 billion of the $7 billion added to the federal higher education budget in the brief period from fiscal 1968 to 1977 and (excluding tax expenditures) represented 62 percent of total outlays in the latter year, compared to 33 percent in the former (see table 1-2).

18. Portions of the following analysis are taken from Chester E. Finn, Jr., "Federal Patronage of Universities in the United States: A Rose by Many Other Names?" *Minerva*, vol. 14 (Winter 1976–77), pp. 496–529 (Brookings Reprint 330).

---

potential full cost to the government of a loan is not realized until years after the loan is actually made to a student.

e. Author's estimate, derived by taking the Office of Education student aid totals shown in *Budget 1979*, table J-9 (for undergraduate and graduate students combined), and subtracting the outlays for specific programs listed above.

f. *Budget 1979*, table J-2. It should be noted that the social security student grant program also includes $314 million at the precollegiate level and $138 million in adult and continuing education expenditures.

g. *Budget 1979*, table J-9. This figure excludes $36 million for social security student grants at the graduate level, already accounted for.

h. *Budget 1979*, table J-3. It should be noted that this figure considerably understates the cost of the full GI bill program, which also contains $92 million at the precollegiate level and $512 million for adult and continuing education. The program has been shrinking rapidly, however, as eligibility for Vietnam-era veterans has been ending. The corresponding figure in fiscal 1976 was $4,301 million (*Budget 1978*, table I-3). The OMB estimate for fiscal 1979 is $2,009 million.

i. *Budget 1979*, table J-9.

j. *Budget 1979*, table J-9.

k. *Budget 1979*, table J-1. This figure corresponds closely to outlays shown in *Budget 1979*, table P-6. But federal "obligations" for research and development to universities and colleges, which is probably a more accurate gauge of activity in this field, is $232 million greater than "outlays," and $210 million greater than the figure shown in the table.

l. *Budget 1979*, table J-2.

m. *Budget 1979*, table J-2. Only a small portion of federal outlays for vocational and occupational education take place at the level of higher education. Elementary and secondary schools account for another $393 million, and adult and continuing education for $134 million.

n. *Budget 1979*, table J-2.

o. *Budget 1979*, table J-2. This figure includes only the higher educational institutions, such as Howard University and Gallaudet College, and omits an additional $33 million for "special institutions," such as the American Printing House for the Blind.

p. *Budget 1979*, tables J-2 and J-3.

q. *Budget 1979*, table J-3. This excludes the amount assigned above to the Department of Defense for student assistance.

r. *Budget 1979*, tables J-2 and J-3.

s. All these figures except the exclusion of social security benefits are taken directly from *Budget 1979*, table G-1.

t. Author's estimate. Calculating that social security student benefits at the higher education level represent 1.43 percent of all social security OASDI outlays (see *Budget 1979*, tables J-2 and M-1), I applied this percentage to the entry in table G-1 marked "exclusion of social security benefits" (using the total of disability insurance, OASI benefits, and benefits for dependents and survivors).

u. This total is understated because the *Special Analyses* do not include all tax expenditures on behalf of higher education. Sunley estimates that in fiscal 1977 "direct" tax expenditures for higher education totaled $2,360 million. In this figure he includes the deductibility of bequests and unrealized capital gains on gifts and bequests. He also estimates an "indirect" federal tax expenditure for higher education of $1,480 million, resulting from the deductibility of state and local taxes (a portion of which underwrites colleges and universities) and the exemption of interest on state and local debt (including certain capital expenses of state colleges and universities). See Emil M. Sunley, Jr., "Federal and State Tax Policies," in David W. Breneman and Chester E. Finn, Jr., eds., *Public Policy and Private Higher Education* (Brookings Institution, 1978), p. 284.

v. This is a relatively conservative figure because it excludes sizable sums classified by the Office of Management and Budget under "adult and continuing education," but probably spent in part in postsecondary institutions; it excludes campus-based training provided under such large federal programs as comprehensive employment and training; and it ignores revenue sharing, at least some portion of which goes to support state (and community) colleges and universities.

Table 1-2. *Federal Outlays for Higher Education, Fiscal Years 1968 and 1977*

Amounts in millions of dollars

Category	1968		1977		Change in amount, 1968–77
	Amount	As percent of total	Amount	As percent of total	
Student support	1,455	33	7,320	62	5,865
Current operations of institutions	429	10	1,200	10	771
Facilities and equipment	954	22	386	3	−568
Academic research	1,434	33	2,724	23	1,290
Other	92	2	134	1	42
Total	4,364	100	11,764	100	7,400

Sources: *Special Analyses, Budget of the United States Government, Fiscal Year 1970*, p. 123, and *Fiscal Year 1979*, pp. 214, 222. Figures are actual expenditures for the fiscal year indicated; figures are rounded. For tax expenditures in fiscal 1977, see table 1-1.

There are three major reasons for this increase. First, since the peak of the civil rights and antipoverty movements in the early 1960s, presidents and Congress have pursued a "student aid strategy," giving priority to programs that help needy people go to college. Such legislation as the Higher Education Act of 1965, the thoroughgoing amendments to it approved in 1972, and the refinements added in 1976 reflects this emphasis on students generally and on impoverished students in particular.

Second, the decision to revive the GI bill in 1966, combined with the vast increase in veterans' rolls after the Vietnam War, meant a mushrooming of the outlays needed to honor the government's commitment to pay monthly stipends to every veteran pursuing an approved course of study.

Third, the 1965 amendments to the Social Security Act extended benefits to young dependents and survivors of social security recipients enrolled in high school or college who had lost such benefits on reaching their eighteenth birthday.

These three large groups—veterans, the poor, and the children of social security beneficiaries—receive the bulk of federal student aid. But dozens of other categories of people also get assistance. Still, aid is not extended to every college student. In most instances, eligibility for such funds hinges both on being a student *and* on satisfying one or more essentially unrelated conditions. It is largely because of the restrictive nature of present aid programs that tuition tax credits and other forms of assistance to "middle-class" (or, one might say, "ordinary") college students became a popular political cause in 1977–78. This impulse is discussed briefly in chapter 4. Those conditions are not generally within the control of the colleges or the students. Thus two persons enrolled on the same campus and identical in many other respects may be treated quite differently in the parceling out of federal assistance funds. Although certain programs channel resources in the first instance to the college for distribution to its students, federal student aid is generally a volatile and unreliable source of institutional revenue. The university that seeks to maximize and stabilize it may find itself bending its regular admissions criteria to favor people who are entitled to federal support.

Money for Institutions

Although Washington gives higher educational institutions more than $4 billion a year, it did not set out to supply them with unrestricted income or to underwrite their ordinary activities, and, with a few exceptions, it does not do so. Instead, it has deployed resources to purchase particular services and to support designated campus activities. Colleges have always had the right to refuse the funds, but if they accept the money they also accept whatever limitations are attached to it. In that sense, the financial relationship between the federal government and the nation's institutions of higher education is not that of patron and beneficiary so much as that of purchaser and vendor.

It would be an oversimplification, however, to depict these ties as strictly commercial. Shared and high-minded purposes are often involved, as is a vigorous and half-acknowledged, but not especially venal, form of mutual exploitation. The universities crave federal money and the government has a variety of tasks that universities can help accomplish. When the resulting financial arrangements are harmonious and beneficial, it may not matter to the college that concern for its general welfare did not impel the programs that furnish it with funds. Indeed, one of the reasons that Washington long ago slipped into the pattern of payments for specific studies and projects was the academy's fear that excessive federal control would follow if the government defined the institution's composite welfare as its primary interest. Limiting the purposes for which federal funds might be obtained was at once cautious and heedless: acknowledging the university's sovereignty while enabling the government to pay for what it wanted without shouldering any responsibility for the well-being of individual institutions or of higher education as a whole.

So long as the government serves up a smorgasbord of programs, and so long as the university is circumspect in deciding which to partake of, such a relation can be satisfactory for all parties. But several hazards are frequently encountered. First, if the campus needs the income badly, it may distort its own organizational priorities in order to obtain federal funds from programs ill matched to its main interests.

Second, the government's priorities change, rapidly or slowly but seldom with any regard for the effect of those changes on the client institutions. When a particular federal interest is growing, the ready availability of funds serves as an amiable bribe or "carrot" to lure universities into that area of interest. But when the interest wanes, and the funds for it shrink or are diverted into another area, the universities frequently find themselves left with continuing expenses but without the resources to meet them.

Third, the money supplied by the federal government directly to the nation's campuses has not kept pace with the increase in enrollments, in federal student aid programs, or in the cost of a college education. Hence, as shown in table 1-3, the federal portion of institutional revenues has fallen somewhat since 1970—not precipitously, to be sure, but enough to raise questions in the mind of anyone worried about the future financial health of colleges and universities.

Fourth, federal institutional funds are unevenly distributed among the colleges and universities. This is not accidental, nor has it gone unre-

Table 1-3. *Federal Funds*[a] *as a Percentage of the Total Current Fund Income of Colleges and Universities, Selected Academic Years, 1939–40 to 1975–76*

Institution	1939–40	1949–50	1959–60[b]	1969–70	1973–74	1974–75[c]	1975–76[c]
Private	0.7	8.6	19.6	22.5	20.1	19.5	19.2
Public	10.3	9.6	17.3	17.3	16.0	15.8	14.9

Sources: Data for 1939–60, June A. O'Neill, *Sources of Funds to Colleges and Universities* (New York: Carnegie Foundation for the Advancement of Teaching, 1973); data for 1969–76, National Center for Education Statistics, *Financial Statistics of Institutions of Higher Education, Fiscal Year 1976* (GPO, 1978), and relevant preceding issues.

a. Receipts from federal sources for all purposes (including federally funded research and development centers) except hospitals.

b. Includes student aid from all public sources since data are not disaggregated. The federal share accounted for most of this category.

c. Starting in 1974–75, the National Center for Education Statistics changed and simplified its method of reporting current fund revenues and expenditures.

marked over the years, and in many cases there are sound reasons for it. But the fact remains that one hundred of the approximately three thousand institutions of higher education in the United States regularly obtain two-thirds of all federal payments to colleges and universities.[19]

Tax Benefits

The least recognized form of federal support for higher education is embedded in the tax code, not in the education laws. In 1977, as a result of taxpayers availing themselves of provisions associated with higher education, the Treasury received approximately $3.8 billion less in revenue than it could otherwise have expected.[20]

The entire subject of tax expenditures is controversial. Many "reformers" consider some or all of these provisions to be "loopholes" whose "cost" to the government should be tabulated and whose wisdom should undergo severe legislative scrutiny. But others object even to listing them, arguing that the action implies that the funds somehow belong to the federal government when in fact the revenue "loss" is simply a by-product of legislation that spared certain types of income and expenditure from taxation.

In any event, the Budget Act of 1974 required that tax expenditures be included, and they are now a regular feature of the President's annual budget submission and of Congress' own calculations. Three types of provisions account for most of the tax expenditures ordinarily associated with higher education.

First, scholarships, fellowships, and kindred benefits to students are exempt from taxation. This applies to veterans' benefits and social security benefits as well as to conventional student aid from public and private sources. These exclusions reduced federal revenues in 1977 by

19. National Science Foundation, "Federal Support to Universities, Colleges, and Selected Nonprofit Institutions, Fiscal Year 1974," A Report to the President and Congress (NSF, 1975; processed), pp. 26–27, and previous editions.

20. Sunley, "Federal and State Tax Policies," p. 284. It may be noted that the figure estimated here is almost $1.8 billion more than the sum ascribed to 1977 "tax expenditures" in table 1-1 above. As indicated in the table notes, the yearly special analyses of the federal budget on which the lower sum is based do not separately identify all the tax expenditures that Sunley associates with higher education. Sunley's more comprehensive tally includes such items as the deductibility of state and local taxes, of which an estimated 9.5 percent goes to support higher education. Ibid., p. 291.

$578 million, and may be regarded as an indirect form of student assistance; if students had paid taxes on this income a commensurate increase in overt student aid would have been needed to attain the same level of educational purchasing power.

Second, parents providing more than half the support of a child may continue to claim the $750 dependent's exemption for that child so long as he is a full-time student, even if his own income exceeds $750 and thus would normally disqualify him for that parental exemption. This "double exemption" cost the Treasury $750 million in 1977. The provision dates to 1954, when the gross income test was eliminated for student dependents. It serves to increase the disposable income of families with tax liability whose children are students with earnings of their own.

Third, individuals and corporations making charitable contributions to colleges and universities may, within certain limits, deduct those contributions from their taxable income. In 1977 such deductions cost the Treasury about $760 million.[21] The charitable deduction differs from the other higher education tax expenditures in several respects. The transaction entitled to favorable tax treatment in this instance is one that yields resources directly to the college rather than to students or their parents. The operative provision of the tax law, however, is much broader than higher education, which accounts for just one dollar out of every seven lost to the Treasury through the charitable deduction. This provision is even more controversial than the exclusion of scholarships or the "double exemption" for parents: people who share a strong devotion to higher education find themselves divided by their attitudes toward the charitable deduction, primarily because of its inequitable features.[22]

From the academy's standpoint the effect of the deduction is intimately bound up with the effect of private philanthropy on institutional well-being. This is not negligible. Although the proportion of the nation's higher education budget supplied by voluntary support has shrunk somewhat in recent years, such gifts remain well in excess of $2

21. See table 1-1. This figure includes a small sum for elementary and secondary schools but excludes the inheritance tax expenditure associated with charitable bequests.

22. In "Federal and State Tax Policies" (pp. 295–97), Sunley examines this problem. The main point at issue is that the charitable deduction confers greatest benefit on the wealthiest taxpayer, less on those in lower brackets, and none at all on donors who do not itemize their deductions.

billion a year.[23] And when combined with the returns on endowment, which is reasonably viewed as the accumulation of earlier gifts, it provided 14.6 percent of private sector income in 1975–76 and 2.6 percent of public sector income.[24]

The averages are deceptive, however, for philanthropy confers markedly uneven benefits on various campuses. Some institutions get many millions, others practically nothing. A few schools obtain three-quarters of their "educational and general" revenues from current gifts and endowment income, and hundreds of them receive more than one-third of such income from those sources.[25] At institutions like Claremont College, the University of Chicago, and Princeton University, voluntary support in 1974–75 came to more than $3,000 per student. Were it to disappear, those campuses would be forced to increase their tuitions or other revenues drastically in order to maintain their accustomed standards of institutional living. On the other hand, philanthropy yielded less than $100 per student in 1974–75 to universities like Northeastern, Duquesne, and Villanova.[26]

The reason for this varied distribution of philanthropic funds and of the tax expenditures associated with them is self-evident: the federal government has no control over *which* colleges and universities (and other eleemosynary organizations) benefit from voluntary support. Such funds go to institutions that by dint of history, hard work, or good fortune have succeeded in attracting donors and benefactors, and they do not go in such quantity to others, however worthy of public or private support.

Mechanisms and Intentions

This brief look at the three principal modes of federal financial support for higher education has stressed their uneven, almost capricious

23. The Council for Financial Aid to Education estimated that total voluntary support received by institutions of higher education in 1974–75 was $2,160 billion. *Voluntary Support of Education 1974–75* (New York: CFAE, 1976), p. 3.

24. National Center for Education Statistics, *Financial Statistics of Institutions of Higher Education, Fiscal Year 1976* (GPO, 1978), pp. 4–5.

25. Patricia Smith and Cathy Henderson, "A Financial Taxonomy of Institutions of Higher Education" (American Council on Education, Policy Analysis Service, April 1976; processed), p. 8.

26. Council for Financial Aid to Education, *Voluntary Support of Education 1974–75*, pp. 10–12. These annual per-student figures are exaggerated, in that total voluntary support was considered, including capital gifts as well as donations for current operating support.

effects on the economic well-being of colleges and universities. One does not have to look far to find the reason for this: none of the major mechanisms can be linked to a single government program or to a well-considered objective. Billions of federal dollars flow into higher education by way of individuals, and assistance for designated classes of students is certainly an identifiable government purpose, but because eligibility is carefully delimited and because the "ordinary" college student has no claim to federal aid, campuses benefit from these programs only insofar as they enroll students who do.

Much the same can be said of the many programs that supply funds directly to colleges and universities for "categorical" purposes. Schools that for some reason are not qualified for or interested in helping carry out those purposes have no claim to the revenues associated with them.

Likewise, though billions of dollars for higher education take the form of federal tax expenditures of several kinds, the financial benefits accrue in the first instance to the students, their parents, and philanthropists who devote some of their own funds to higher education. The campuses profit from these expenditures, too, but only to the extent that they attract the attention of the initial beneficiaries.[27]

The financial mechanisms, then, do not line up neatly alongside the numerous discrete objectives the federal government has set for its higher education expenditures. Though nearly every campus is touched by all three forms of federal support, their importance varies according to the nature of the institution and its income pattern. It follows, too, that the averages displayed in table 1-3 mask extraordinary differences among individual campuses. Some could accurately be described as heavily dependent on federal funds; others derive only a modest fraction of their financial support from direct and indirect federal expenditures.

Much the same observation could also be made of federal agencies and their missions. Some rely on colleges and universities to conduct a sizable portion of their work or to help achieve goals that no other social institution is equipped to handle. Still others may look to the campuses for assistance with discrete and limited projects that may fairly be described as useful but not central to the accomplishment of agency assignments. And some, of course, have virtually no contact with educational

27. To be sure, colleges and universities are themselves exempt from federal income taxation, which means that any so fortunate or well managed as to end the year with a surplus do not have to share it with Washington.

institutions or their students, except possibly for engaging a professor as consultant from time to time.

For all its apparent confusion and seeming inadvertence, however, there is much to be said for the piecemeal nature of federal involvement with higher education as it has developed since the Morrill Act. Though Washington has failed to provide much by way of unrestricted income for the institutions, it has nevertheless managed to provide something for nearly all of them, and to do so in ways that silently acknowledge both the diversity of the academic enterprise and the wide-ranging endeavors of the government. The lack of a systematic federal policy toward higher education is thus a strength as well as a weakness—although clearly it makes for a flimsy framework on which to attach policy modifications aimed at helping higher education overcome the difficulties that lie ahead.

Chapter Two

The Once and Future Crisis

WHAT IS the condition of higher education today and what are its prospects for the future? Is higher education—as many of its spokesmen maintain—headed for a new crisis?

Unfortunately, in appraising the health of individual colleges and universities, and of higher education as a whole, it is often necessary to use crude quantitative measures instead of the sensitive gauges of quality that would be most helpful to the policymaker. For these gauges either do not exist or the conclusions to be drawn from them are subject to intense dispute within the academy, particularly when "outsiders" seek to draw policy guidance from them.

This chapter illustrates the analyst's dilemma as it moves from an account of the remarkable expansion of higher education in the 1950s and 1960s, to an examination of the perceived "crisis" of the early 1970s, to a look at some of the forces at work on the academic enterprise as it nears 1980.

The Educational Boom

Whatever the future, there is no denying the scale of the higher education industry in the United States today or its remarkable explosion over the past thirty-odd years. Table 2-1 shows the number of public and private institutions and the number of students in selected years from 1950 to 1975; these numbers are still growing.

Fueled by mounting student demand, the boom began immediately after World War II, slowed a bit as the first GI bill ran out, then picked up in the mid-fifties as Korean War veterans returned to college and enrollments began to grow by 200,000 a year. In the late fifties and through most of the sixties—a period sometimes referred to as the

20

Table 2-1. *Private and Public Institutions of Higher Education and Degree and Nondegree Students, Selected Years, 1950–75*

Item	1950	1955	1960	1965	1970[a]	1975[a]
All institutions	1,859	1,886	2,040	2,207	2,573 (2,855)	3,055
Private	1,221	1,225	1,319	1,417	1,472 (1,520)	1,601
Public	638	661	721	790	1,101 (1,335)	1,454
Percent private	*66*	*65*	*65*	*64*	*57* *(53)*	*52*
Percent public	*34*	*35*	*35*	*36*	*43* *(47)*	*48*
Students (thousands)						
Degree-credit	2,297	2,679	3,610	5,570	7,986	9,420
Private	1,142	1,180	1,474	1,916	2,141	2,246
Public	1,154	1,499	2,136	3,655	5,845	7,174
Percent private	*50*	*44*	*41*	*34*	*27*	*24*
Percent public	*50*	*56*	*59*	*66*	*73*	*76*
Degree plus nondegree	n.a.	n.a.	n.a.	5,967	8,649	11,323
Private	n.a.	n.a.	n.a.	1,967	2,173	2,385
Public	n.a.	n.a.	n.a.	4,000	6,476	8,938
Percent private	n.a.	n.a.	n.a.	*33*	*25*	*21*
Percent public	n.a.	n.a.	n.a.	*67*	*75*	*79*

Sources: American Council on Education, *A Fact Book on Higher Education*, issue 3 (1975), table 75.125, and issue 2 (1975), table 75.65; National Center for Education Statistics, *Education Directory: Colleges and Universities, 1975–76* (GPO, 1976).

n.a. Not available.

a. Beginning with its 1974–75 compilation, the National Center for Education Statistics began to count "branch campuses" separately, whereas previously they were combined for statistical purposes with their parent institutions. To demonstrate the transition, the tallies for 1970 give the "new method" figures in parentheses. Of the 282 institutions added in 1970 by virtue of the change in methodology, all but 48 were public campuses.

"golden years"—both public and private colleges and universities grew and prospered as never before.[1] By 1975 higher education had transformed itself into a $45 billion enterprise, with more than 11 million students—there were only 1.5 million at the time of Pearl Harbor—hundreds of new campuses, thousands of additional professors, and scores of intricate new governance and financing arrangements.[2]

The challenge of the fifties and sixties was how to accommodate the unexpected hordes of new students. In 1958, as Congress was passing the National Defense Education Act, the American Council on Education

1. See Hans H. Jenny and G. Richard Wynn, *The Golden Years* (Wooster, Ohio: College of Wooster, n.d.).

2. National Center for Education Statistics, *The Condition of Education, 1977*, vol. 3, pt. 1 (GPO, 1977), p. 181.

published projections—designed to argue the case for public funds to construct new college facilities—that forecast 1970 enrollments of 5 million to 6 million students.[3] But even the larger estimate proved too low by a third, for in 1958 few could have anticipated that during the ensuing decade enrollments would grow by an unprecedented 300,000 to 600,000 students a year.[4]

No simple explanation adequately accounts for this remarkable development, but several factors clearly contributed to it: the post–World War II "baby boom"; the increasing proportion of high school students receiving diplomas; the rising percentage of high school graduates who chose to pursue their educations further; a growing demand for highly skilled (or at least well-credentialed) employees in commerce, industry, and technology; economic prosperity that allowed many families to pay for their children's advanced schooling; and public policies at both the state and federal levels that helped to underwrite the education of millions more.

To accommodate these students, postsecondary institutions opened at a rate of almost one a week. In 1955 there were 1,886 colleges and universities in the United States; by 1970—some 780 weeks later—there were 2,573.

Existing campuses also grew. In 1950 more than three-quarters of American colleges and universities enrolled fewer than 1,000 students apiece; two decades later, fewer than half did, and one in six boasted more than 5,000 students. Such enlargement cost dearly, but society paid: higher education's share of the gross national product rose from 0.9 percent to 2.5 percent between 1955 and 1970.

The federal government contributed heavily to academic growth and aggrandizement, launching the multitudinous domestic and international programs of the period with the expectation, fully justified at the time, that colleges and universities would eagerly partake of as many of them as possible. Using funds requested by the President and appropriated by

3. John D. Long, *Needed Expansion of Facilities for Higher Education, 1958–70* (American Council on Education, 1958), p. 10.

4. NCES, *Condition of Education, 1977*, p. 177. David Henry stated that in fact these increases were anticipated by some demographers and planners as early as 1953, but that their forecasts were only slowly understood and accepted. He explained that "public interest and concern did not jell until after the Second Report of the President's Committee on Education Beyond the High School" in 1957. See David D. Henry, *Challenges Past, Challenges Present* (Jossey-Bass, 1975), pp. 99–100.

the Congress, educational institutions erected buildings, enlarged their professional staffs, enriched their course offerings, added to their research agendas, and substantially increased their range of services to students, local communities, and state and federal agencies. Such undertakings invariably added to the institutions' fixed costs for many years to come, without being accompanied by any assurances that the government that stimulated them would continue to underwrite them.[5]

Federal student aid programs also encouraged institutional expansion by intensifying the demand for higher education. Many who were attracted to higher education by the new assistance programs of the mid–1960s were "disadvantaged," meaning both that they had few financial resources of their own and that they were apt to require supplementary instruction, counseling, and other services. Enthusiastically sharing in the national fervor for equal opportunity and social mobility through education, colleges and universities nevertheless found themselves enlarging their institutional capacities—a costly undertaking in its own right—and committing themselves to the education of people who could not pay the associated costs and whose government aid was often not sufficient to cover those costs. Consequently, colleges and universities became more dependent for general revenues on the enrollment of large numbers of students able to pay the full "posted price."

There were signs of trouble ahead. By the mid-sixties it was obvious that the birthrate was declining: the number of eighteen- to twenty-one-year-olds in 1985 would be much smaller than in 1975. In the summer of 1965, Allan Cartter cautioned that soon there would be too few college students to afford faculty employment to all the Ph.D.'s emerging from the nation's flourishing graduate programs.[6] But higher education was too busy growing to heed warnings that such growth could not continue. And indeed, in the fall enrollments were up 576,000 from twelve months earlier.[7] In the mid-sixties, the "crisis" of higher education was still the one identified by Rivlin in 1961: the need for "the resources de-

5. The government's role in "overinvestment" by colleges and other nonprofit institutions, and the fiscal travail that predictably follows, are examined by Bruce C. Vladeck, "Why Non-Profits Go Broke," *The Public Interest*, no. 42 (Winter 1976), pp. 86–101. See also William G. Bowen, *The Economics of the Major Private Universities* (Carnegie Commission on Higher Education, 1968), p. 11.

6. Allan M. Cartter, "A New Look at the Supply of College Teachers," *Educational Record*, vol. 46 (Summer 1965), pp. 267–77.

7. U.S. Office of Education, *Digest of Educational Statistics, 1967* (GPO, 1967), p. 68.

voted to higher education . . . to increase considerably faster in the next decade than national output is likely to increase, unless the American people are prepared to allow either a deterioration in the quality, or stricter limits on the availability, of higher education."[8]

The "New Depression"

Within three or four years, the situation had changed. When Earl Cheit visited a selection of colleges and universities in 1970, he found 71 percent of them "headed for financial trouble or . . . in financial difficulty."[9] In 1971 William W. Jellema of the Association of American Colleges testified before Congresswoman Edith Green's subcommittee on education that "colleges and universities are apprehensive, and . . . have reason to be. Most colleges in the red are staying in the red and many are getting redder while colleges in the black generally are growing grayer. . . . Taken collectively," Jellema warned, "these institutions will not long be able to serve higher education and the Nation with strength unless significant aid is soon forthcoming."[10] "Crisis Hits Private Colleges" proclaimed the *Washington Post* on May 30, 1970. The Association of American Universities, the major organization of elite research campuses, stated as early as 1968 that "American higher education is experiencing critical and widespread financial pressures. . . . These pressures constitute a threat to the nature and vitality of American higher education and are therefore a cause for national concern."[11] In somewhat calmer tones President Nixon's Task Force on Higher Education reported in 1970 that "present levels of public and private support of higher education do not provide an adequate base for maintaining existing institutions and developing expanded capacity."[12]

The celebrated "new depression in higher education," as Cheit called it, had arrived. Its main symptoms were deficit budgets, declining appli-

8. Alice M. Rivlin, *The Role of the Federal Government in Financing Higher Education* (Brookings Institution, 1961), p. 2.

9. Earl F. Cheit, *The New Depression in Higher Education* (McGraw-Hill, 1971), p. 139.

10. *Higher Education Amendments of 1971*, pt. 1, Hearings before the House Education and Labor Committee, 92:1 (GPO, 1971), p. 150.

11. Association of American Universities, *The Federal Financing of Higher Education* (AAU, 1968), p. 6.

12. *Priorities in Higher Education*, Report of the President's Task Force on Higher Education (GPO, 1970), p. 2.

cations, unsteady enrollments, painful cost reductions, fading educational quality, and an apparent inability to gain control of the situation so as to set matters right. It was rendered still more depressing by the campus turmoil of the late sixties, by the punitive legislation sailing through one state legislature after another, by the creeping politicization of the academic enterprise, and by mounting popular skepticism, reflected in a startling Gallup poll of May 1970 that found campus unrest perceived as the nation's most serious problem, well ahead of the Vietnam War, racial strife, and the high cost of living.[13]

Specifically, three gross measures of higher education's material well-being caused concern. First, the number of colleges and universities rose at a much slower rate between 1968 and 1970 than it had previously; the private sector actually contracted, as the number of campus closings exceeded the number of openings.[14] Second, although total enrollments continued to rise, the annual growth was much less than before; 356,000 more degree-credit students enrolled in 1972 than in 1970, whereas the previous biennium had seen an increase of more than 1 million. The combined enrollments of private colleges and universities actually fell slightly between 1970 and 1971. And total "first-time degree-credit enrollments" —a fair proxy for the size of the freshman class—declined in 1971 and again in 1972.[15]

Third, the deficits that Cheit, Jellema, and others had found in the ac-

13. *The Gallup Opinion Index,* Report no. 61 (July 1970), p. 3. See also Special Committee on Campus Tensions, *Campus Tensions: Analysis and Recommendations* (American Council on Education, 1970); Carnegie Commission on Higher Education, *Dissent and Disruption* (McGraw-Hill, 1971); Richard E. Peterson and John A. Bilorusky, *May 1970* (Carnegie Commission on Higher Education, 1971); Urban Research Corporation, "Student Protests 1969: Summary" (Chicago, 1970; processed); Alan E. Bayer and Alexander W. Astin, *Campus Disruption During 1968–1969,* ACE Research Reports (American Council on Education, 1969); Robert A. Nisbet, "The Twilight of Authority," *The Public Interest,* no. 15 (Spring 1969); Robert Brustein, "The Case for Professionalism," *The New Republic,* April 26, 1969, pp. 16–18.

14. American Council on Education, *A Fact Book on Higher Education,* issue 3 (1975), table 75.125. By "openings" and "closings" I mean colleges and universities added to, or subtracted from, the annual *Education Directory* compiled by the National Center for Education Statistics (and previously by the Office of Education). A number of criteria are involved, some of them tied to the institution's accreditation status; hence being added does not necessarily mean the college is brand new, and being deleted may not mean it has actually shut its doors. See the appendix titled "Changes" in *Education Directory: Colleges and Universities 1975–76,* and similar listings in earlier editions.

15. ACE, *Fact Book on Higher Education,* issue 2 (1975), tables 75.65 and 75.87.

count books of selected higher education institutions were common in the private sector.[16] In school year 1969–70 the nation's private colleges and universities ran a combined deficit in their current fund accounts of $44 million, and the following year they fell short by $27 million.[17] The poor fiscal health of particular campuses drew much attention in the press, and when renowned institutions such as Columbia and New York University reported financial travail it was front-page news.

Understandably concerned, higher education leaders looked for help. But their quest for federal relief in the form of general operating subsidies came to nothing, and most state capitals responded slowly if at all.[18] The colleges fared better, however, in such self-help efforts as recruiting students, curbing costs, and increasing private revenues; and in a remarkably short time the "new depression" was all but over. Revisiting his sample campuses in 1973, Cheit found a "fragile stability" in their account books, which he attributed more to heroic cost reduction than to increased revenues.[19] Jellema reported that the picture, though still gloomy, was less frightening than before.[20] The number of colleges and the number of students both began to rise again. Even the beleaguered private sector raised its campus complement almost as much between 1972 and 1975 as it had from 1964 to 1967. Degree-credit enrollments

16. Public campuses may encounter severe fiscal distress, but "deficits" are not a very satisfactory guide, since the state supplies such a large portion of their income, including supplemental appropriations when required, and since in some jurisdictions it is not permissible for state agencies to incur deficits.

17. NCES, *Financial Statistics of Institutions of Higher Education, Fiscal Year 1970* (GPO, 1972); National Center for Educational Statistics, *Digest of Educational Statistics, 1974* (GPO, 1975), pp. 109–15. It should be noted that a comparison of current revenues and expenditures for all colleges and universities, or even for just all private or all public campuses, is a somewhat simplistic way to analyze their financial condition. Furthermore, educational institutions do not invariably follow the behavioral norms and accounting practices of business establishments, which usually seek to maximize profits. Indeed, colleges and universities are impelled by diverse motives, such as the desire for academic prestige, and constrained by distinctive customs and idiosyncratic procedures. Nevertheless, since few colleges can afford large, recurrent deficits, aggregating their income and outlays offers at least a clue to their fiscal stability as a group. For a much more sophisticated analysis of institutional finances, though confined to a sample of private campuses, see Howard R. Bowen and W. John Minter, *Private Higher Education, 1975* (Association of American Colleges, 1975), and succeeding editions.

18. The 1969–72 campaign for federal institutional aid is reviewed in chapter 5.

19. Earl F. Cheit, *The New Depression in Higher Education—Two Years Later* (Carnegie Commission on Higher Education, 1973).

20. William W. Jellema, *From Red to Black?* (Jossey-Bass, 1973).

rose by 260,000 from 1972 to 1973, by 500,000 the following year, and by 310,000 the year after that.[21] Taken as a whole, private higher education moved back into the black. By 1975–76 its composite (current fund) surplus had reached $153 million and the next year it was $228 million.[22] When Bowen and Minter completed the first of their detailed sample surveys of four-year private campuses in 1975, they found most colleges and universities "solvent even though not highly prosperous," and hailed the private sector for its "enormous staying power."[23]

In sum, the new depression was real enough, but for higher education as a whole, and for most colleges and universities, it appears to have been a temporary phenomenon, a period of painful adjustment followed by signs of renewed stability and some fresh vigor.

Higher education had simply grown faster than the demand for it. In a 1974 survey of college and university presidents, more than half of them stated that the enrollments at their institutions that year were smaller than their own projections made in the late 1960s. Among church-related junior colleges (admittedly a small group) these "fewer-than-expected" confessions reached 78 percent, but they were almost as frequent—65 percent—within the important category of state universities.[24] Since many of these institutions had erected the buildings and hired the staff they would need to accommodate the students they anticipated, a number of them faced a painful readjustment when the matriculants failed to appear. Nor were college presidents the only ones surprised. In 1968, basing their projections on a straightforward extrapolation of enrollment trends up to that year, statisticians at the National Center for Educational Statistics had forecast that first-time degree-credit students in 1973 would number 1,889,000, but only 1,775,000 registered. Similar projections showed private colleges and universities with a total of 2,377,000 degree-credit students in 1973; just 2,160,000 actually enrolled.[25]

21. ACE, *Fact Book on Higher Education*, issue 2 (1975), table 75.65.

22. NCES, *Financial Statistics of Institutions of Higher Education, Fiscal Year 1976* (GPO, 1978). Preliminary figure for 1976–77 is from the staff of the National Center for Education Statistics.

23. *Private Higher Education, 1975*, pp. 78–79.

24. Lyman A. Glenny and others, *Presidents Confront Reality* (Jossey-Bass, 1976), p. 144.

25. *Projections of Educational Statistics to 1977–78* (GPO, 1969), pp. 13, 16; ACE, *Fact Book on Higher Education*, issue 2 (1975), tables 75.65 and 75.87.

Problems Ahead

Although the "crisis" of the early seventies is over, many higher education leaders fear that a new one is at hand. Four matters evoke particular concern: demographic changes that may result in fewer—or different kinds of—students; a decrease in the number of good applicants at many colleges; a possible decline in the overall quality of higher education; and the prospective demise of some institutions.

Demography and Dollars

Whereas the number of students found on a given campus is the product of many forces, for higher education as a whole enrollments obey a firm and simple law. They are the mathematical product of the size of a given population (that from which students are drawn) multiplied by the percentage of that population that chooses to attend college.

Although the postsecondary population is not necessarily found in any particular age group, in the United States enrolling in college is something one generally does soon after graduating from high school. The pattern has modified somewhat; nevertheless, as recently as 1975 nearly three-quarters of all freshmen surveyed by the American Council on Education were eighteen years old, and 96 percent of them were between their seventeenth and twenty-first birthdays.[26] This has long been the conventional time for matriculating; hence the size of that age group has long functioned as the first factor in the enrollment equation. During the 1960s the college-age population ballooned to remarkable proportions, a corollary of what Daniel P. Moynihan has termed "a profound demographic change . . . in American society which was a one-time change, a growth in population vaster than any that had ever occurred before, or any that will ever occur again, with respect to a particular subgroup in the population, namely those persons fourteen to twenty-four years of age."[27] That age group, which had grown by

26. Alexander W. Astin, Margo R. King, and Gerald T. Richardson, *The American Freshman: National Norms for Fall 1975* (Cooperative Institutional Research Program, American Council on Education and the University of California at Los Angeles, 1975), p. 41.

27. Daniel P. Moynihan, *Coping: On the Practice of Government* (Random House, 1973), pp. 422–23.

12.5 million during the seventy years from 1890 to 1960, increased by 13.8 million in a single decade.

But the extraordinary birthrates of the late 1940s and early 1950s that underlay this growth did not last. The annual number of live births in the United States stopped rising in 1957, leveling off for the next four years and then beginning a major decline between 1961 and 1962.[28] During the years of higher education's fastest enrollment growth in the mid-1960s, the number of births each year was shrinking. Already this is beginning to cause a series of institutional dislocations. Elementary school enrollments reached their zenith in 1969, and have now shrunk by more than 4 million.[29] Barring extraordinary teenage immigration, the eighteen-year-old population will begin to shrink in 1979 and, except for a brief and modest upturn in the mid-eighties, will continue downward until 1991.[30] The eighteen- to twenty-one-year-old group will consist of 2.5 million *fewer* people in 1990 than in 1980, an erosion of about one-seventh. The twenty-two- to twenty-four-year-old group will be nearly 2 million smaller in 1990 than in 1985.[31]

An essential difference between grammar schools and colleges is that the former, being compulsory, find their enrollments almost perfectly correlated with the size of a specific age group, whereas the latter may draw upon diverse age groups and may also hope to vary the second factor in the enrollment equation by attracting larger percentages of the traditional college population.

From the standpoint of higher education planners in the late sixties, it was evident that for three decades the percentage of young adults attending college had been steadily increasing. In 1940, 7.3 percent of eighteen- to twenty-four-year-olds were undergraduates; in 1950, 10 percent; in 1960, 13.3 percent. By 1969 the proportion had escalated to 24.9 percent, by far the highest in American history and, one presumes, the highest of any nation at any time.[32] The rhetoric of the era spoke of

28. *Statistical Abstract of the United States, 1976* (GPO, 1976), p. 51.

29. National Center for Education Statistics, *Projections of Education Statistics to 1984–85* (GPO, 1976), p. 18.

30. For a graphic illustration, see David W. Breneman and Chester E. Finn, Jr., "An Uncertain Future," in Breneman and Finn, eds., *Public Policy and Private Higher Education* (Brookings Institution, 1978), p. 4.

31. *Statistical Abstract of the United States, 1976*, pp. 6–7.

32. U.S. Office of Management and Budget, *Social Indicators, 1973* (GPO, 1974), p. 105.

universal higher education, and most enrollment forecasts assumed that the percentage of young people going to college would continue to rise.[33]

It proved not to be so. The proportion of eighteen- to twenty-four-year-olds enrolled as undergraduates declined slightly to 23.3 percent in 1970.[34] The percentage of male high school graduates going directly into postsecondary education fell from a 1968 peak of 63 percent to 55 percent in 1970, and continued downward to 49 percent in 1974.[35]

Multiple explanations have been offered, ranging from the mounting cost of college to evidence that lifetime earnings were no longer so greatly enhanced by a university degree as they once had been. Another possibility is that more young people—perhaps, in the case of males, abetted by the end of the military draft—were delaying their entry into college rather than proceeding straight from high school. The essential points are, first, that a college planner in the late sixties could not antici-pate this decline and, second, that this break in the decades-old pattern of rising matriculation rates signals more serious enrollment woes ahead. It means that the simplest solution to the problem of a dwindling eighteen-year-old population—luring a larger percentage of the re-mainder into college—may not be realistic.

In the mid-seventies, however, another surprise befell higher educa-tion planners: students showed up in greater numbers than almost any-one expected. Just about the time many forecasters were altering their projections in light of changing reality, reality changed again. Thus, as table 2-2 shows, 1974 enrollments surpassed by more than half a million students the government projections made only a year earlier and in 1976 they remained well ahead of the forecasts. In 1977 they again ex-ceeded expectations.[36]

33. The 1968 edition of the Office of Education enrollment projections, fore-casting the years through 1977, included the straightforward "assumption that first-time enrollment, expressed as a percentage of the population averaging 18 years of age, will follow the 1957–67 trend." (*Projections of Educational Statistics to 1977–78*, p. 14n.) It is noteworthy that the theme of the American Council on Education's annual meeting in 1970 was Higher Education for Everybody? and the following year it was Universal Higher Education. See W. Todd Furniss, ed., *Higher Education for Everybody?* (ACE, 1971), and Logan Wilson, ed., *Universal Higher Education* (ACE, 1972).

34. OMB, *Social Indicators, 1973*, p. 105.

35. Joseph Froomkin, "Recent Developments in Post-Secondary Education, 1970–1975" (Washington, D.C., January 1976; processed), p. 61.

36. It should be noted, however, that total 1976 enrollments, though still ahead of those projected, were down 1.5 percent from those of fall 1975—the first such

Table 2-2. *Projected and Actual Enrollment in Higher Education,*
1972, 1974, 1976

Thousands

Students	1972 Projected	1972 Actual	1974 Projected	1974 Actual	1976 Projected	1976 Actual
Degree and nondegree, public and private	9,213	9,215	9,568	10,223	10,964	11,122
Public, degree and nondegree	7,001	7,070	7,402	7,988	8,683	8,713
Public, degree only	6,262	6,158	6,361	6,838	7,361	n.a.
Private, degree and nondegree	2,212	2,145	2,166	2,235	2,281	2,409
Private, degree only	2,171	2,107	2,130	2,185	2,224	n.a.

Sources: National Center for Educational Statistics, *Projections of Educational Statistics to 1979–80* (GPO, 1971), pp. 15–18; *Projections of Educational Statistics to 1982–83* (GPO, 1974), pp. 25, 28; *Projections of Education Statistics to 1984–85* (GPO, 1976), pp. 22, 26; Andrew J. Pepin, "1976 Opening Fall Enrollment in Higher Education—Final Count" (National Center for Education Statistics, August 1977; processed).
n.a. Not available.

Why the sudden surge? No one really knows. The most persuasive explanation is that the weak job market afforded few attractive alternatives to young people who might otherwise not have gone to college. Whatever the reasons, one can understand the puzzlement of observers who, amid widespread accounts of retrenchment, cutbacks, and campus closings, also found the *Chronicle of Higher Education* in November 1975 headlining "Enrollment Increase: Biggest in a Decade . . . Both Public and Private Institutions Gain."

Despite the gains, changes in the student population attest to the volatility of the major variables and the difficulty of planning around them. A profound alteration has taken place, for example, in the college enrollment rates of eighteen- to twenty-four-year-old males and females.[37] Whereas in 1967, men in this age group were significantly more likely to be found in college than were women of the same age group—

decline in memory. Enrollments increased slightly at private colleges and universities and shrank more than 2 percent at public institutions. In the fall of 1977, however, enrollments rose in both sectors, 0.8 percent more in private institutions than in public. (Women accounted for 93 percent of this rise.) See "Opening Fall Enrollment in College and Universities, 1977," National Center for Education Statistics *Bulletin*, December 1977, and *Chronicle of Higher Education*, vol. 15 (January 9, 1978), p. 1.

37. The reference here is to "dependent family members" aged eighteen to twenty-four.

rates of 42.9 and 34.9 percent, respectively—nine years later the situation had virtually reversed: in 1976 43.2 percent of eighteen- to twenty-four-year-old women were enrolled in college, compared with 35.3 percent of men. During the same period older people (of both sexes) increased their college participation rates: from 6.6 to 10.0 percent for twenty-five- to twenty-nine-year-olds, and from 4.0 to 6.0 percent for thirty- to thirty-four-year-olds. Minority group members also showed marked improvement in their college participation rates. Among blacks aged twenty and twenty-one, for example, 11.6 percent were attending school or college in 1966; a decade later the rate was 28.2 percent.[38]

Some colleges and universities are well situated to capitalize on these changes; others have difficulty holding their own. Thus Froomkin estimates that, between 1970 and 1975, 31.7 percent of all private campuses and 14.2 percent of public institutions lost more than 10 percent of their enrollments.[39] On the other hand, the one hundred private campuses surveyed by Bowen and Minter added 8 percent to their aggregate enrollments between 1969 and 1976. They actually experienced a slight drop in the number of undergraduates, but this was more than offset by a 27 percent increase in their graduate students and an extraordinary 79 percent rise in professional students.[40]

College and university administrators may be forgiven their preoccupation with enrollments, for on most campuses there is a firm link between the number of students registered and the financial well-being of the institution. "When institutions finally falter economically," veteran analyst Hans Jenny writes, "the primary reason is that their enrollment foundation has eroded."[41] In the private sector students provide tuition revenue, which supplies more than a third of institutional income, as well as sizable sums in room and board payments and other fees. Although tuitions and fees supply a much smaller part of the income of public colleges and universities—about 12.9 percent in 1975–76—the state sub-

38. U.S. Bureau of the Census, *Current Population Reports*, Series P-20, no. 319 (GPO, 1978), pp. 63–64.

39. Joseph Froomkin and Clinton McCully, "A Review of Financial Developments in Higher Education, 1970/71–1974/75, and a Prognosis for 1980–1985" (Washington, D.C., February 1977; processed), table 11.

40. Howard R. Bowen and W. John Minter, *Private Higher Education, 1977* (Association of American Colleges, 1977), p. 8.

41. Hans H. Jenny, *Higher Education and the Economy*, ERIC/Higher Education Research Report no. 2 (American Association of Higher Education, 1976), p. 12.

sidies that account for 44.8 percent of institutional revenues are ordinarily calculated with enrollment-based formulas.[42]

By far the easiest way to raise revenues is to add students, and since the income produced by an additional student usually exceeds the marginal cost of equipping him with an education, expansion is also a proven means of bettering a college's financial position.[43] Moreover, an expensive physical plant and heavily tenured faculty make for high fixed costs and for difficulty in adding new educational programs or more professors, except when revenues are growing faster than inflation. Thus most colleges and universities grew accustomed in the 1950s and 1960s to innovating by growing.

This was a risky habit. The Carnegie Commission warned in 1972 that "a confrontation has developed between institutional expectations and the hard realities of the national situation" and urged stern self-discipline upon the campuses.[44] The commission, of course, was right, as events of the early 1970s proved, particularly for campuses that found themselves losing students. Costs per student rose faster in shrinking institutions than in those with stable or growing enrollments, and, in order to cover those costs, tuitions rose faster, too, particularly in the private sector. Often the result has been a vicious circle wherein colleges and universities with enrollment problems are obliged to raise their prices, thus making themselves even less attractive to the students they seek to register.

Selectivity

Selectivity, or the ability to pick and choose among many applicants, is prized by the colleges that have it and coveted by most that do not. A campus that cannot or will not expand is nonetheless gratified when the number of people seeking admission exceeds the number it has room for. Only in that way can it accommodate the faculty's desire to teach the

---

42. NCES, *Financial Statistics of Institutions . . . 1976*, pp. 4–5.

43. To be sure, a college that already makes full use of its physical facilities and that does not want to worsen its faculty–student ratio would find additional students more expensive and perhaps would end up worse off. It may be noted that some states have recently begun to adjust their college subsidy formulas in an attempt to match only the actual marginal costs per added (or subtracted) student. This will curb the temptation to expand enrollments and will mitigate the fiscal damage of reduced enrollments on public campuses.

44. Carnegie Commission on Higher Education, *The More Effective Use of Resources* (McGraw-Hill, 1972), p. 3.

brightest students, the admissions office's fondness for a "well-rounded" student body, and the trustees' ambition to attain a fine reputation.

Many institutions, of course, have always been denied the luxury of selectivity. A number of public campuses, particularly community colleges, practice "open admissions"—or something close to it. At some private institutions the ability to choose among applicants has never been the practice. Indeed, one of the defining characteristics of the nearly 500 private colleges—attended by half a million students—that Astin and Lee termed "invisible" is their low level of selectivity.[45]

Many factors contribute to a college's attractiveness and thus to its ability to choose among applicants. Since the institutions differ greatly, it must be assumed that some have characteristics—a distinguished faculty, a choice location, low tuitions—that render them more attractive to more prospective students, and it must also be assumed that if total demand slackens the least atractive schools will suffer most. Nationwide enrollment totals would have to plummet before the hundred campuses whose names are household words would face an absolute shortfall in their freshman classes (though they may have to accept a larger percentage of their applicants), whereas many less prestigious institutions would encounter serious trouble much sooner, even if they were prepared to lower their accustomed standards.

Bowen and Minter examined selectivity in their sample of one hundred private campuses and found that between 1969 and 1976 the number of completed freshman applications fell by 4 percent and the percentage of applicants offered admission rose slightly, from 70 to 71 percent. This modest decrease in applications was paralleled by a slight deterioration in the quality of students applying, accepted, and enrolled, if one judges by test results and high school rank. The percentage of entering freshmen who had graduated in the top two-fifths of their high school class declined from 78 to 75, and a small fall-off in freshman college-board scores matched the much discussed—and yet unexplained—national erosion in those scores for all high school seniors.[46] At the same time, it is important to remember that undergraduates were beginning to constitute a smaller fraction of total enrollments at these institutions, and that private colleges and universities were generally finding their numbers of "first time" students (that is, freshmen) static, even while their complement of upper division, graduate, and professional students was growing.

45. Alexander W. Astin and Calvin B. T. Lee, *The Invisible Colleges* (McGraw-Hill, 1972), pp. 31–34.
46. *Private Higher Education, 1977*, p. 10.

Thus freshmen admissions could become less selective, but also less important to the composition of the entire student body.

On many campuses maintaining enrollments calls for more effort with each passing year. Between 1969 and 1976 Bowen and Minter's sample colleges enlarged their admissions office staffs by 42 percent, and the number of students admitted per staff member fell from 104 to 76.[47] Many schools have begun actively to recruit students, a practice that is the virtual obverse of the traditional function of admissions offices and that implies a near absence of selectivity.[48] Also colleges are often not able to draw their applicants and recruits from the accustomed locales. Finding themselves squeezed out of their traditional student markets by rival institutions, some scour high schools thousands of miles away. But most have put a renewed emphasis on nearby communities, particularly as a source of older and part-time students who cannot travel far to enroll. With many state scholarship programs confined to residents of the sponsoring state, and with public universities in other jurisdictions levying heavier charges on nonresidents, students often find it more economical to attend a school near home; many colleges find the geographic range of their entering freshmen has shrunk. Out-of-state students enrolled in Ohio colleges and universities, for example, declined from 61,000 in 1968 to 43,000 five years later.[49]

Finally, it is not uncommon for institutions of higher education to ease their former admissions standards in order to attract and accept more students. A 1974 poll of college presidents revealed that 41 percent of the respondents' institutions had modified their standards since 1968 so as to increase undergraduate enrollments, and two-thirds indicated a heightened emphasis on "active recruitment" of traditional students.[50]

Quantity, Quality, and Productivity

If colleges and universities were susceptible to greater productivity, they would be less vulnerable to enrollment fluctuations. Resources could

47. Ibid., p. 13.

48. "Admissions recruiters" may also be hired in the name of equal educational opportunity. And, of course, a college may both recruit and select, seeking certain kinds of students while rigorously weeding out surplus applicants in other categories.

49. Association of Independent Colleges and Universities of Ohio, "Fact-File 1975–76" (n.d.; processed).

50. Lyman A. Glenny and others, Presidents Confront Reality, app. A.

diminish without educational quality suffering. Improvements could be made in curriculums without students having to pay more. But higher education's record in this regard is not encouraging.

In 1959 Seymour Harris noted that while consumer prices in the United States increased about 50 percent from 1919 to 1956, the income per (resident) student to American colleges and universities rose by some 250 percent.[51] A Carnegie Commission study found that between 1929 and 1960, the cost per credit hour in postsecondary institutions rose at an average rate that was 2.5 percent a year faster than the consumer price index.[52] Such facts led the commission to observe in its peroration of 1973: "Higher education does not lend itself very readily to permanent increases in productivity. Thus its rising costs . . . are directly reflected in the prices it must charge . . . whereas in industrial sectors of the economy cost increases are offset by an average annual rate of increase in productivity of 2.5 percent." Apparently willing to accept the past as prologue, the commission insisted that "if quality is to be maintained and if salary increases are to match those elsewhere, we must expect expenditures per student to rise as rapidly as the cost of living plus about 2.5 percent."[53]

The National Commission on the Financing of Postsecondary Education (established by Congress in 1972) was less sanguine about higher education's immunity from improved productivity, saying that even if it had been immune in the past, the public would not permit such a luxury in the future. The commission warned, however, that "it will be extremely difficult for educators to demonstrate productivity gains with the analytical tools now at hand."[54]

It is indeed difficult to determine whether colleges and universities (and other labor-intensive, nonprofit service institutions) are susceptible to productivity gains and, if so, how they should be measured. There is little agreement as to what the "outputs" of a college are, or should be,

51. Seymour E. Harris, "Financing of Higher Education: Broad Issues," in Dexter M. Keezer, ed., *Financing Higher Education 1960–70* (McGraw-Hill, 1959), p. 42.

52. June O'Neill, *Resource Use in Higher Education* (Carnegie Commission on Higher Education, 1971), pp. 37–38.

53. Carnegie Commission on Higher Education, *Priorities for Action: Final Report of the Carnegie Commission on Higher Education* (McGraw-Hill, 1973), pp. 63–64. Much the same point was made earlier in Carnegie Commission on Higher Education, *Quality and Equality: New Levels of Federal Responsibility for Higher Education* (McGraw-Hill, 1968), p. 6.

54. *Financing Postsecondary Education in the United States* (GPO, 1974), p. 44.

and how to compare the products of diverse institutions. But it is essential to recognize that one person's evidence of heightened productivity is another's cause for alarm over the deteriorating faculty-student ratio. Reduced costs per student—a good—is the flip side of shrunken resources per student—an evil. From some perspectives colleges improve when conventional indexes of productivity in higher education are heading *down*.

Measuring higher education's output so as to match it against inputs is further bedeviled by the difficulty of gauging quality among colleges and universities; without solid indicators of either one it is not possible to speak confidently about institutional health. A college may well be moving toward bankruptcy because its expenditures exceed its income, and presumably its trustees have the right to continue on that course. But if, as is increasingly the case, government officials are asked to adopt policies designed to fend off that eventuality, it is reasonable for them to demand objective measures of institutional performance and financial condition. Yet no such measures enjoy widespread acceptance, and efforts to create them have met with general opposition from higher education leaders, who insist—not without reason—that campuses differ so widely that any standard measures of their performance will be at best crude and unhelpful, at worst damaging to academic diversity, quality, and independence.

Congress bluntly stated its dismay in 1972, after three years of pleas by educational leaders for unrestricted federal aid to ease growing fiscal distress: "Various proposals have been presented to the Congress ... for providing financial assistance to the Nation's institutions of higher education but ... insufficient information is available on the basis of which the Congress can determine, with any degree of certainty, the nature and causes of such financial distress or the most appropriate means with which present and future conditions of financial distress may be dealt."[55]

To remedy this situation, the National Commission on Financing Postsecondary Education was charged with suggesting "national uniform standards for determining the annual per student costs of providing postsecondary education for students in attendance at various types and classes of institutions of higher education" and with developing "alternative models for the long range solutions to the problems of financing postsecondary education."[56] But after considerable effort, the

55. 86 Stat. 245.
56. 87 Stat. 72.

commission all but admitted failure, reporting that "no generally accepted standards or uniform criteria are available to ascertain the existence or extent of financial distress in postsecondary education," and recommended that "national standard indicators should be developed."[57] But despite further effort by many analysts, little progress has been made, leading Jenny, in 1976, to conclude correctly that "the single most serious defect" in appraisals of the academic condition is "the absence of nationally credible indicators of institutional health."[58]

Consequently, both hopeful and worrisome conclusions about higher education can be drawn from the experience of the past several years, depending on the choice of data and perspective. In a study conducted for the American Council on Education, for example, Lanier and Andersen found "negative growth rates" in "constant dollar expenditures per student" in every classification of public and private institution in 1974–75, and concluded that "progressive deterioration has been occurring in the financial condition of higher education as a whole in recent years."[59]

Others, such as Joseph Froomkin, conclude that from 1970 to 1975 higher education was able to hold its per-student outlays practically level by keeping its own inflation rate slightly below that of the economy as a whole. Thus current dollar expenditures per student rose from $3,462 to $4,476 from 1970–71 to 1974–75, but when rendered into constant (1967) dollars, using a deflator specifically tailored to the costs of colleges and universities, the corresponding figures are $2,735 and $2,724.[60] These figures stand in marked contrast to those of the late 1960s, when the "higher education price index" rose considerably faster than the consumer price index and other general indicators of the inflation rate.

Even though resources per student may be declining, it does not necessarily follow that academic quality is too. It is noteworthy that Bowen and Minter found "virtually no evidence of qualitative deterioration" in the private institutions they examined. Their sample campuses offered, on the average, 29 percent more undergraduate courses in 1975–76 than they had in 1969–70. Fifty-five percent of chief academic officers reported that overall faculty performance was generally improving in

57. *Financing Postsecondary Education*, p. 351.
58. *Higher Education and the Economy*, p. 50.
59. Lyle H. Lanier and Charles J. Andersen, *A Study of the Financial Condition of Colleges and Universities: 1972–1975* (American Council on Education, 1975), pp. 75–76.
60. Froomkin, *Review of Financial Developments*, p. 59.

quality, and only 2 percent found it diminishing. The average class size was growing on nearly half these campuses, but the "overall quality of the learning environment" was eroding in just 5 percent. Half the college presidents judged their schools to be gaining ground in "capacity for self-renewal"; only 5 percent felt they were backsliding.[61]

Of course, such surveys should be read with skepticism, for senior college administrators must cultivate the images of their institutions and it is hard to know whether they feel themselves better served by stating that everything is fine and getting finer or by singing the blues in order to lend credence to appeals for help. Yet lacking sound objective measures of educational quality, one has little else to go by. Certainly it would be shortsighted to allow resources per student to serve as the only proxy for educational quality or institutional well-being, particularly when the point of comparison is the "golden years." That era was a lofty plateau in postsecondary finances, a decade and a half in which growth rates were significantly above their historic levels, a period in which the standard of living of many colleges and universities reached an unprecedented high. It was most assuredly not a period in which efficiency, productivity, and cost-minimizing behavior characterized American higher education, public or private. Thus a leveling off, even a slight decline in resources per student, especially in a time when enrollments are again rising and inflation is rapid, though undeniably painful for the institutions living with it, could also be termed an overdue belt-tightening, a readjustment to earlier standards of living, and a much-delayed sign that greater cost effectiveness and productivity either are being or must be achieved.

Closings and Openings

Of the many indicators used to substantiate claims of a "crisis" in higher education, none is more vivid and seemingly incontrovertible than the demise of entire institutions. For observers and partisans of higher education, nothing is more poignant than to read of a century-old college forced by dwindling enrollments and rising deficits to shut its doors and sell or auction off its earthly remains. Between 1970 and 1976 some 113 private postsecondary institutions (and branch campuses)

61. Howard R. Bowen and W. John Minter, *Private Higher Education, 1976* (Association of American Colleges, 1976), pp. 32, 39, 50.

Table 2-3. *Public and Private Institutions of Higher Education and Branches, 1969–70 to 1976–77*[a]

Number of Institutional Units

Category	1969–70	1970–71	1971–72	1972–73	1973–74	1974–75	1975–76	1976–77	1969–70 to 1976–77
All institutions and branches	2,836	2,855	2,902	2,951	3,018	3,038	3,055	3,075	239
Four-year	1,773	1,799	1,806	1,834	1,867	1,887	1,914	1,928	155
Two-year	1,063	1,056	1,096	1,117	1,151	1,151	1,141	1,147	84
Public	1,312	1,335	1,381	1,414	1,445	1,453	1,454	1,467	155
Four-year	519	530	536	541	549	552	553	558	39
Two-year	793	805	845	873	896	901	901	909	116
Private	1,524	1,520	1,521	1,537	1,573	1,585	1,601	1,608	84
Four-year	1,254	1,269	1,270	1,293	1,318	1,335	1,361	1,370	116
Two-year	270	251	251	244	255	250	240	238	−32

Source: National Center for Education Statistics, *Education Directory: Colleges and Universities, 1975–76* (GPO, 1976), p. xxvii, and *Education Directory . . . 1976–77* (GPO, 1977), p. xxvii.

a. As explained in the note to table 2-1, the figures shown here are "new method," that is, each branch is counted separately. It should be repeated, however, that being added to or dropped from these listings is not identical to "opening" or "closing," since various criteria must be met in order to be listed and retained in subsequent years. Unfortunately, these criteria have changed from time to time, but they center on accreditation, or some facsimile thereof, such as having credits accepted by other institutions that are accredited. Thus a college or university is listed when it meets the criteria, although it may have existed for some time.

Fadil has analyzed these data for the private sector, and concludes that during the period 1970–76, 46 colleges (and branch campuses) were founded that satisfied federal criteria for inclusion in the *Education Directory* and that 262 preexisting institutions satisfied the criteria and were therefore also added to the *Directory*. Virginia Fadil, "Openings, Closings, Mergers and Accreditation Status of Independent Colleges and Universities" (National Association of Independent Colleges and Universities, November 1977; processed), pp. 3–4.

For additional information on genuinely "new" postsecondary institutions, see Paul L. Dressel, ed., *The New Colleges: Toward an Appraisal* (Iowa City: American College Testing Program, 1971); and *New Academic Institutions: A Survey* (American Council on Education, 1972).

closed down; and their collapse has received widespread attention as an unmistakable symptom of higher education's malaise.[62]

At the same time, however, higher education has been renewing itself, with colleges and universities growing and changing, and with a surprising number of institutions *adding* their names to the lists each year. As shown in table 2-3 there were 239 more institutions of higher education in 1976–77 than during the "new depression" year of 1969–70, including a net increase of 84 in the private sector (116 more four-year schools and 32 fewer junior colleges). During the same period the public sector grew by 155 institutions, three-quarters of them two-year "community" colleges.

The new arrivals are undeniably a mixed assortment. Included are institutions whose very names imply quality, stability, and respectability, such as the Mayo Medical School of Rochester, Minnesota, and the Rand Graduate Institute for Policy Studies of Santa Monica, California. Also listed are others that stand well outside the traditional mainstream: the Maharishi International University (Los Angeles) and the Vermont Institute of Community Involvement. A number are church-related institutions, many of them self-proclaimed "bible colleges," an increase that supports David Riesman's observation that fundamentalist churches are tilling one of the most fertile fields in American higher education.[63] Still others are specialized professional schools—chiropractic medicine, embalming, engineering, theology, and institutions devoted to the arts. In the public sector most recent arrivals are community colleges, usually little known outside their immediate locales. In neither sector do these newcomers bear much resemblance to Wellesley, Vanderbilt, or Michigan State. On the other hand, most of today's eminent colleges and universities were also small, specialized, and obscure at the time of their founding. Certainly higher education shows signs of continuing dynamism, of being an industry in which marginal institutions fail but are replaced by new entrants perhaps better attuned to the changing demands of the educational marketplace.

So long as the industry as a whole retains this vibrancy and capacity for self-renewal, the demise of individual campuses need not be a matter

62. Virginia Fadil, "Openings, Closings, Mergers and Accreditation Status of Independent Colleges and Universities" (National Association of Independent Colleges and Universities, November 1977; processed), p. 1.

63. David Riesman, "The Future of Diversity in a Time of Retrenchment," *Higher Education*, vol. 4 (November 1975), pp. 461–82.

for concern. To imply that government policy, whether state or federal, should seek to sustain in perpetuity every institution that styles itself a college or university borders on the absurd, not least because it suggests that anyone wishing to go out and found one should be able to do so with the assurance that the society will maintain it. This is a recipe for educational stagnation, as the mere existence of an institution comes to take precedence over its quality and its responsiveness to educational needs as reflected in a changing student marketplace.

It may even be necessary to entertain the unsettling thought that the mortality rate in private higher education is too *low* to make room for the entry of the new institutions needed for a truly dynamic industry. Bowen and Minter suggest that the pace of recent closings—half of 1 percent a year between 1970 and 1975—among accredited four-year institutions should be compared with similar indicators from earlier times, observing that "of the 891 institutions (public and private) founded between 1770 and 1870, 650 had disappeared by 1870, an average mortality of 6.5 per year," and that 19 percent of the private four-year colleges started between 1940 and 1970 were gone by 1970.[64]

Taking Stock in 1978

In higher education it is hard to know when a "crisis" exists. The dearth of sound measures of educational quality and institutional health, the stubborn disputes over such gauges as productivity, the unreliability of the data base, the volatility that has crept into such key indicators as enrollments, and the folly of drawing policy guidance from the demise of individual campuses all make for a perplexing situation in the present and for legitimate uncertainty about the future.

No one can deny that American higher education today boasts more institutions, more students, and greater resources than ever before. Inflation has taken its toll and resources per student are no longer increasing in "real" terms, but there is little hard evidence of qualitative decay. Some colleges and universities have shut their doors, primarily in the private sector, and such sad events have attracted much notice, but probably more than they deserve. Some postsecondary subspecies, such as the private two-year college, would appear to be in serious trouble,

64. *Private Higher Education, 1975*, pp. 72–73.

but others, such as the public two-year college, are flourishing. Costs and prices are rising, and the "gap" between public and private tuitions is widening,[65] yet enrollments are more than keeping pace.

Despite vast amounts of analysis and prognostication, the future remains unclear. The one certainty is that the traditional college-age population will soon begin to shrink. From the student's standpoint, this means wider choice among colleges and universities that will be eager to enroll him. From the institutions' point of view, the effects will vary greatly. The competition for students will intensify and, as in any "buyer's market," the sellers with a high-priced or poor-quality product will have more difficulty attracting business.[66] The state subsidies that underwrite low tuitions in public colleges and universities, and the unwillingness of state legislatures to allow the marketplace to take its toll among them, certainly give a competitive edge to the public campuses and create a high probability that the private sector will absorb more than "its share" of whatever retrenchment takes place.[67]

Fewer students mean less income, and less income carries an obvious threat to educational quality, particularly in the absence of improved productivity. Colleges and universities that mastered the challenges of growth in the "golden years" are institutionally ill equipped to shrink. Despite stronger management on many campuses and a greater willingness to face tough choices, postsecondary institutions remain ponderous creatures with decentralized decisionmaking, high fixed costs, and personnel practices that make it hard to replace weak employees or to eliminate superfluous ones.

Attached to such obvious problems is a host of more subtle ones. Will higher education become more diverse, in order to attract students, or more homogeneous as a consequence of its growing dependence on state and federal funding and the uniform standards and detailed regulations that accompany it? Will the cessation of institutional expansion lead to educational stagnation and to the loss of an entire generation of young scholars who might enliven the academy but who cannot get jobs on heavily tenured campuses that have no room for additional pro-

65. This issue is examined in chapter 3.

66. The "price" and "nonprice" factors in the student marketplace are explored at length in Michael S. McPherson, "The Demand for Private Higher Education," in Breneman and Finn, eds., *Public Policy and Private Higher Education.*

67. These and related issues are examined fully in Breneman and Finn, eds., *Public Policy and Private Higher Education.*

fessors?[68] Will institutional independence and academic freedom be eroded by the compromises colleges and universities make in order to keep their doors open?

There is a poor fit between higher education's perceived problems and the sorts of solutions most easily undertaken by the federal government. The government cannot readily change the demographic patterns that lie at the heart of higher education's most acute problems. It cannot require colleges to become more productive or to reduce their costs—and if it tried to it would be charged with heinous offenses. It cannot impose quality standards that the academy rejects. It cannot make more people want to avail themselves of higher education—although it can make it easier for more to afford it. It cannot dictate the elimination of obsolete educational practices and programs. It cannot compel the states to adopt new patterns of financial support for higher education—although it can tempt them. It cannot arrogate to itself the responsibility for institutional triage, choosing to revive some campuses while leaving others to their fate.

Still, myriad federal programs and practices will influence the fate of individual colleges and universities, and of higher education as a whole. In the following chapters the implications of that involvement are examined, beginning with the dominant form of federal support for higher education: aid to students.

68. For a general background discussion of the manpower problem, see Bruce L. R. Smith and Joseph J. Karlesky, *The State of Academic Science: The Universities in the Nation's Research Effort* (Change Magazine Press, 1977), pp. 179–89.

Chapter Three

College Prices
and the Student Aid Muddle

THE LARGE and growing federal involvement in financial assistance to college and university students bespeaks an increasing national interest in the ability of individuals to obtain the benefits of higher education for themselves and their society (see table 1-2). A wide array of specific goals underlies the dozens of federal programs that provide aid to individual students, but all of them are also addressed to one common condition: higher education is expensive, and if people wishing to avail themselves of it had to pay the full costs, many would not be able to attend college at all.

Although actual costs vary among institutions and among students, by almost any measure equipping a person with a college education is an expensive undertaking: it is labor intensive, the key workers are highly skilled and generally well-paid professionals, and it is a slow process that usually takes four years or more, during which time the student must also subsist.

Colleges and universities spent an average of $3,040 to teach each student in 1977–78;[1] a student's noninstructional expenses (for room, board, transportation, books, and the like) averaged an additional $1,900 to $2,300 (see table 3-1). Thus the basic "social costs" of higher education come to about $5,000 per student a year, or $20,000 in the course of a conventional bachelor's degree—without taking into account such institutional expenses as research and community service, or such personal sacrifices as the income a person forgoes when he or she attends college rather than holds a job.

The obvious question is who should pay these costs, but it is not one

1. The figure comes from the staff at the National Center for Education Statistics.

45

Table 3-1. *Average Annual Costs at Public and Private Institutions, 1977–78*[a]

Dollars

Type of institution and student	Tuition and fees	Room and board	Books and supplies	Transportation	Personal and miscellaneous	Total
Public						
Two-year, commuter	389	864	190	411	460	2,314
Four-year, commuter	621	780	201	404	480	2,486
Four-year, resident[b]	621	1,383	201	204	497	2,906
Private						
Two-year, resident[b]	1,812	1,346	204	232	421	4,015
Four-year, commuter	2,476	842	215	348	450	4,331
Four-year, resident[b]	2,476	1,430	215	244	446	4,811

Source: Elizabeth W. Suchar, Stephen H. Ivens, and Edmund C. Jacobson, *Student Expenses at Postsecondary Institutions 1977–78* (College Entrance Examination Board, 1977), pp. v–vii.

a. Costs shown are means reported by institutions in each classification for resident or commuter students as indicated. They are not weighted by size of institution.

b. Resident refers to a student residing in housing provided by the institution. Living in private off-campus housing increases total costs by $100 to $300.

for which American society has devised any clear or consistent answer. Two opposing doctrines have vied for acceptance: one holds that higher education is like elementary and secondary schooling, a public good whose benefits accrue to the entire nation and whose costs should therefore be written into the social contract and financed by the public sector through taxation; the other asserts that because higher education enhances the lives of those receiving it, they should pay for it themselves. The crazy-quilt pattern of financing higher education today reflects the inability to agree on either doctrine and the resultant compromises that have been made. Postsecondary schooling, it appears, is regarded as both a public good and a private investment, and is paid for accordingly.

Almost never is the student or his family asked to meet the entire cost of his education, for nearly every college and university benefits from various institutional subsidies that underwrite these expenses; in other words, the "posted price" of a college is discounted well below the true cost of attendance. John Harvard started one tradition with a bequest to the infant college that would take his name; private philanthropy now contributes more than $2 billion a year to higher education. A second tradition also began in seventeenth-century Massachusetts, when the general court granted Harvard the income generated by the Charlestown ferry. It has been thought appropriate ever since for the populace at large, acting through one or another level of government, to channel "public" monies into colleges and universities.

Although the federal government supplies billions of dollars directly to colleges and universities, almost never does it do so for the purpose of subsidizing the instruction of ordinary students or assisting the institution to offer a lower posted price to all its applicants. Insofar as public funds are involved, that task has fallen primarily to the states. The chief purpose of state support is to maintain educational institutions in such a way that they can make their benefits available to students at a uniformly low price. As far as they have gone, the states have succeeded admirably in this objective, not only in helping millions of people acquire college degrees who could not have paid the full costs, but also in making higher education a widely available "public" good, thus encouraging postsecondary study by millions more who could, but perhaps would not, pay a higher price for it.

The Price of College

State subventions give rise to several problems. Even at their most generous, that is, when they fully underwrite the instructional costs of a college and allow it to provide free tuition, they do not cover all the costs a person contemplating higher education must consider, such as room and board, books, and transportation.[2] In requiring some outlay of funds by the student, they do not bring college within the financial grasp of all who might wish to partake of it. Table 3-1 shows how much

2. In practice, very few state colleges or universities provide free tuition. With the recent imposition of tuition charges at the City University of New York, the community colleges of California remain among the few "free" institutions, and in the aftermath of the state referendum known as Proposition 13 it is unclear how long they can retain that distinction. Moreover, nearly all institutions impose student fees of various kinds, often amounting to hundreds of dollars a year. Since many state campuses are allowed to keep these fees, while being obliged to turn over tuition payments to the state treasury, it is not surprising that they would rather increase fees than tuitions, although, from the student's standpoint, the distinction is inconsequential.

Table 3-2. *Distribution of Current Fund Income of Private and Public Institutions of Higher Education, by Source, Fiscal Year 1976*

Source	Private institutions		Public institutions	
	Millions of dollars	As percent of total	Millions of dollars	As percent of total
Tuition and fees	4,749	36.7	3,488	12.9
Federal government[a]	2,483	19.2	4,029	14.9
State governments	298	2.3	12,097	44.8
Local governments	117	0.9	1,505	5.6
Private gifts	1,301	10.1	618	2.3
Endowment earnings	591	4.6	97	0.4
Sales and services of educational activities, and hospitals	1,343	10.4	1,797	6.6
Auxiliary enterprises	1,662	12.8	2,895	10.7
Other	392	3.0	497	1.8
Total	12,936	100.0	27,023	100.0

Source: National Center for Education Statistics, *Financial Statistics of Institutions of Higher Education, Fiscal Year 1976* (GPO, 1978), pp. 4–5.
a. Includes federally funded research and development centers.

the several different types of colleges cost the unaided student in 1977–78; the *least* expensive of them amounted to more than $2,300 a year.[3]

As a result of conscious policy decisions, state subsidies are meted out with exceptional unevenness among colleges and universities (see table 3-2). And because the state subsidies are so large, their unevenness translates into sizable differences in the unsubsidized portions of college budgets and thus into marked disparities in the prices the institutions must charge their students. The best known of these disparities is the celebrated "tuition gap" between private and public colleges, the recent history of which is shown in table 3-3, where figures are given in both current and constant (1967) dollars. Although the gap has figured in college costs ever since a clear distinction between public and private began to emerge in the nineteenth century, it has widened considerably in the past decade and a half.

3. These are unweighted average figures. Of course, some colleges and universities are much more expensive than others; tuition and fees, for example, can vary from less than $100 to upward of $5,000 a year. It should be noted, too, that the College Scholarship Service, which compiles these figures, includes institutional estimates of room, board, transportation, and other costs for commuter students, items that an individual family may pay without realizing they are part of the cost of attendance for a student living at home.

Table 3-3. *Average Tuition and Fees at Public and Private Institutions of Higher Education, and Tuition Gap, in Current and Constant Dollars, Selected Academic Years, 1929–30 to 1976–77*

	Current dollars			Constant (1967) dollars		
	Average tuition and fees[a]			Average tuition and fees[a]		
Year	Public institutions	Private institutions	Tuition gap	Public institutions	Private institutions	Tuition gap
1929–30	63	226	163	123	441	318
1933–34	65	227	162	167	585	418
1939–40	64	147	83	154	353	199
1941–42	78	251	173	177	569	392
1945–46	91	273	182	169	506	337
1949–50	177	416	239	248	583	335
1953–54	139	464	325	174	579	405
1957–58	162	584	422	192	693	501
1961–62	194	796	602	217	888	671
1965–66	241	1,045	804	255	1,106	851
1966–67	254	1,078	824	261	1,109	848
1967–68	279	1,152	873	279	1,152	873
1969–70	334	1,348	1,014	304	1,228	924
1971–72	385	1,591	1,206	317	1,312	995
1972–73	407	1,705	1,298	325	1,361	1,036
1973–74	428	1,815	1,387	322	1,364	1,042
1974–75	460	1,995	1,535	311	1,351	1,040
1975–76	473	2,146	1,673	293	1,331	1,038
1976–77	526	2,365	1,839	309	1,387	1,078

Sources: Data for 1929–68, June A. O'Neill, *Sources of Funds to Colleges and Universities* (Carnegie Foundation for the Advancement of Teaching, 1973), p. 44; later data from yearly reports in NCES, *Financial Statistics of Institutions of Higher Education: Current Funds Revenues and Expenditures* (GPO, 1970–77); and NCES, *Fall Enrollment in Higher Education* (GPO, 1971–77).

a. Because of differences in calculating enrollments, a deflator of 1.13 was applied to the 1969–70 series to link it to the earlier series. This deflator brings both methods of calculating 1967–68 data into agreement.

Prices also vary within the public sector. Public campuses in different states levy unequal charges as a result of dissimilar state-funding formulas. The public colleges and universities of California, for example, charged (home-state) students tuition and fees averaging just $133 in 1973–74, whereas those of Pennsylvania charged $832 and those of Vermont, $1,000. Actual expenditure differences account for some of this range, but the crucial factor is the lavishness of the public subsidy, that is, the portion of education costs borne by the state rather than by the student. This varies a good deal from one jurisdiction to the next. Tuition charges in California are equivalent to just 8 percent of state (and local) expenditure per student; in Pennsylvania they are equivalent to 55 percent, and in Vermont to 92.5 percent.[4]

Because states do not ordinarily subsidize the education of people from other states as generously as that of their own residents, most public colleges and universities must impose surcharges on out-of-state students. These requirements have been the subject of much litigation. Colleges and states have developed elaborate procedures for judging student residency, and a determined student today can usually qualify for home-state rates after one year of paying the higher tuitions. Nevertheless, these surcharges touch many people—463,000 students in four-year public colleges and universities were "nonresidents" in 1971—and they are not trivial. The College Scholarship Service estimated that in 1977–78 they would average $930 at four-year public institutions, enough to raise the total tuition to $1,551, about midway between the private sector and home-state public sector averages.[5]

Collegiate price differences are not entirely the result of state financing patterns. The private sector gets some subsidies—principally gifts—in greater measure than the public sector, and private tuitions are thus lower than they would otherwise be. Also, private sector costs (per student) are generally somewhat greater than public sector costs; there is an "expenditure gap" alongside the tuition gap. Thus even if all institutions set out to raise the same portion of their income from students, actual tuition rates would still differ. Finally, though most colleges and universities engage in "price discounting"—allowing some students to pay less than the posted price—not all have an equal desire or capacity to do so. Often the burden is simply transferred from needy students to those better able to pay, by means of tuitions pegged at a higher level than they would have to be if all students actually paid the same amount.

In one sense, these price differences attest to the heterogeneity that a decentralized higher education system has produced in the United States. Just as colleges and universities vary in their pedagogical style, curricular offerings, and expenditures per student, so do they range widely in the

4. Carnegie Foundation for the Advancement of Teaching, *The States and Higher Education: Supplement* (CFAT, 1976), figs. A-18 and A-19.

5. Elizabeth W. Suchar, Stephen H. Ivens, and Edmund C. Jacobson, *Student Expenses at Postsecondary Institutions 1977–78* (College Entrance Examination Board, 1977), p. v. For additional insight into the "out-of-state tuition" issue, see Robert F. Carbone, *Alternative Tuition Systems* (Iowa City: American College Testing Program, 1974), and Carbone, "Voting Rights and the Nonresident Student" (National Association of State Universities and Land-Grant Colleges, n.d.; processed).

tuitions they charge. This is a form of diversity, too, and in its way it enhances the choices available to people contemplating college attendance, though perhaps not in ways many of them like.

But because the price differences result at least as much from an uncoordinated assortment of public and private subsidies as from true differences in the cost (and quality) of the educational products being offered, they make for a warped marketplace in which two institutions offering much the same education end up charging widely differing prices for it. This condition does not enhance equality of opportunity, nor does it foster educationally motivated choices on the part of the college-bound student, and in a time of declining enrollments it compounds the difficulties faced by some colleges and universities. For although many factors enter into the selection of colleges by students (and of students by colleges), the cost of attendance is not inconsequential.[6]

Though the federal government is not responsible for the uneven institutional subsidies that lead to variegated college prices, and though it has generally refrained from attempts to influence college tuitions per se, its heavy investment in student aid has entangled it with the consequences of these subsidies and their effects on prices. For Washington— and for state and private suppliers of student aid as well—the task of helping students pay for college is vastly complicated by the diversity of college and university tuitions, and by the conflicting values that bedevil efforts to make clear policy decisions.

Whom to Help, and How Much to Help Them?

Not all student aid is related to financial need. A "scholarship" once meant an award of funds in recognition of superior academic promise. Based on merit, scholarships sought to ensure that their recipients could get a good education without having to work their way through college. Thus the celebrated New York State Regents Scholarships, the National Merit Scholarships, and others like them have been both a financial boon and a prize for talent and accomplishment.

6. For a discussion of the effects of "price and nonprice" variables on student choices among colleges—and of the limits of our understanding of those effects— see Michael S. McPherson, "The Demand for Higher Education," in David W. Breneman and Chester E. Finn, Jr., eds., *Public Policy and Private Higher Education* (Brookings Institution, 1978).

A number of merit scholarships of various kinds endure, some still underwritten by public funds,[7] but a second important form of student aid overshadows them: assistance to particular categories of people deemed worthy of a subsidy for essentially noneducational reasons. The best known example is the immense federal program of benefits for military veterans, but smaller schemes of this sort abound. Faculty children often qualify for educational subsidies; the children of policemen may, too. Handicapped people receive certain benefits, as do American Indians and Cuban refugees. At the campus level, there are endowed fellowships whose income may be granted only to the residents of particular towns, the descendants of families with specific names, the graduates of certain secondary schools, or the progeny of alumni of designated years.

A third type of student subsidy aims to attract people to particular careers or fields of study. Graduates who teach in urban slums or who practice medicine in rural areas may get their loans forgiven. Certain fellowships are confined to future scientists, others to humanists. Graduate students in public administration get one type of subsidy; army officers willing to study accounting or engineering get another. Nascent dental technicians may obtain a federal grant-in-aid, prison guards willing to upgrade their skills may qualify for state assistance, and budding classicists may receive fellowships from century-old funds held by a single university department.

The fourth major kind of student subsidy—for the past decade perhaps the best known—is aid for people whose qualifying characteristic is poverty, that is, those considered unable to pay for college without assistance. Such programs are sponsored by the universities themselves, by state and federal governments, and by sundry private organizations. Sometimes the subsidies become available only to a low-income person able to satisfy a second, narrower criterion: one who seeks to study medicine, one who enrolls at a traditionally black college, one who plans to teach mathematics, or whatever. Other schemes require simply proof of poverty, acceptance by some college or university, and, perhaps, residency in a particular jurisdiction.

Whatever its rationale, the subsidy itself may take many forms: a straightforward cash grant to the student; a waiver or remission of tui-

7. Recent attempts to introduce meritocratic factors into the determination of eligibility for federal student aid programs at the undergraduate level have encountered sharp opposition from civil rights groups and student groups and from some college and university spokesmen as well. See testimony and discussion in *The Student Financial Aid Act of 1975*, Hearings before the House Education and Labor Committee, 94:1 (GPO, 1975), especially pp. 171–74, 337–53, 377–93, 414–29.

tion by the college; a loan with interest payments held below the "market rate"; a job with wages paid from aid funds; a teaching fellowship or research assistantship that demands work but also helps cover the recipient's own educational costs; a "matching payment" by a private employer. What unites these student subsidies, and distinguishes them from institutional subsidies, is that their purpose is not to reduce the posted price a college charges, but rather to assist individual students who meet the requisite criteria to pay that price.

In designing programs to meet these objectives, providers of student aid face vexing policy choices: how broadly to extend the categories of persons eligible for assistance; how much to expect students (and their families) at various income levels to pay for their college educations; whether to equip those receiving aid with the minimum resource level that would allow them to attend the lowest-priced institutions, or to provide larger sums in order to give them wider choice among colleges and universities; whether to provide the subsidy directly to the student himself, so that he can shop among institutions, or to channel it through the colleges so that they can shop for students.

For the federal government, several other issues arise from the complex interaction of national and state policies. Should Washington continue to take the college pricing structure as a given and simply help students deal with it, or should it try to alter the institutional subsidy patterns that lead to such erratic prices, knowing that to do so entails changing established state practices? Should aid programs ignore state borders and act as if the student marketplace were truly national, or should they be tailored to the dimensions of each jurisdiction's higher education system?

Because student assistance is also a form of income redistribution, those giving it must attend to larger issues of social policy. Whose income is to be redirected to whom, and in what amounts?[8] Is higher education sufficiently important to justify subsidies to people in middle-income brackets, when less prosperous people who do not attend college get no such subsidies—and may, indeed, help pay for them with their taxes? Should there be an obligation attached to the recipient of student aid to do something in return, whether it be national service of some sort or the repayment of the funds supplied him, or should student assistance be an unencumbered gift?

8. Not the least among many perplexing aspects of this question is the issue of intergenerational income transfers caused by programs that generally take revenues from the "parents' generation" and bestow them upon the children.

Need and Aid

To understand student aid, one must reckon with the concept of "need." Most people can muster at least part of the cost of their education. In the argot of the student aid profession, "need" is the amount that remains to be paid when the sum that the student and his family can contribute is subtracted from his total cost of attendance. But this basically simple idea has become enormously complex, since those dispensing the aid, whether government officials or college scholarship officers, naturally want a uniform and equitable basis for assessing the need of different students. It will not do simply to ask the individual or his parents how much they are prepared to pay.

Merit schemes, categorical payments, and manpower-training incentives of course ignore these calculations and allot their funds according to altogether different criteria. But aid plans intended to compensate for poverty generally employ a "means test" that estimates the contribution a family can reasonably be expected to make toward the higher education of one of its members. Accordingly, a number of "need analysis" systems have been devised, and the financial aid officer's task is to apply one of them to the circumstances of the student and then to assemble an assistance package tailored to his or her actual situation.

The heart of a need analysis system is a set of assumptions about household incomes and budgets. Some of these assumptions relate to objective differences among families, such as the number of dependents they must support. Others stem from subjective judgments about personal standards of living and spending priorities. All can be and are modified from time to time by those responsible for the system.[9]

Means tests are familiar features of American social policy, and it is not unusual for them to consider individual circumstances as well as such absolute norms as the "poverty line." (The federal poverty line itself varies with family size, farm or nonfarm residence, and so on.) Less characteristic of most means-tested programs, but central to student aid need analysis, is reliance on a second independent variable: the cost of education at a particular institution. This is readily visualized by analogy to the food stamp program, which, if it operated the same way,

9. Regardless of the assumptions, the "expected family contributions" that result may have little resemblance to what families are willing to spend. For evidence of a sizable discrepancy here, see James E. Nelson, William D. Van Dusen, and Edmund C. Jacobson, "The Willingness of Parents to Contribute to Postsecondary Educational Expenses" (CEEB, March 1978; processed).

Table 3-4. *Estimated Average Costs of Attendance at Public and Private Colleges, and Family Income Needed to Pay Those Costs, by CSS Need Analysis, 1977–78*

Dollars

Type of college and student	Cost	Gross income needed by a family (two children)
Low-cost community, commuter	1,200	16,900
Average public two-year, commuter	2,300	21,700
Average public four-year, commuter	2,500	22,200
Average public four-year, resident[a]	2,900	23,700
Average private two-year, resident[a]	4,000	27,400
Average private, four-year, commuter	4,300	28,400
Average private four-year, resident[a]	4,800	30,200
High-cost private, resident[a]	6,000	34,900

Source: College Scholarship Service, *CSS Need Analysis: Theory and Computation Procedures for the 1977–78 PCS and FAF* (CEEB, 1976), table F.
a. Resident refers to a student living in housing provided by the institution.

would calculate a family's subsidy by relating its income to its dinner table preferences and the cost of groceries in its vicinity. A household favoring steak would have greater "need" than an otherwise identical family that is content with macaroni; or two families that want meat loaf would qualify for differential subsidies because one of them must pay more for ground beef than the other.

Thus a person's need for student aid varies with his choice of college as, of course, does the amount of income that his family must earn before it is expected to pay for college without help.[10] According to the College Scholarship Service, one of the foremost sources of need analysis in the United States, not until income exceeds $30,000 should a family of four be expected to pay the $4,800 a year that represents the average cost of attendance at a four-year private college, whereas the same size family would be expected to pay the entire average cost of a community college when its income neared $22,000.

Table 3-4 forges a crude link between gross family income and aver-

10. I refer frequently to "family contribution" and "family income," since traditional need analysis assumes that a student is his parents' dependent and that their income—and other circumstances—forms the proper basis for calculating his need. The increasing number of "emancipated" nineteen-year-olds and independent older students has elicited additional assumptions and tables. A student, earning far less than his parents, can usually increase his need and probable aid by going to the trouble of achieving "independent" status.

Table 3-5. *Percentage Distribution of Undergraduate Students, Aged Eighteen to Twenty-Four, by Type of Institution and Family Income,[a] October 1976*

Category	Number of students (in thousands)	Family income (dollars)						
		Under 5,000	5,000– 9,999	10,000– 14,999	15,000– 19,999	20,000– 24,999	25,000 and over	Not reported
All institutions	5,266	6	11	17	17	16	25	9
Public	4,075	7	11	17	17	16	23	8
Private	1,191	2	9	15	16	15	31	12
Two-year[b]	1,279	7	15	19	18	15	18	9
Four-year[b]	3,838	6	9	16	17	16	28	9
Public	2,780	7	9	16	17	17	26	7
Private	1,058	2	9	15	16	15	32	12

Source: U.S. Bureau of the Census, *Current Population Reports*, Series P-20, No. 319 (GPO, 1978), p. 62. Percentages are rounded.

a. Omits another 554,000 undergraduate students between the ages of eighteen and twenty-four who are married and live with their spouses, that is, who may be presumed to be independent of their parents.

b. Figures are slightly low because not all students reported whether they attended two-year or four-year institutions.

age college costs, using the assumptions built into the CSS need analysis system for 1977–78. In any individual case, of course, more variables are considered. And need analysis systems making different assumptions would show different family contributions at the various income levels. But the table serves to illustrate the "steak and macaroni" problem inherent in any means test that tries to reconcile personal resources with variable costs.

The fact remains, however, that if ability to pay is judged by the norms of table 3-4, many students are in college today whose families are seemingly unable to pay for it. In 1976–77, for example, 51 percent of (dependent undergraduate) students between the ages of eighteen and twenty-four came from families earning less than $20,000 a year (see table 3-5).

One plausible explanation is that existing student aid programs are having their intended effect, and in part this is surely the case. But very little is known about how much price–aid–net cost calculations influence a person's choice of a college—or how many people they deter from going to college at all. The available studies take two forms: polls that ask students why they picked the colleges they did, and statistical analyses employing regression techniques to gauge the weight of one factor—price—in decisions involving many factors. Neither is entirely satisfactory, particularly if one is trying to anticipate the effects on student behavior of prospective changes in aid programs.[11] Still, it is interesting to inspect the replies of freshmen asked in 1975 to indicate which reasons were "very important" to them in selecting their college. The most common response, marked by 51 percent of the students, was: "will help to get a better job." Second, marked by 47 percent (students could check more than one item) was: "has a good academic reputation." Students considered price-related factors much less important: "low tuition" was in fourth place (25 percent) and "financial

11. These studies are reviewed in McPherson, "Demand for Higher Education." See also National Commission on the Financing of Postsecondary Education, *Financing Postsecondary Education in the United States* (GPO, 1973); Sloan Study Consortium, *Paying for College* (Hanover, N.H.: University Press of New England, 1974); Illinois State Scholarship Commission, "A Longitudinal Study of Illinois State Scholarship Commission Monetary Award Recipients 1967–1974" (June 1975; processed); Daryl Carlson, "Student Price Response Coefficients for Grants, Loans, Work-Study Aid, and Tuition Changes: An Analysis of Student Surveys" (November 1974; processed).

assistance" in fifth (17 percent).[12] But one cannot be certain that the respondents were candid, and in any case such polls say nothing about the possible deterrent effect of prices on the millions of their high school classmates who for some reason did not go on to college. Table 3-5 shows that regardless of student aid programs, people from low-income families are less likely to matriculate than are those from more prosperous ones. People from families earning less than $10,000 constituted 30 percent of the population in 1976, but only 17 percent of college undergraduates; people from families earning more than $25,000 accounted for 25 percent of the undergraduates and just 18 percent of the population.[13]

The people from low-income families who do enroll are somehow managing to bridge the gap between their costs of attendance and the resources supposedly available to them. In 1975–76 the College Entrance Examination Board estimated that gap at $2 billion, when from the aggregate costs of attendance for full-time students were subtracted parental contributions and financial aid from all known sources.[14] One has to assume that these students mustered resources—larger family contributions, jobs, helpful relatives, savings, loans, and so on—in excess of what the compilers of the need analysis tables said they should be expected to find.

Income levels also continue to be associated, though loosely, with the type of college attended. As shown in table 3-5, private institutions have a generally wealthier student body than do public ones, four-year colleges have a concentration of students from families earning more than $25,000, and two-year schools—overwhelmingly community colleges—have the most low- and moderate-income students. Presumably the different costs of attendance at these various institutions account for part of the variation in student income levels, and presumably the present aid schemes do not entirely compensate for those cost differences.

12. Alexander W. Astin, Margo R. King, and Gerald T. Richardson, *The American Freshman: National Norms for Fall 1975* (Cooperative Institutional Research Program, American Council on Education and University of California at Los Angeles, 1975), p. 42.

13. Table 3-5 and *Statistical Abstract of the United States, 1977* (GPO, 1977), p. 440.

14. "Estimating the Unknown: Unmet Financial Needs of 1975–76 College Students" (CEEB, March 1975; processed).

The Federal Role in Student Aid

In federal student aid programs, the principle of parsimony clashes with the ideal of choice. If government does not endeavor to provide steak to its food stamp recipients, or a lavish standard of living for its social security beneficiaries, why should it assist a needy eighteen-year-old to enroll at Harvard or Sarah Lawrence, particularly when quite satisfactory educational institutions are available at markedly lower prices?

But in American society, need-based student aid serves a dual purpose. It brings college within reach of people who might not otherwise be able—or willing—to enroll, and it also brings students to colleges that might not otherwise have enough students, at least not enough of the sort they favor. This second purpose should not be ignored, for, though student aid is most often discussed in the high-minded language of equal educational opportunity, from the viewpoint of institutions whose well-being depends on having enough students it plays a more utilitarian role, not very different from the discounts, rebates, and bargain days encountered in the commercial world.

Aiding students is not a recent development. Princeton cut its tuition (and its faculty salaries!) in 1827 in order, suggested the historian Frederick Rudolph, "to attract students and dispel its reputation as a rich man's college." President Francis Wayland of Brown University complained in 1842 that "we cannot induce men to pursue a collegiate course unless we offer it vastly below its cost, if we do not give it away altogether." Throughout the nineteenth century, Rudolph observed, the "endless multiplication of colleges without regard to the nature of the collegiate market" produced a situation in which institutions "found themselves bidding even more highly for students."[15] Thus, although it is frequently argued that student aid is properly society's task, in that its primary purpose is to help the needy go to college, in reality such discounts have long been a customary marketing strategy of colleges looking for students. The perplexing public policy question is how heavily should the society tax itself on behalf of this second objective in a time when many colleges anticipate difficulty in keeping their classrooms full.

15. Frederick Rudolph, *The American College and University* (Vintage Books, 1962), pp. 198–99.

The federal government's involvement with student aid began during World War I, when it began to pay for the training of federal dependents—both military personnel and disabled veterans—in civilian institutions. It grew enormously when Congress passed the Servicemen's Readjustment Act of 1944, authorizing educational benefits for millions of World War II veterans.

As new research agencies sprang up—the National Cancer Institute in 1937, the Atomic Energy Commission in 1946, the National Science Foundation in 1950, and many others—they provided training grants and fellowships, primarily at the graduate level, to foster the production of skilled manpower in the requisite specialties. The National Defense Education Act of 1958 included within its ten provisions another program of graduate fellowships and—an important precedent—the beginning of assistance (long term, low-interest loans) for needy undergraduate students.[16]

The idea that poverty or need justifies federal help for college students was strengthened in the early 1960s, when the civil rights movement, the war on poverty, and the long-standing quest for federal aid to higher education came together in a string of new programs, notably the college work-study program (1964), educational opportunity grants (1965), and a second set of partly subsidized guaranteed loans (1965). In addition, the Social Security Amendments of 1965 extended benefits to student dependents (and survivors) of workers covered by social security.

By the mid–1960s the lineaments of federal student assistance were reasonably clear. Three broad categories of people could look to Washington for help: the poor, who could not otherwise afford to matriculate; those pursuing particular disciplines and professions that the government wanted to emphasize or expand; and federal "dependents" of several types, ranging from army veterans to American Indians and the children of social security recipients.

By the early 1970s the federal government's role in higher education was undergoing intense scrutiny. The debate leading up to the Education Amendments of 1972 indicated that both interest groups and policymakers wanted a clearer answer to a fundamental question of strategy:

16. This book does not attempt to deal separately with the complex issues of graduate student support. For a discussion of these issues, see National Board on Graduate Education, *Federal Policy Alternatives Toward Graduate Education* (National Academy of Sciences, 1974).

should the federal government henceforth concentrate its higher education efforts on programs that assisted institutions or on those that provided aid primarily to students?

Congress did not explicitly deny federal funds to the colleges and universities, but the landmark 1972 legislation strongly favored the students, and was accurately regarded as a defeat for those whose prime objective was institutional aid. Thereafter the Nixon administration clung to what became known as the "student aid strategy" and the Ford administration followed suit, observing in its 1977 budget message that "the Administration's program for higher education will place major emphasis on providing assistance directly to students rather than to educational institutions." Although Congress has been less eager to embrace the notion of a "higher education marketplace," the House Education and Labor Committee noted in 1976 that "there is a consensus today that the proper Federal concern is for the student."[17]

The political appeal of student aid is straightforward. Several million people attend college and graduate school each year with federal aid.[18] Such numbers are not inconsequential in the eyes of elected officials, particularly now that eighteen-year-olds are enfranchised. And, channeling funds to higher education by way of the students has other advantages: It skirts the church-state issue, since it does not subsidize sectarian institutions per se.[19] While respecting the First Amendment, it also honors the Tenth, for in aiding students Washington is not intruding into the state domain of institutional maintenance, nor is student assistance as directly menacing to collegiate autonomy. Differences among states and regions can also be disregarded, since eligible students are defined on a national basis. Finally, student aid avoids the need for

17. *The United States Budget in Brief, Fiscal Year 1977* (GPO, 1976), p. 37; *Higher Education Amendments of 1976*, H. Rept. 94-1086, 94:2 (GPO, 1976), p. 4.

18. See, for example, *Special Analyses, Budget of the United States Government, Fiscal Year 1979*, p. 223. Because many students receive aid from more than one program, it is not possible to obtain an accurate unduplicated count.

19. A bit of history is illuminating. What emerged from Congress in 1958 as the graduate fellowship program of the National Defense Education Act was originally intended by the Eisenhower administration to supply grants-in-aid to universities for purposes of expanding their graduate schools. Since some institutions that would qualify were church-related, Babbidge and Rosenzweig explained, "it raised the controversy in unavoidable terms," and therefore never reached the House or Senate floor. Instead it was transformed in committee and "emerged as a program of fellowship aid to individual students." Homer D. Babbidge, Jr., and Robert M. Rosenzweig, *The Federal Interest in Higher Education* (McGraw-Hill, 1962), pp. 143–44.

government officials to pick and choose among universities, with all the attendant political pressures and problems of evenhandedness.

Such benefits carry their costs. The foremost of these are the insensitivity of student aid programs to the varied needs and requirements of colleges and universities, particularly to their differing tuition levels, and the special difficulty of tailoring student aid policies so as to benefit institutions that lack state subsidies and therefore charge high prices.

The size of a student's subsidy depends on many factors of which the colleges' posted charges are not the most important, if indeed they figure at all. In most federal assistance programs, the sums going to individual recipients are sharply constrained by law, so that a high-priced (typically private) college collects little more per aided student than a public community college and risks losing the student altogether because of the gap between what it charges and what the program supplies.

It was not always so. The World War II GI bill, the first important expression of federal assistance to college and university students, split a veteran's education benefits in two parts: a fixed stipend to cover his living expenses and incidentals, and a separate payment (up to $500 a year) that went directly to the college to meet its tuition charges. Since tuitions in 1945–46 averaged just $91 a year in (four-year) public institutions and $273 in private ones (see table 3-3), the program provided the wherewithal for a student to choose between the public and private sectors without regard to their price difference. Thus it was common in the late forties to find veterans enrolled in private institutions in the same proportions as in nearby public colleges. Rivlin estimated that "at the peak of the World War II program, slightly more than half of the total veterans' payments went to private institutions, which obtained 29 percent of their educational and general income from this source, as contrasted with 20 percent for all public institutions."[20]

Unfortunately the separate tuition payment provision proved unworkable, as colleges raised their charges to exploit it and the Veterans Administration found itself having to negotiate rates and fees with hundreds of institutions. A survey by the General Accounting Office disclosed that "questionable practices existed at approximately 65 percent of the institutions and establishments examined." Among the principal offenders were thousands of profitmaking proprietary schools that sprang into existence, some of which were patronized solely by veterans,

20. Alice M. Rivlin, *The Role of the Federal Government in Financing Higher Education* (Brookings Institution, 1961), p. 69.

and too many of which were found to be falsifying their records, over-stating their charges, and generally abusing the federal program.[21]

As this situation grew into a major scandal, Congressman Olin E. Teague's special investigating committee insisted that the Korean War version of the GI bill curb these unsavory practices. The most important reform was the decision to pay all benefits directly to the veteran in the form of a fixed stipend that he would use to meet both his living expenses and the cost of education at the institution of his choice.

The new arrangement created an obvious incentive for the veteran to search out a low-priced college, since he could literally pocket the difference. Moreover, the benefit levels—$1,000 to $1,200 a year—were not high enough to trivialize the several hundred dollar public-private tuition gap that had emerged by the mid-fifties. Not surprisingly, by 1958 some 62 percent of GI bill beneficiaries were enrolled in public institutions.[22]

Some private colleges and universities fought the 1952 reforms, warning that the Teague proposals would not only "remove from the veteran freedom of choice of institutions as enjoyed under the current GI bill, but will also tend, through economic compulsion, to discriminate against the Korean GI veteran who chooses to attend a privately controlled institution of higher learning." With admirable prescience, their spokesmen anticipated that "if the Teague bill is passed, without amendment, it may at a later date become the pattern for Federal scholarships."[23]

Some public institutions also opposed the bill on grounds that complemented the fears of the private colleges. Testifying on behalf of the City and State universities of New York, Dean John J. Meng of Hunter College observed that the proposed reforms would bring about an "influx of veterans," all seeking to stretch their GI benefits by availing themselves of the massive educational subsidies that the state governments provided to matriculants at public colleges and universities. Faced

21. *Veterans' Readjustment Assistance Act of 1952*, Hearings before the Senate Labor and Public Welfare Committee, 82:2 (GPO, 1952), pp. 131–32. See also *Report of the House Select Committee to Investigate Educational and Training Programs under the G.I. Bill*, H. Rept. 81-3253, 81:2 (GPO, 1951).

22. *Final Report on Educational Assistance to Veterans: A Comparative Study of Three G.I. Bills*, submitted to the Senate Veterans' Affairs Committee by the Educational Testing Service, 93:1 (GPO, 1973), p. 36. Total enrollments had also shifted toward the public sector, but not as dramatically. In 1957–58 private colleges and universities still enrolled 42 percent of the total student population.

23. *Veterans' Readjustment Assistance Act of 1952*, Hearings, pp. 171–73.

with such an onslaught, Meng warned, "we would be forced to curtail our services for nonveteran students."[24]

But Congressman Teague was able to demonstrate that his reforms had the support of the principal college associations (including the umbrella American Council on Education), of the comptroller general, and of Commissioner of Education Earl J. McGrath, who stated that "the vast majority of administrative officers in colleges and universities, even in the private institutions, consider the Teague bill good legislation."[25]

The bill became law, and with it the principle that federal payments meant for student aid should go to students, not to institutions. Fairness and economy dictated that each individual get the same amount, except where his personal circumstances warranted otherwise—but his preference for a higher-priced college did not qualify as such a circumstance. Payments to colleges had become associated with waste and profiteering. Payments to students were something else; up to a point individuals could be allowed to squander the government's money so long as they did so through personal decisions for which public officials were not answerable. To minimize that waste and to moderate the total federal cost, the stipend was fixed at a level that would permit the veteran to attend *some* college, not to have the luxury of indulging his educational preference at any institution, however expensive, that appealed to him.

Although the student aid programs enacted in 1958 and in the mid–1960s allowed the costs of attending a particular school again to figure in the amount of a student's federal subsidy, they also introduced a means test that the GI bill never had: a student seeking aid under these new programs had to be needy. Thus Washington stumbled into need analysis, for there had to be a way of comparing a student's personal resources with the cost of attending his chosen college in order to determine the amount of aid he required.

This meant hundreds of thousands, eventually millions, of separate calculations and payments, and a sensitivity to individual circumstances that the Office of Education could not manage. So Congress chose to entrust the handling of these new student aid funds to the colleges, and the executive branch entrusted need analysis to the colleges as well.[26]

But that delegation of power left the federal government with a fresh

24. Ibid., p. 176.
25. Ibid., p. 68.
26. John F. Morse, "How We Got Here from There—A Personal Reminiscence of the Early Days," in Lois D. Rice, ed., *Student Loans: Problems and Policy Alternatives* (CEEB, 1977), pp. 3–15.

dilemma. As in consigning food stamp eligibility to the grocers, the question of what amounts to allot each distributor arose. A costly private university could use up large sums of federal money, yet aid fewer— and possibly less-impoverished—students than a community college with a different price structure and clientele. Complex and inconsistent state allocation formulas and appeal procedures were devised to ration funds among the campuses, and federal regulations set limits on who might be aided and in what amount, but the problem refused to go away. The proliferation of separate programs deepened the confusion without adding much equity. A low-income high school senior considering college had no assurance of financial help from the federal government, since his access to those funds depended on campus decisions. Surveying the array of federal programs in the last year of the Johnson administration, Rivlin and her colleagues discerned a "fundamental limitation which cannot be removed without changes in their structure: They do not dramatically and clearly indicate that the Federal Government has established a policy of removing financial barriers to college attendance. Under existing programs lower income students must first apply to specific schools in order to try to qualify for aid, yet we know that high school performance (and graduation) is affected by students' perceptions of college costs while they are still in the early grades of high school."[27]

In the early 1970s the Nixon administration and the Congress undertook to rationalize the aid structure so that a needy student could count on a minimum resource level, wherever he chose to matriculate.[28] This intention led away from reliance on campus-based aid and toward the establishment of a single, national "foundation" program, similar to the GI bill except that need rather than prior military service would determine eligibility. All students would be subject to a uniform, nationwide standard for family contributions, which would be the basis for a homogeneous system of outright federal subsidies awarded directly to individual students rather than to the colleges.

The amount of the subsidy would vary according to individual need and, as before, need would be defined as the gap between the family

27. Department of Health, Education, and Welfare, Assistant Secretary for Planning and Evaluation, *Toward a Long-Range Plan for Federal Financial Support for Higher Education* (GPO, 1969), pp. 8–9.

28. For general accounts of developments leading to the 1972 Education Amendments, see Lawrence E. Gladieux and Thomas R. Wolanin, *Congress and the Colleges* (D. C. Heath, 1976), and Chester E. Finn, Jr., *Education and the Presidency* (D. C. Heath, 1977).

contribution and the cost of attending a particular college. But a ceiling was placed on the maximum federal subsidy and on the portion of college-going costs that Washington would assume. The new basic grants program would provide an assured resource floor, but it would not entitle any student to a "free ride" to college, courtesy of Uncle Sam, nor would it alone pay for high-priced colleges. Thus the program began with two important constraints: no student could obtain a grant larger than $1,400, nor could he receive more than one-half the cost of his college education.

For the institutions, this was a mixed blessing. Since the tuition and fees alone in private colleges and universities averaged more than $1,800 the year the program was enacted, a resource level of $1,400 would not get anyone through the front door, even with the addition of self-help funds such as those a recipient might reasonably be expected to earn during the summer. Like the GI bill, the basic grants scheme was sufficient to provide access to higher education for a category within the population—in this case low-income people—that had been defined as a federal responsibility. But, again like the reformed veterans' program, Washington was not going to make the full range of postsecondary institutions equally accessible to every recipient.

To offset the threat that state colleges would thus be favored by basic grant recipients, private college partisans successfully inserted into the 1972 legislation several provisions deemed favorable to their institutions. The half-cost limitation on basic grants curbed the financial incentive for recipients to elect a public campus, since Washington would furnish no more than half their educational costs, even at a low-tuition college. More important, the old campus-based programs were also retained, even though no one was sure how comfortably they would sit atop the new foundation program. This meant that the higher-priced institutions could still use a more flexible definition of need to package federal aid in ways that served their interests. But in a large sense the Education Amendments of 1972 reaffirmed the tenets established in the GI bill reforms twenty years earlier: in the name of economy, evenhandedness, and rationality, federal subsidies designed to help students attend college were not well calibrated to the varied pricing structure of American higher education. A social policy of landmark significance had been enacted into law: the nation had at last undertaken to ensure that poverty would not bar a potential student from securing a college education. The effect of that policy on the well-being of institutions whose function was to deliver that education was a secondary consideration.

Appraising the Major Student Aid Programs

Federal student aid expenditures amounted to more than $7.3 billion in 1978 (see table 1-1); about 90 percent of these outlays were made through eight major programs. Individually and collectively, these programs benefit a vast number of students—and many institutions. But at the same time they are complex and confusing, sometimes difficult to administer, and notably uneven in their effects.

The Direct Payment Programs

By the mid–1970s the lion's share of federal student assistance was concentrated in three big programs that paid their stipends directly to individual students.[29] But that is the only salient characteristic they have in common, for they are aimed at three different groups and are run by separate agencies along distinctive lines.

BASIC EDUCATIONAL OPPORTUNITY GRANTS. The new "foundation" program got under way in school year 1973–74, and for the first two years stayed modest in size. Appropriations totaled $122 million in the first year, $475 million in the second. Through 1974–75 the participation of eligible students in the basic grants program (BEOG) was so far below expectations that sizable sums remained unspent at the end of each school year.[30] In 1975–76, however, participation greatly exceeded predictions,

29. Whereas the veterans' and the social security programs entail monthly federal checks to individual recipients, most recipients of basic educational opportunity grants never see the money, because it is sent to their colleges and deducted from their term bills or other college charges. In other cases, the individual student may receive some or all of his grant directly. But whether the institution serves as disbursing agent for the government or not, the basic grants program is properly viewed as a "direct payment" program, in that the college has no influence on a student's eligibility for aid or on the size of his grant. In this important respect the basic grants program is different from "campus-based" aid schemes.

30. There were several reasons for the surplus. The program was poorly publicized at the outset, and many students did not know that it was available, or were deterred by complex and unfamiliar procedures that their campus financial aid officers also had no experience with. Grants were relatively small in the first two years—a maximum of $450 in 1973–74 and $1,050 in 1974–75—and the program announcements were made late, in the first year just weeks before the fall semester opened. Because the program was initially confined to full-time freshmen, and added just one class a year, it was inaccessible to students already on college campuses, who are most easily reached with information and assistance. Finally, the Office of Education had no sound basis on which to forecast the percentage of eligible students that might take advantage of the program, or the new enrollment patterns that it might induce. Without that information it was also difficult to estimate the number of awards that could be provided on a fixed appropriation.

Table 3-6. *Expenditures for Student Assistance, Selected Federal Programs, Fiscal Years 1973–79*

Millions of dollars

Fiscal year	Basic grants[a]	Veterans' education benefits[b]	Social security, student benefits[b]
1973	. . .	2,016	638
1974	49	2,309	618
1975	342	3,479	840
1976	905	4,301	998
1977	1,387	2,802	1,181
1978	1,529	2,316	1,338
1979	1,936	2,009	1,505

Sources: *Special Analyses, Budget of the United States Government, Fiscal Year 1975*, pp. 113, 115; *Fiscal Year 1976*, p. 144; *Fiscal Year 1977*, pp. 165, 167; *Fiscal Year 1979*, pp. 214, 217, and 219. Data through 1977 are actual expenditures. Data for 1978 and 1979 are estimates as reported in *Special Analyses*.

a. The basic grants program is "forward funded," meaning that funds spent in one fiscal year had been appropriated in the previous year's budget.

b. The GI bill and social security benefits program both provide assistance not only to students in higher education but also to high school students and others. The figures shown here include just the higher education portion of those expenditures.

and by midyear the Office of Education, its appropriation exhausted, was back on Capitol Hill asking for supplemental funds.

Basic grants has grown rapidly. Its funding history (and that of the other two direct payment programs) is shown in table 3-6. The total cost of the program can be expected to rise sharply if it, rather than tuition tax credits or some other scheme, becomes the principle mechanism by which Congress decides to aid middle-income students. In February 1978 the Carter administration proposed such an expansion (beginning in school year 1979–80), which would increase the cost by about $1 billion a year.

The colleges may serve as disbursing agents for basic grants, but the essential relation is between the Office of Education and the individual student. Neither the state nor the institution has a role in determining the student's allotment, which is fixed by a national need analysis system promulgated by the commissioner of education. This functions as a means test that has served to cut off eligibility for most students when family income nears $15,000. Below that limit, the poorer the family, the larger the potential grant, but in no case does current law permit it to exceed $1,800.[31] The minimum grant permitted is $200. In practice, the

31. Although at first a basic grant was limited to $1,400, the 1976 amendments authorized this figure to rise to $1,800 beginning in fiscal 1978, but appropriations for that year were sufficient to permit an increase only to $1,600. The Carter admin-

average basic grant in 1976–77 was $820 and will be about $900 in 1978–79.

From the standpoint of the colleges, several features of the BEOG program are particularly significant. Because colleges do not control the allocation of aid funds to students, they have no say over which students receive assistance and which do not. On the institutions' account books, BEOG money is indistinguishable from ordinary student-supplied income. The relatively modest size of individual grants makes them markedly less beneficial to students in the higher-priced colleges and universities: the maximum stipend affords a student roughly one-half the resources he needs to attend an average-tuition public institution (in his own state), but the same amount supplies less than one-third of the funds required to attend a comparable private institution. Moreover, many students do not qualify for the maximum. A more typical grant of $800 would cover about 30 percent of average public college costs (including all the tuition) compared with roughly 18 percent of private college costs. And, of course, many students are not eligible for basic grants at all, because their income (and presumed family contribution) is too high. Table 3-5 shows that almost 60 percent of (dependent) undergraduates have family incomes in excess of $15,000. Yet as may be noted by reference to table 3-4, another widely accepted need analysis system estimates that not until family income approaches $22,000, far above the effective cutoff of the basic grants program, should the student be expected to pay the cost of attendance even at a typical community college.

Though basic grants would thus appear well tailored to the lowest-income students attending the lowest-priced colleges, the provision limiting a student's grant to half his cost of attendance has what could fairly be termed a punitive effect on precisely those students. With a grant ceiling of $1,600 (in 1978–79), this restriction affects people en-

---

istration's initial budget request for fiscal 1979 envisioned raising the figure to the full $1,800 authorized. As the program is "forward-funded," that change would not affect student recipients until school year 1979–80. Even with the increased maximum payment for low-income students, the basic grants need analysis system would still bar all but a smattering of aid to persons with family incomes above $16,000. The main element of the "middle income" addition to the program proposed in early 1978 was a significant change in the need analysis tables, designed to permit small grants to students with family incomes as high as $25,000. This change would cost a great deal but would not affect the maximum grant available to low-income students.

rolled in schools where the cost is less than $3,200 a year.[32] Consider a low-income student. If he or she is poor enough to qualify for the maximum grant, then for every dollar *less* than $3,200 that it costs to attend the college of his or her choice, the half-cost limitation will serve to reduce the grant by fifty cents. Perversely, the main impact of this provision is felt by students otherwise eligible for the largest grants, that is those with the slenderest personal resources, and it is felt by them *only* if they select a relatively low-priced college or university.

Although this feature may increase the incentive for recipients to attend higher-priced colleges, if only by making it financially less attractive for them to matriculate in low-tuition schools, the basic grants stipends themselves are too small to narrow the public-private tuition gap significantly or to bring higher-priced colleges within reach of people with no resources except their basic grants and family contributions. Even though about one-fifth of all basic grants recipients do enroll in private colleges and universities,[33] it is widely believed, as the head of the Pennsylvania state scholarship program wrote, that "the BEOG treatment of educational costs is, unintended or not, a form of federal policy that favors the institutions supported by state tax dollars to the detriment of the unsubsidized, full-charge independent institutions."[34]

THE GI BILL. Still the largest of all federal student assistance schemes, veterans' education benefits helped more than 2.8 million people pay for schooling or other training in 1975–76, including 1.9 million veterans enrolled in college-level programs.[35] Expenditures totaled $4.3 billion that year—the year of maximum outlays under the Vietnam-era program.[36]

32. The term "actual cost of attendance" in the statute authorizing basic grants is defined as "actual per-student charges for tuition, fees, room and board (or expenses related to reasonable commuting), books, and an allowance for such other expenses as the Commissioner determines by regulation to be reasonably related to attendance at the institution at which the student is in attendance." 20 USC 1070a.

33. Frank J. Atelsek and Irene L. Gomberg, *Estimated Number of Student Aid Recipients, 1976–77* (American Council on Education, 1977), p. 12.

34. Kenneth R. Reeher and Earl R. Fielder, *A Critical Review and Analysis of the Federal Basic Educational Opportunity Grants Program and Its Effect on the Pennsylvania Higher Education Grant Program* (Harrisburg: Pennsylvania Higher Education Assistance Agency, 1976).

35. *G.I. Bill Improvement Act of 1977*, S. Rept. 95-468, 95:1 (GPO, 1978), p. 21. In addition to the veterans, some 100,000 of their survivors and dependents also received GI bill assistance that year, chiefly at the college level.

36. See table 3-6. Expenditure figures represent only the higher education portion of GI bill payments.

This figure has since been heading downward, and will continue to fall as the peacetime army shrinks and as Vietnam-era veterans use up their benefits—or lose their eligibility for such benefits.[37] Budget projections for fiscal 1979 anticipate the expenditure of $2 billion at the college level. A drastically altered program of education benefits passed by Congress in late 1976 pertains to men and women who entered the armed forces after January 1, 1977; under this scheme the federal contribution will "match" (two for one) monies voluntarily withheld from their pay while they are on active duty.[38]

The effect of this change will not be evident for some time, although it would seem to encourage the education-minded serviceman to aim for a low-priced college. For the present, the distinguishing feature of the GI bill, still following the course charted in 1952, is that the size of a veteran's stipend bears no relation to the cost of education at the college he selects. An unmarried veteran who was a full-time student in 1976–77 could expect to receive $292 a month, or $2,920 in the course of a ten-month school year. A spouse and children would entitle him to larger benefits, but once his monthly check is computed according to such non-educational variables, the amount remains fixed, whether he attends a community college or an Ivy League university, and from it he is expected to pay all his educational and living expenses.

The program thus maintains a double incentive for the veteran to

37. The law contains a "delimiting period"—ten years in most situations—after the conclusion of military service during which the veteran must use his GI bill entitlement or lose eligibility for benefits.

38. To participate in this "contributory vesting program," a serviceman (or servicewoman) must agree to have $50 to $75 per month withheld from his pay while on active duty, for a minimum of twelve months; he can contribute up to $2,700. Upon subsequently enrolling in an approved educational institution or program, he will receive these funds plus the "two for one" supplement provided by the Veterans Administration. Participation is voluntary. (Post-Vietnam Era Veterans' Educational Assistance Act of 1977, 90 Stat. 2392.) As of June 1977, just 7,000 servicemen had elected to take part. As Veterans Administrator Max Cleland stated in congressional testimony that month, "When you have to pay in advance for your educational opportunity that you are going to get 2 or 3 years later, I don't think there is all that much incentive there to participate in the program, especially if you are a person who came into the military for the purpose of getting a job and some money. . . . It requires, I think, a pretty sizable degree of maturity and willingness to defer $50 to $75 a month out of your paycheck, and if you are a young enlisted man in the military, $50 to $75 out of your paycheck a month means a lot more to you now than it may later." *Oversight Hearings on All Forms of Federal Student Financial Assistance*, Hearings before the House Education and Labor Committee, 95:1 (GPO, 1977), pp. 522–23.

choose a low-tuition college. Since his total annual benefits roughly correspond to the cost of attending a moderately priced public institution in his own state, he can elect a more expensive school only if he has access to additional resources. Moreover, if he chooses a school that costs *less* than his veteran's stipend, he can still pocket the difference, in effect turning a profit by going to college.

Not surprisingly, as the public-private tuition gap has grown, so has the tendency of veterans to enroll in public colleges and universities. "The Vietnam veteran desiring to attend a private institution," the Educational Testing Service reported to the Senate Veterans' Affairs Committee, "is severely disadvantaged with respect to the veteran of World War II."[39] In recent years, fewer than 19 percent of college-level GI bill recipients have enrolled in private institutions, a marked contrast with the 50-50 split in the late 1940s when the original GI bill was in force.[40]

Within the public sector, too, the GI bill has had a markedly uneven effect. Although 33 percent of all eligible Vietnam-era veterans had used their benefits to pursue college-level study by April 1976, the participation rates varied from more than 50 percent in Arizona and California to less than 20 percent in Vermont, Pennsylvania, and Indiana. The explanation of the Senate Veterans' Affairs Committee is as plausible as any:

The failure of some States to provide significant support for postsecondary education has meant that many veterans do not have access to low-cost institutions in which to enroll. The Committee concludes (as it did in 1974) that higher school costs in certain States make it less easy and less attractive for veterans to enroll which, in turn, is reflected in state participation rates.[41]

39. *Final Report on Educational Assistance to Veterans*, p. 31.

40. Ibid., p. 36, and *Chronicle of Higher Education*, October 14, 1975, p. 11. Of course, the percentage of all college students enrolled in private institutions had also fallen, but not as much. In 1974–75 it was 24 percent for degree-credit students and 22 percent for all students. American Council on Education, *A Fact Book on Higher Education*, issue 2 (1976), table 76.81.

41. *Veterans' Education and Employment Assistance Act of 1976*, S. Rept. 94-1243, 94:2 (GPO, 1976), p. 37. The committee set about the following year to do something about this problem, proposing to allow "acceleration" of benefits so that, although no veteran would get an increase in his total forty-five-month entitlement to educational assistance, he would be able to expend that total at a more rapid rate and thus augment the resources available to him in any given school year. The Senate accepted this proposal, while defeating a more radical amendment by senators from high-tuition northeastern states to institute an actual tuition differential similar to that of the post–World War II program, but it vanished in conference. Instead the conferees agreed only to a very limited loan forgiveness scheme. For background on the Senate action, and the Veterans' Affairs Committee rationale, see *G.I. Bill Improvement Act of 1977*, especially pp. 32–43.

Consequently, those public institutions with higher tuitions—whether because of meager state support or greater expenditures per student— fare the worst in the competition for veterans and for the federal funds they bring with them. It is no coincidence that the two high-participation states cited have average public sector tuitions that are among the lowest in the nation, and the three low-participation states rank among the five jurisdictions with the highest charges.[42]

SOCIAL SECURITY BENEFITS. Seldom regarded as a student aid program,[43] the massive outlays of the Social Security Administration in 1976–77 included approximately $1.2 billion in benefits for eighteen- to twenty-one-year-olds attending colleges and universities. The 700,000 recipients are the dependents or survivors of social security beneficiaries, and to qualify for these supplements they must be unmarried and enrolled in a full-time program of study.[44] Their monthly stipends averaged $143 in fiscal 1976.[45] Although the calculation of social security benefits is quite complex, one variable excluded from these formulas is the cost of attending college. With student benefits averaging just $1,716 a year, clearly this program is insufficient to cover even the costs of most low-priced state and community colleges.

Unlike basic grants, no means test is associated with the social security program. Still, most recipients come from more modest circumstances than those of their classmates. "The 1972 median family income of the social security students attending college," reports the Congressional Budget Office, "was $9,690, which was 89 percent of the median income for all families with 18- to 24-year-old members, and only 71

42. Carnegie Foundation for the Advancement of Teaching, *The States and Higher Education* (Jossey-Bass, 1976), p. 78. Tuition data from 1973–74.

43. The Social Security Administration insists that its expenditures are nothing of the sort, observing that "unfortunately, the student benefit is sometimes misunderstood to be a form of aid rather than a component of family income. Despite its name and the requirement for school attendance, the student benefit program is not a grant, scholarship, loan or aid program. The distinction is fundamental." Quoted in Congressional Budget Office, *Social Security Benefits for Students*, p. 14.

44. In one sense, these are not supplements, since the student's family does not ordinarily receive any more benefits than it got when the student was seventeen years old. But if he does not remain in school after his eighteenth birthday, the family's aggregate social security payments would, in most instances, decline. For the exceptions, and other complexities and fine points of the program, see CBO, *Social Security Benefits for Students*.

45. These average payments varied according to the program category under which a student was covered. Children of disabled workers, for example, averaged $87, while survivors of deceased workers averaged $158. Ibid., p. 5.

percent of the median for all such families with children in college."[46] Yet not all beneficiaries are poor. In 1972–73, 31 percent of them came from families with incomes (exclusive of the student benefits) above that year's median for all families with eighteen- to twenty-four-year-old members.[47] Though this may help to explain why 29 percent of all college-level social security student beneficiaries that year—a higher fraction than for college students generally—enrolled in private institutions of higher education, it also raises a question of equity. Roughly one-third of these benefits (in 1972–73) were paid to students whose family income would have rendered them ineligible for basic grants and who thus do not qualify as needy under the terms of the principal federal need-tested student aid program.[48] Moreover, as one might expect of an income replacement program, but not of a student assistance program, the larger grants tend to go to the wealthier beneficiaries. Whereas students from families with incomes below $5,000 received average payments of less than $1,050 in 1972–73, those from families with total incomes above $10,000 received benefits averaging more than $1,227.[49]

EVALUATION. None of the three direct payment programs was designed to aid higher education per se, or the ordinary college student. Each was intended for a particular group of federal dependents and, although the benefits become available only if these dependents pursue a course of study, eligibility itself hinges on factors wholly external to the higher education system: previous military service, family ties to a social security recipient, or, in the case of basic grants, poverty. Because the funds flow from Washington to millions of students, the money can play no reliable part in the budgetary calculations of colleges and universities, nor are these federal programs in any useful sense within the control of the institutions delivering the services they are intended to pay for. In none of these programs does the stipend approach the amount needed to attend most private, or out-of-state public, colleges and universities and, aside from the minor inhibition of the BEOG half-cost rule, all three programs create some economic incentive for students lacking other

46. Ibid., p. 7. Unfortunately, the only data on student characteristics are from school year 1972–73. See also Philip Springer, "Characteristics of Student OASDI Beneficiaries in 1973: An Overview," *Social Security Bulletin*, November 1976, pp. 3–32.
47. CBO, *Social Security Benefits for Students*, p. 8.
48. Ibid. Of course the basic grants program was not yet in effect that year.
49. Ibid.

resources to select a low-priced institution.[50] Moreover, though only basic grants links its payments to an analysis of student need, most participants in all three programs come from modest circumstances and are unlikely to have ready access to substantial extra funds, except from other student aid programs or by working while they study.

The Campus-Based Programs

All three of what are known as campus-based programs are holdovers from the 1950s or 1960s when need-based student aid was a new federal activity and when Washington tended to entrust the parceling out of assistance funds to the colleges and universities. Although the three pro-

50. This is a controversial and largely unprovable point, but not an implausible one. Assume, for example, a prospective college student attempting to choose between the average four-year public and private colleges whose attendance costs are shown in table 3-4; that is, between about $2,900 a year in the former, and $4,800 in the latter. The price differential for an unaided student is $1,900, and the ratio between the two costs of attendance is 1:1.66. Now assume that $1,000 in student aid is made available to that student, regardless of his choice of institution. The "net" prices fall to $1,900 and $3,800. A rational economic being would see that the actual gap is still $1,900; but a prospective student worried about the high price of college might notice instead that now the private institution costs him twice as much to attend as does the public. Moreover, the aid has covered 34 percent of the gross attendance costs of the public campus, compared with just 21 percent at the private institution.

Now assume also that the same prospective student has in hand $1,000 a year in family resources available to help pay for college. This will leave him with just $900 in "uncovered" costs if he chooses the state institution, a sum he can reasonably expect to earn during the summer and school year, but to attend the private college he will have to come up with $2,800—more than three times as much—a year, even though the nominal gap is still just $1,900.

Does this mean that the presence of student aid in the flat amount of $1,000 serves to "encourage" the prospective student to select the public institution by giving him an economic incentive to do so? Certainly he would weigh other factors as well. But it is at least reasonable to state that a person who would not be able to attend college at all if it were not for student aid will find it easier to make ends meet at the public institution.

Still, it is also necessary to point out that the aid funds, even when "fixed" in amount, also reduce the net cost of attendance at private institutions, and thus make them more affordable than if there were no such aid. Although the perception of the situation may be altered, the aid introduces no *new* economic incentives for public sector enrollment, and thus may not "encourage" the choice of either type of college. Perhaps the strongest criticism that can confidently be leveled at flat grant programs is that they fail to change the incentive structure that was already in the marketplace, one that is properly described as "biased" in favor of public institutions.

grams collectively received more than a billion dollars in federal appropriations for the 1978–79 school year, none of them is as large as any of the direct payment schemes.

SUPPLEMENTAL EDUCATIONAL OPPORTUNITY GRANTS. SEOG is the lineal descendant of the first sizable federal scholarship program for low-income students, enacted in 1965. It provides stipends of up to $1,500 a year for "exceptionally needy" undergraduates, with both need and grant size calculated by the college (or one of the national need analysis services) in accordance with certain government stipulations. The program appropriation (for school year 1976–77) totaled $240 million, a mere 14 percent increase over the sum voted four years earlier. SEOG funds are first distributed among the states on the basis of their total enrollments and are then divided among colleges and universities on the basis of applications submitted by them.[51] In 1976–77, SEOG provided 432,000 awards averaging $550 each. Private college students made up 36.7 percent of the recipients and their grants averaged $610; the average public sector student received $510. The program is moderately well focused on low-income students: 48 percent of the (dependent) recipients (in 1976–77) came from families earning less than $7,500 and 25 percent went to those with incomes in excess of $12,000.[52]

COLLEGE WORK-STUDY. This program springs from the Economic Opportunity Act of 1964 and was initially meant more as an antipoverty measure than as a conventional student aid program.[53] Transferred to the Office of Education and altered several times in successive years, it now furnishes 80 percent of the funds used to pay the wages of needy students employed by the college or in nonprofit activities off campus.

51. Ninety percent of the appropriation is distributed by formula, with the remaining 10 percent reserved to the commissioner of education to apportion among states whose allotments would otherwise decline.

52. Calculated from Atelsek and Gomberg, *Estimated Number of Student Aid Recipients*, pp. 16–17. It should be noted that these figures refer only to SEOG recipients deemed dependent on their families. Among all SEOG recipients, 25.6 percent in 1976–77 were independent students.

53. Testifying before the House Special Subcommittee on Education in 1974, John D. Phillips, then acting associate commissioner for student assistance in the Office of Education, gave this statement of the program's origins: "The college work-study program was enacted in 1964 as Title I, Part C, of the Economic Opportunity Act. From the effective date of that act until passage of the Higher Education Act of 1965, the college work-study program operated as one of the Office of Economic Opportunity's delegated programs and was seen as an integral part of the war on poverty." *Student Financial Assistance*, pt. 2, *Work Programs*, Hearings before the House Education and Labor Committee, 93:2 (GPO, 1974), p. 95.

The college or employer must supply the remaining 20 percent, with student eligibility and individual earnings again governed by an approved need analysis system. Appropriations for 1976–77 came to $390 million. The program aided 698,000 people that year, 36 percent of them in private institutions. But average payments under this program were somewhat lower in private colleges and universities than in public ones. Moreover, college work-study is less clearly focused on the poor than are the grant programs. Among dependent undergraduates receiving funds from it, 38 percent came from families earning more than $12,000, the same as the percentage from families with incomes below $7,500.[54]

NATIONAL DIRECT STUDENT LOANS. The NDSL program traces its antecedents to the National Defense Education Act of 1958. It provides the colleges with capital that they lend to needy students at exceptionally low interest rates (3 percent, starting after the borrower ends his studies). The federal share of the capital is 90 percent, and the institution provides the remainder. In addition, the college may recycle the principal and interest repaid on earlier loans. In fiscal 1976 the federal appropriation totaled $319 million. A sizable number of students receive aid from this program—757,000 of them in 1976–77—and 39 percent of them were enrolled in private colleges and universities, where awards averaged $840, compared to $690 in public institutions. Nearly 44 percent of the dependent undergraduates receiving these loans came from families earning more than $12,000;[55] only 31 percent had family incomes below $7,500.

EVALUATION. The three campus-based programs continue to be popular with college and university leaders—particularly those in the private sector—for several reasons. Far more than the direct payment schemes, they are within the control of the institutions themselves. Funds come to the campus in a lump sum and can be figured into the school's financial aid budget. Although the amount may change from one year to the next, once allotted it is definite and does not depend on the college's admission of aid-bearing students. Moreover, the campuses are permitted to retain a small percentage of the funds awarded to them, ostensibly to cover the administrative costs of the programs. Because the need analysis systems that ration campus-based aid are substantially within the control of the colleges as well, they are more sensitive to the actual gaps between college-going costs and family resources than are programs that rely on a

54. Atelsek and Gomberg, *Estimated Number of Student Aid Recipients*, p. 18.
55. Ibid., pp. 15, 19.

simple poverty test. This means that the campus-based programs are better tailored to institutional pricing policies and more responsive to the higher tuitions of private and out-of-state public colleges. Since assistance from the campus-based programs can be layered atop the direct grants, individual aid packages can be assembled that begin to approximate the actual cost of attending the higher-priced institutions. Moreover, students ineligible for basic grants, the GI bill, and the social security program, yet unable to cover college costs out of their own resources, can often qualify for some assistance from the campus-based programs.

Despite their flexibility and their popularity with college administrators, the campus-based programs have several shortcomings.[56] They have never been coordinated with one another or with the newer basic grants program, and thus their interworkings make for considerable confusion. The fund allotment procedures create inequities among states and lasting uncertainty over the fair treatment of diverse institutions with different price structures. Despite numerous safeguards, the programs reward skillful campus grantsmanship, one reason why private colleges and universities, with their large and practiced financial aid staffs, have fared well under the campus-based programs, while less experienced institutions—notably the community colleges—receive less money from them than the income distribution of their students might indicate.

From the standpoint of the federal government, the campus-based programs have two main faults. Since the analysis of student need for these programs remains largely in private hands, federal officials cannot be certain that their funds are being "targeted" according to the government's social policies of the moment; a lower-middle-class student may end up with more federal aid than an impoverished one at a nearby college. And since the funds flow through the colleges, students can rarely distinguish them from the institutions' own aid programs; hence the programs confer little of the political reward associated with a student opening his mailbox to find a Treasury check.

56. These issues are explored further in Robert W. Hartman, "Federal Options for Student Aid," in Breneman and Finn, eds., *Public Policy and Private Education;* Lawrence E. Gladieux, *Distribution of Federal Student Assistance: The Enigma of the Two-Year Colleges* (CEEB, 1975); Consortium on Financing Higher Education, *Federal Student Assistance: A Review of Title IV of the Higher Education Act* (Hanover, N.H., April 1975; processed); and CEEB, "Title IV of the Higher Education Act," in *Student Financial Assistance,* Seminars before the House Education and Labor Committee, 93:2 (GPO, 1974), pt. 9, pp. 156–68.

Other Student Aid Programs

Although a perusal of the *Catalog of Federal Domestic Assistance* reveals dozens more titles, ranging from Drug Abuse Fellowships to loans for Cuban refugees, two entries round out the list of programs that now account for the bulk of the federal government's investment in student assistance.

GUARANTEED STUDENT LOANS. The GSL program commits the federal government to insure loans made by private lenders—banks and colleges —to students and to subsidize (though much less than the NDSL program) the interest on most such loans. Another part of the program provides partial federal reinsurance of loans guaranteed by state or private nonprofit agencies.[57]

Government officials have little control over appropriations for this program. The volume of loans—and the rate of default, money market conditions, borrower death and disability, and so on—determines the sums necessary to fulfill the federal obligation. Moreover, these costs are cumulative; most of them do not appear in the budget in the year a loan is made but show up later, when it is being repaid.[58]

From the student's standpoint, the program is equally unpredictable, for Washington gives him no assurance that he will be able to find a willing lender, only that his loan will be guaranteed if he does. If banks and other sources of capital do not wish to tie up their money in student loans, they are under no obligation to do so. If they choose to favor regular customers and to deny others, perhaps including those in greatest financial need, they are free to do so. And many do.

The federal subsidies built into the program are but crudely related to individual need. Under amendments passed in 1976, any student borrower whose adjusted family income is less than $25,000 is entitled to an interest subsidy.[59] That covers more than 90 percent of all borrowers, but the size of the subsidy is the same for every one of them, whether very poor or solidly middle class. And the largest subsidies of all—full

57. This program and the national direct student loans program are examined in Rice, ed., *Student Loans.*

58. Still, these costs are rapidly mounting. President Carter's 1979 budget request sought $757 million to cover them, more than twice the amount required two years earlier.

59. Those with higher incomes may also receive that subsidy if their colleges certify them to be in need of it. Moreover, the Carter administration's middle-income student aid proposals of 1978 included lifting that ceiling to $45,000. The Senate and House education committees chose to eliminate it altogether.

government repayment of the principal—are entirely unrelated to need and go to any borrower who cannot or chooses not to repay his loan. It is not surprising that this program has been plagued with a high rate of default.[60]

In spite of its problems, the guaranteed loans program supplies sizable amounts of capital to a large number of college students, including many enrolled in the higher-tuition institutions. In 1976–77 approximately 695,000 people received such loans—44 percent of them so that they could attend private colleges and universities—in amounts averaging $1,350 apiece.[61]

STATE STUDENT INCENTIVE GRANTS. The SSIG program was enacted in 1972. Far smaller than the other major federal aid programs, it provides federal "matching" funds for state scholarship programs, but because these programs have grown much faster than Washington's appropriations the match has been unequal. In 1976–77, with federal SSIG funding at $44 million, state need-based scholarship programs awarded $645 million to more than one million students.[62] SSIG funds are allotted to the states according to a formula tied to total enrollments. Although individual grants are limited to $1,500, and must be based on need, the states have wide latitude in the design and management of their programs. Before 1978, for example, states could confine their federally matched scholarships to students attending public colleges (or to those attending private institutions), and several did so. Even now the states are free to deny aid to students attending college in other jurisdictions. In spite of its modest size and other idiosyncrasies, however, SSIG has considerable significance as the one federal student aid program that attempts purposefully to mesh national and state efforts.[63]

60. Arthur M. Hauptman, "Student Loan Defaults: Toward a Better Understanding of the Problem," in Rice, ed., *Student Loans*. See also the discussion of institutional eligibility in chapter 6, below.

61. Atelsek and Gomberg, *Estimated Number of Student Aid Recipients*, pp. 15, 20.

62. Joseph D. Boyd, "National Association of State Scholarship and Grant Programs, 8th Annual Survey, 1976–77 Academic Year" (Deerfield: Illinois State Scholarship Commission, 1976; processed).

63. Strengthening that link between state and nation is one of the principal options available to policymakers wishing to rationalize the confusing array of individual and institutional subsidies sketched in the previous pages. For a thorough and sympathetic appraisal of this option, see Breneman and Finn, eds., *Public Policy and Private Higher Education*, especially chaps. 5 and 10.

Chapter Four

Toward the Reform
of Student Assistance

THE JERRY-BUILT structure of federal student aid described in the previous chapter would seem ripe for a complete overhaul. It is irrational, confusing, and cumbersome from practically every standpoint. Yet the obstacles to reform in this policy domain are at least as formidable as the reasons why reform appears so necessary. This chapter explains why.

Uncertainties and Inequities of the Programs

Although the federal student aid programs overlap and conflict, there is something to be said for the latitude they grant the determined student and the adroit financial aid officer to assemble an assistance package from multiple sources. Indeed, such a package may even provide the resources needed for a low-income student to attend a high-priced college: a family contribution of, say, $600; a basic grant of $800; a supplemental grant of $1,000; a summer job yielding $700; a term-time work-study job paying $900; a $1,000 loan; and $5,000 have been accumulated without using the college's own resources or presuming eligibility for veterans' or social security benefits.[1] Perhaps Great Aunt Marcella can lend a hand with books, clothing, and spending money. Maybe the state has a substantial need-based program of its own, partially financed with federal SSIG funds, from which the student can seek additional aid. Or possibly he can obtain a second loan with the help of whichever federal loan program he did not avail himself of the first time.

1. Strictly speaking, the college would probably have spent $180 as its 20 percent of the work-study payment.

But it is all so uncertain. Does the state in fact have a scholarship scheme that the student is eligible for and can use at the university of his choice? Is his family's income low enough to warrant a basic grant? Have the federal assistance funds been appropriated in time, and in sufficient amount, or are the administration and Congress still wrangling over "tradeoffs" between basic grants and campus-based aid? What about next year? How adroitly has the college maneuvered for an allocation of campus-based funds? Is there a bank willing to make the loan, and at what interest rate? Is the student capable of working at paid jobs year-round without neglecting his studies? And if he is not really poor, if he comes from a middle-class family earning $15,000 to $25,000 a year, how many sources of aid will he find closed to him?

If the prospective student has not yet enrolled anywhere—or perhaps is still deciding whether or not to go to college—he will find that the very features that make campus-based aid helpful and flexible from the standpoint of the institution make it incomprehensible from his own. As with the college's own assistance programs, he has no way of knowing how much help he might get until he has applied, been accepted, had his request evaluated, and been run through the mixer where colleges blend their budgetary calculations, their own notion of equal opportunity, their success or failure at obtaining outside funds, and their requests from other students. The basic grants, veterans', and social security programs at least offer some foreknowledge about the benefits he may be entitled to. But any aid from the campus-based programs will come as part of a package that is not assembled until long after the prospective student has paid the application fee. He has no satisfactory way of building this aid into his "net price" calculations. And if his college has fared poorly in the annual battle for fund allocations, he will be more than inconvenienced by the delay; he may well find himself without the federal aid money he would have received had he selected another school. Helpful and flexible though campus-based aid monies from Washington are to the colleges, therefore, they are not always equitable, and even when they are they contribute little to student "choice" at the point where an individual must make his first important set of decisions.

It is clear that many prospective students lack adequate information about the net cost of various colleges and the availability of financial assistance from diverse sources.[2] It is less clear that all colleges and uni-

---

2. George Weathersby tells of a student who wrote all the colleges and universities in Boston to obtain the costs of attendance and the amount of aid she might expect to receive if she enrolled in each. "It seemed," said Weathersby, "like a nice,

versities want them to have such information. "There is an indication," reported the College Entrance Examination Board, "that many post-secondary institutions withhold information about cost and aid for strategic, policy, or procedural reasons. Some believe that 'the truth will scare them away.' "[3] Even though the Education Amendments of 1976 require institutions receiving federal student aid funds to "carry out information dissemination activities regarding financial assistance,"[4] colleges that find it in their interest to provide minimal cost and aid data to potential students will probably continue to do just that.[5] In any case, the complexity of the aid programs themselves, and the relatively late date at which most institutions make their assistance awards for the following year, render these federal programs less useful to the student than to the college.

From the colleges' standpoint, the federal aid programs show other inequities and uncertainties. Because the campus-based programs compete with basic grants, guaranteed loans, and state incentive grants (as well as with one another) for funds, schools find themselves at odds in each year's appropriation hearings. The incompatible formulas by which funds are allocated among states and then among institutions are a lasting source of discontent, for they have little relation to the distribution of student "need" across the country. Thus, for example, in 1973–74 Utah's allotment for direct student loans met 100 percent of its institutional requests, while Maine's met less than 20 percent.[6]

Wealthy colleges may also be affected differently from poor ones. If

---

straightforward question." But none of them provided the information sought, leading Weathersby to conclude that "it is impossible in the city of Boston to find out the net price of attending postsecondary education." He observed, however, that if she had actually applied, been accepted, and paid the tuition deposit, she would then have been advised about her financial aid, if any. With application fees and deposits averaging $100 per college, and with sixty-eight colleges in Boston, the enterprising student could make a "rational" net price calculation by investing a mere $6,800! *Higher Education Daily*, April 26, 1976, pp. 5–6. For the student's own findings, see Sandra L. Willett, "Information on Federal Student Assistance: Its Availability, Price, and Other Unfinished Business" (Kennedy School of Government, Harvard University, March 1976; processed).

3. College Scholarship Service, College Entrance Examination Board, and others, *Making It Count* (CEEB, 1977), p. 13.

4. 90 Stat. 2148.

5. It is possible that similar motives lie behind the "early admission" policies of some private colleges and universities, policies that encourage students to make their choices before all the relevant alternatives are known.

6. Figures refer to percentages of "panel approved requests." See *Student Financial Assistance*, Seminars before the House Education and Labor Committee, 93:2 (GPO, 1974), pt. 9, p. 168.

a school has sizable student aid resources of its own, it is better able to fill in the chinks among the federal programs and tailor its assistance to individual situations. An impoverished institution that does not have many affluent applicants is inevitably more dependent on the vagaries of the federal programs and consequently may even find itself revising its program offerings, recruitment techniques, and admissions procedures to lure students who bring federal resources with them. If the cost of attendance at a particular college is $5,000, for example, a veteran with $2,700 a year in GI bill benefits need worry only about the remaining $2,300, but a basic grant recipient with $1,400 in (personal and federal) resources would need $3,600 more, and a student not eligible for any federal aid would need whatever portion of the $5,000 he and his family cannot provide.

Another problem for colleges is the complexity of helping the federal government run so many different programs. Even the veterans' program, which would appear to be fairly simple from the college's point of view—the funds go directly to the student and come into the college in the form of tuition payments—has entangled the institutions in a web of certification and compliance procedures, since the Veterans Administration, confronted with overpayments so large as to verge on the scandalous, has been told by Congress to enlist the colleges in policing the educational progress and assistance claims of its recipients.

From the federal policy perspective, these programs have other problems. By entrusting part of its student aid monies to the colleges and universities, Washington has sacrificed some of its ability to target resources on students in greatest need of assistance. A student from a family earning $25,000 can easily qualify as "needy" if he attends a high-tuition college and thus obtains federal aid that a less affluent student at another university does not qualify for. If he is a veteran or the child of a social security beneficiary, he may receive aid that he does not need at all. If he qualifies for a basic grant, on the other hand, he must be needy according to the federal definition, but that does not assure him access to college if none within his "price range" will have him, if he lives in a state where tuitions are high, or if the subject he wants to study is available only at a private or out-of-state university. The more uniformly the federal programs treat students, the less sensitive the programs become to the differences in cost of attendance among colleges and universities and to the goal of student choice. But insofar as Washington tries to respond to those variations and to maximize the opportunities available to students, the more certainly it finds itself redistributing income according to imprecise criteria and paying for the postsecondary equivalent of luxury goods for some without providing the bare essentials to others.

Common sense and social equity would both suggest that the structure of federal student aid should be renovated. Two similarly situated persons should be treated similarly by the federal government. A prospective student should be able to learn the amount of his aggregate federal subsidy at a time when that knowledge will be most useful to him. Some types of institutions should not be favored over others. Requirements and eligibility criteria should be uniform and easily understood. The programs should be simple for federal agencies and colleges to administer and equitable in their treatment of states and regions. They should be neutral in their effect on the ability of colleges to recruit and select the students they want and on the ability of students to gain admission to, and pay for, the colleges of their choice.

As with many social policy domains, however, it is easier to list goals than to carry them out, particularly when an elaborate array of ongoing programs and institutional interests is involved.

Political Obstacles to Reform

Each of the programs described in chapter 3 benefits certain types of postsecondary institutions and students more than it does others. Thus it is not surprising that each has both zealous defenders and jealous critics. Although the multiplicity of programs and the complexity of the system diffuse some of the conflict that would otherwise develop, student aid is the area of federal policy in which the fiercest battles are waged among colleges and universities. If enrollments begin to dwindle and college costs continue to rise, these battles will intensify as institutional leaders see the survival of their campuses inextricably linked to their ability to attract students, which in turn is linked to their ability to bend the terms of federal aid to the financial contours of their schools.

The sharpest differences are those that divide public higher education from private. Believing passionately in the importance of low tuitions, and therefore in the institutional subsidies that make them possible, leaders of the public sector have been somewhat ambivalent about aid to students. They fear that if the federal government makes it easy for students to pay high prices, the states will lose their incentive to keep prices low. Even worse, from their viewpoint, is a heavy emphasis on student loans, which implies that the individual rather than society should pay the cost of his or her own higher education.

As early as the debates about the National Defense Education Act (NDEA) of 1958, spokesmen for the state universities explained to the Senate Committee on Labor and Public Welfare:

Basing payment to institutions on the amount of their customary fees to all students discriminates against those institutions which, through private or non-Federal public resources, make it possible for many students to attend college without outside help. Large-scale Federal programs which pay institutions their customary fees produce strong pressures toward raising those fees, making it necessary for more and more students to have scholarships and fellowships in order to attend college. . . . There should be no special bonus to an institution because it charges high fees.[7]

This attitude did not disappear rapidly. Three years later, the NDEA having been enacted and the Kennedy administration having proposed a broad new scholarship program, John D. Millett presented the following argument to Wayne Morse's Senate subcommittee on behalf of the two major associations of state colleges and universities:

Unless funds are provided to help meet operating costs and facilities costs for colleges and universities—other than passing them on to the student and his family through tuition charges—there will be no end to the demand for more and more scholarships. We believe that if the central problem of support is attacked first, and attacked vigorously, the need for scholarships will be minimized rather than maximized, and that otherwise no conceivable scholarship program will perform the task of keeping educational opportunity open.[8]

By the mid-sixties, spokesmen for the public sector were more ready to embrace federal aid for low-income students, but they have steadfastly opposed measures, such as expanded access by students to large loans, that invite higher tuition charges or that imply that students should be expected to pay a bigger share of their educational costs.[9]

7. Testimony of John T. Caldwell, representing the American Association of Land-Grant Colleges and State Universities, and the State Universities Association, in *Science and Education for National Defense*, Hearings before the Senate Labor and Public Welfare Committee, 85:2 (GPO, 1958), p. 685.

8. *Aid for Higher Education*, Hearings before the Senate Labor and Public Welfare Committee, 87:1 (GPO, 1961), p. 298.

9. See, for example, the vehement opposition of the two major state university associations to the proposal for an "Education Opportunity Bank," described by them as the "Student Loan Indenture Proposal": National Association of State Universities and Land-Grant Colleges, and American Association of State Colleges

But they were favorably disposed to the basic grants program enacted in 1972, once they had reconciled themselves to the futility of their quest for general institutional assistance, and have been steadfast supporters of the GI bill. If federal aid is to go to students, these leaders reason, it is best that it take the form of grants (or work-study jobs) rather than loans, that it be given out in amounts that encourage recipients to attend low-tuition institutions, and that it be channeled through programs carefully designed not to tempt the states to cut back on institutional support or raise tuition rates. Not surprisingly, they have been staunch advocates of eliminating the half-cost ceiling in the basic grants program, arguing that it penalizes schools with modest charges and pushes students toward higher-priced institutions. They have also been ambivalent about continuing the supplemental grants program in its present form, and have feared that the state student incentive grants program may encourage states to shift funds from institutional support to student aid.

For their part, leaders in the private sector have generally opposed federal programs that make low-tuition colleges economically attractive and that do not supply enough resources for recipients to meet the cost of higher-priced schools. They prefer programs that, singly or in combination, allow students to assemble large resource packages and that are sensitive to the price differences within higher education. Accordingly, private sector leaders have strongly favored the campus-based programs, with their flexible definition of "need." They have supported the state student incentive grants program as a laudable federal effort to stimulate the states to help residents who need other educational assistance than that provided by subsidized tuition. They have welcomed the continuation of loan programs, if not in principle then at least on the basis that grants and other straightforward subsidies will never be adequate to bring private colleges within the financial reach of all who might wish to attend them. And they have fought to retain the half-cost limit in the basic grants program, apparently reasoning that even if it does not make attending private colleges easier, at least it makes matriculation at public colleges somewhat less attractive economically.

These conflicting values and self-interests account for much of the confusion in present federal student aid policy. They explain the pressures on Congress in 1972 that led to retention of the campus-based

and Universities, "Recommendations for National Action Affecting Higher Education," in *Higher Education Amendments of 1970*, pt. 2, Hearings before the Senate Labor and Public Welfare Committee, 91:2 (GPO, 1971), pp. 1223-24.

programs even when the new basic grants and state student incentive grants programs might have been thought to make them superfluous.[10] They help to explain why we have two federally sponsored loan programs instead of one. They are the main reason that Congress has annually reshaped the President's student aid budget requests. And they account for the remarkable legislative stalemate that resulted in 1976 after two years of laborious effort in the executive branch and on Capitol Hill to rationalize and simplify the government's student aid offerings.[11]

Analytical Dilemmas

The pitfalls to student aid reform are many, and neither politics nor the vested program interests of colleges and universities account for all of them. The reformers' goals themselves tend to work at cross-purposes, and the rationales of some existing programs are, if not incompatible, at least unrelated to one another and thus difficult to embrace within a single new structure.

The most obvious misfits are the large student aid programs run by the Veterans Administration and the Social Security Administration. Although they serve to help students pay for college, they are unrelated to need and therefore cannot easily be embedded in a comprehensive assistance scheme. Such a comprehensive program, however, would vitiate the rationale for separate student aid arrangements for veterans and social security recipients—at least it would if their ability to pay for college were judged to be the dominant federal policy objective.[12]

10. For an excellent account of the legislative battles that resulted in the 1972 amendments, see Lawrence E. Gladieux and Thomas R. Wolanin, *Congress and the Colleges* (D. C. Heath, 1976).

11. For an account of the 1976 events, see Lawrence E. Gladieux and Thomas R. Wolanin, "Federal Politics," in David W. Breneman and Chester E. Finn, Jr., *Public Policy and Private Higher Education* (Brookings Institution, 1978).

12. In its 1977 budget proposals, the Ford administration suggested phasing out the social security student benefits program and terminating the GI bill for veterans of the post-Vietnam "peacetime army." In the first instance, the White House argument included the fact that need-based student aid programs are available and that funds meant to help people pay for college are better channeled through student aid programs than through income maintenance programs. In the second instance, no explicit link was made between the termination of the veterans' benefits and the existence of other student aid programs. The higher education associations, however, were quick to note the connection. In criticizing the President for budget recommendations "so inadequate as to endanger our national commitment to the extension of postsecondary opportunities," the American Council on Education

This logic may be more compelling in the case of the social security program, which is arguably intended to help people pay for college who probably could not otherwise do so, than in the case of the GI bill, which is also a form of delayed compensation for military service. But before either program could reasonably be merged with, or eliminated in consequence of, a national student aid scheme keyed to individual need, its rationale would have to be made congruent with the conventional goals of federal student aid. Although the savings that would result from a program consolidation would help offset the added costs of the larger need-based scheme,[13] the difficulty of redefining long-established policy goals and of ending present benefits militates against the success of such a proposal. Perhaps the most that should be expected is to exclude social security and veterans' benefits from the category of student aid programs, to regard their payments as income supplements awarded for entirely different reasons, and to treat them the same way as other income for purposes of determining a student's need for assistance.

A Parsimonious "Solution"

If the quest for comprehensiveness is confined to the federal need-based programs administered by the Office of Education, a simple and economical plan for reform is not difficult to devise.[14] But it is one that

cited as particularly egregious examples the proposal "to phase out the two largest Federal programs providing educational benefits for students; those for veterans and for children of deceased, disabled, or retired social security beneficiaries," without at least making compensating increases in the Office of Education student aid programs. Quoted in *Higher Education and National Affairs*, March 19, 1976, p. 2.

13. "Savings" from phasing out the social security program require a complex set of budgetary assumptions, since it is financed from trust funds rather than general revenues. Ending that billion dollar annual drain on the trust funds would slightly ease the pressure on those funds—and on the payroll tax that replenishes them—but some of the costs would then have to be assumed by need-based student aid programs that would expand to help those formerly assisted by social security. In the case of both the social security and veterans' programs, any real savings would result from the denial of benefits to some who would have received them under the extant programs, presumably those veterans and social security dependents and survivors who would not qualify for assistance if it were based on need.

14. Indeed, one version of such a program was devised by the Nixon administration and presented to Congress in 1971, where it had a chilly reception. See "Statement by Sidney P. Marland, Commissioner of Education" in *Higher Education Amendments of 1971*, pt. 2, Hearings before the House Education and Labor Committee, 92:1 (GPO, 1971), pp. 131–40.

will inevitably have adverse effects on many students and institutions. Such a program would undertake to raise all prospective college students to a uniform resource level, much as the basic grants program does now.[15] Similarly situated people would be treated in exactly the same way.[16] Anyone wishing to attend a more expensive college or university would receive no additional federal subsidy, but he could borrow the funds needed. The result would be just two federal student aid programs, one providing subsidies to the poor, the other providing (or insuring) loans to everyone else. State governments, private donors, and the colleges themselves would, of course, be free to augment these federal offerings with their own student aid programs.

Such a scheme is rational, easily understood, simply administered, and economical. It takes full advantage of state subsidies and says to the prospective student that the federal obligation to subsidize his college education is discharged when he is assured enough resources to enroll in a low-priced public institution. Should he wish to go to a more expensive school, he is free to do so, but he will have to pay the difference himself.

The defects of such a proposal are also readily apparent. By doing nothing to counteract the distortions of the present higher education marketplace, it leaves students with an economic incentive to select a low-tuition college, and denies low-income students a degree of educational choice that their wealthier classmates enjoy. It would make it difficult for a federally aided student to select a private, or out-of-state public, university even if he felt his educational interests were best served there. It would tend to "reward" students fortunate enough to live in states with a well-developed system of low-tuition higher education and to "punish" those who live elsewhere. It would mark a step backward from present programs that attempt, however imperfectly, to give geographic mobility and institutional choice to many students.

15. The analogy is valid only if one eliminates the half-cost constraint from basic grants and treats that program as an entitlement to $1,800 (or whatever) in postsecondary purchasing power.

16. It would be necessary to decide how to handle the student who enrolled in a college costing less than the uniform resource level. If his grant were scaled down accordingly, the program would in fact be need tested (within its limits) rather than income tested. If it were not reduced, however, the student would find himself with more money than he required. If the states and colleges behaved "rationally," and sought to maximize the share of their costs borne by the federal government, those schools costing less than the uniform resource level would presumably raise their prices until they equaled it.

A program constructed along these lines would also be sharply biased in favor of some colleges and universities and against others, and that bias would have nothing to do with their educational quality or distinctiveness. Instead, it would be related to their success in getting enough institutional subsidies (or cutting their costs enough) to permit them to charge low tuitions.

An Expensive "Solution"

A program that responds to different college prices, however, quickly runs into another set of obstacles. Clearly, the "fairest" approach from the standpoint of the colleges is a program that allows them to compete on an equal basis for federally assisted students; that is, the aid provided would tend to compensate for price differences among institutions, thus enabling students to choose colleges on noneconomic grounds. From the student's perspective, such an arrangement is very nearly ideal, for it allows him the fullest range of educational choices without regard to his financial condition. But this is more easily presented as a goal than put into practice. Four important drawbacks deserve attention.

First, the "steak and macaroni" problem returns. While it is not unheard of for federal income supplement programs to vary their payments according to the cost of living in different parts of the country, there is little precedent for a program that would take two otherwise identical persons and give one of them $2,000, the other $4,000, simply because their tastes or aspirations differed. Although students amassing the benefits from several current student aid programs may achieve much the same result now, the disparities in payments are less visible and —because some parts are entrusted to the colleges—less directly a federal responsibility.

Second, to help a student with no resources of his own attend even an average-priced private college would require subsidies of about $4,800.[17] Assuming that the aid diminished as income rose, and assuming also that there should not be a "notch" where a $100 increase in income resulted in a greater than $100 reduction of subsidies, it would be necessary to devise an equitable schedule of family contributions. If the schedule of

17. Of course there is no need to supply 100 percent of a student's cost of attendance, and as explained below, there is some reason not to. But every step down from that level implies a narrowing of the student's choice among colleges and an associated bias in favor of attendance at lower-priced institutions.

the College Scholarship Service (see table 3-4) were adopted, the final dollar of a $4,800 federal subsidy would not vanish until family income exceeded $30,000. That would mean that more than 90 percent of the families in the United States would be entitled to federal student assistance if their children wished to attend—and were able to gain admission to—a private college or university.[18]

The political pressure apparently being placed on congressmen by middle-income families convinced that they *do* need help with the costs of college suggests that perhaps the society is ready for a program of income supplements (either grants or tax credits) available to practically everyone for this purpose. But if such a program is to furnish more than trivial sums to individual beneficiaries, it will be very costly. Political considerations aside, a serious question of social equity ought not be ignored: should the national government provide such subsidies —even for so worthy and limited a purpose as higher education—to people whose own earnings place them in the top quarter of the income distribution, when it provides no such assistance to millions earning far less whose children cannot, or choose not to, attend college?

Third, the more fully the program serves the student by obliterating college price differences and assuring him the resources to attend the university of his choice, the more it erodes certain desirable features of the higher education marketplace. For despite its defects, that marketplace has much going for it. Potential students choosing a college ordinarily seek value for money. Subsidies aside, the main reason some institutions charge more than others is because their costs are higher, they spend more per student, and in some sense prospective students think their product is *worth* more. This kind of "worth" defies simple analysis, since it has much to do with status, tradition, presumed educational quality, friends who are enrolling, the campus environment, liberal arts versus technical training, the prospects for making the football team, the chances of making valuable "contacts," the presence or absence of coed dormitories, and much more. On balance, choosing a college is not much different from choosing a car. And as with automobiles, price differences are one consideration. Not everyone wants, needs, or can afford a Cadillac.

Price consciousness is healthy for colleges, too, although their spokesmen are obliged to deny it. It serves as their main incentive to hold down

18. Strictly speaking, this is true only if attendance at a particular private campus entails costs equal to, or greater than, the average for all such campuses.

costs and to seek funds from multiple sources. If students were willing and able to pay any price, colleges would have little reason to hold the line on expenditures, seek greater productivity, strengthen management, solicit alumni contributions, or phase out obsolete activities. As has been seen in health care and elsewhere, when government (or other third parties) unhesitatingly reimburses beneficiaries for whatever services they receive at whatever price those services are provided, costs and prices both rise and needless services are rendered. Thus a "price sensitive" student aid scheme would be seized upon by some, if not most, colleges as a "price responsive" reimbursement scheme.

Fourth, once it became clear that the federal government was prepared to provide enough aid to students to enable them to pay higher college prices, state governments and private donors could be expected to reevaluate their own actions. The states would have a powerful incentive to transfer to Washington some of the higher education costs they now pay, through the simple device of reducing their institutional support and forcing their public campuses to raise tuition rates.

That possibility reinforces the old fear, held by public university leaders and others who believe in the doctrine of free tuition, that overly generous student aid creates a strong temptation for those who support institutions to cut back on their support and for the notion to take root that people who can afford to pay for higher education themselves should do so, that the states have no obligation to subsidize their institutions, and that colleges *should* obtain their revenues in the form of tuition payments.

History holds a lesson, for the only time the federal government did equip large numbers of students with purchasing power keyed to private college prices, the states seemingly set out to make the most of it. As the aid was not predicated on student need, the precedent has limits, but the story of the original World War II GI bill is nonetheless instructive.

At the program's peak in 1947–48, approximately a million students —about half the nation's total enrollment—financed their higher education with the help of this program. And by the end of that year, average public sector tuitions, which had hovered between $60 and $90 from the early thirties through the Second World War, had leaped to $194, coming closer to parity with private sector prices (a ratio of 1 to 1.9) than ever before or since. Out-of-state tuitions rose particularly fast, from $193 to $349 between 1940 and 1950 in one sample of public universities, an increase of 81 percent, compared with a 54 percent rise in resident rates at the same schools, and a 53 percent rise in tuitions in a sample group of private institutions. For decades public institutions had lagged behind the private sector in "educational and general income per student," but by 1950 the state schools were taking in (and presumably spending) more per student than their private counterparts. With veterans' benefits also sufficient to cover private sector prices—even to permit rises in those prices—and with enrollments ballooning, the private institutions grew more dependent on tuition income, too; whereas in 1930 and 1940 private higher education had derived 57 to 58 percent of its educational income from student charges, by 1950 it derived 68 percent.[19]

The comptroller general of the United States testified before Congress that "many of the educational and training institutions of this country considered the GI bill as an open invitation to raid the Treasury," and, as described above, in 1952 the legislation was amended to provide a single fixed monthly payment to every beneficiary.[20] By 1953 public sector tuitions had fallen back to $173, and the public-private tuition ratio had widened again to 1 to 3.3.

The experience under the GI bill supports this assumption: if Washington holds out the promise of large enough subsidies to a large enough group of students, colleges and universities will raise their prices to take maximum advantage of their consumers' enhanced ability to pay, and the federal government will shoulder the burden of some educational costs that would have been borne by others or perhaps not incurred at all. Though a shrinking applicant pool in the 1980s would cause enrollment-conscious college administrators to be wary of drastic tuition increases, and though the popularity of low tuition might also give pause to state legislators, the temptation to transfer educational costs to Washington would prove irresistible to many. And undoubtedly alumni, philanthropists, foundations, and corporations would also reconsider their practice of supporting colleges and universities if the federal government made it easier for students to pay high prices.

There are additional reasons why federal higher education policy

19. June A. O'Neill, *Sources of Funds to Colleges and Universities* (Carnegie Foundation for the Advancement of Teaching, 1973), especially p. 44; Rivlin, *Role of the Federal Government*, pp. 63–70; John D. Millett, *Financing Higher Education in the United States* (Columbia University Press, 1952), pp. 290, 292–303.

20. *Veterans' Readjustment Assistance of 1952*, Hearings before the Senate Labor and Public Welfare Committee, 82:2 (GPO, 1952), pp. 131–32.

cannot and perhaps should not attempt to grapple directly with the price structure of the college marketplace. (Some of these are examined in chapter 5.) But if it does not, it is left with the problem described earlier, that is, the immense difficulty of tailoring its student aid in ways that foster individual choice, that do not discriminate against the higher-priced institutions, and that do not exact undesirable consequences of their own.

A Proposal for Reform

Even if grand reform designs appear impracticable—and in some ways undesirable—changes could be made in the need-based federal aid programs that would combine the goals of student "access" to some institution and student "choice" of a particular institution but would not have the perverse side effects of a full-price reimbursement scheme.[21] The distortions of the present college marketplace could be eased, though not eliminated, and the prospective student could be presented with a relatively simple subsidy program in which he could ascertain his benefits (if any) at the point when that knowledge would help him most. A means test could be constructed to provide some assistance to the low- or middle-income student wishing to attend a higher-priced private, or out-of-state public, university—although, of course, the more people made eligible for assistance, the more expensive the program would be.

The present basic grants program provides the obvious starting place, for it already embodies the essential principle: the federal government will assist every needy student to attain a stated level of postsecondary

21. Although it is theoretically possible to design a tax credit to carry out any given set of policy specifications (and in that sense tax credits and grants may be viewed as alternative means to the same ends), the specific tuition tax relief proposals attracting congressional interest in 1978 are not apt to have much effect on student access or choice. A few hundred dollars a year in aid to practically every student, regardless of need, is insufficient either to induce many more people to go to college or to bring higher-priced institutions within reach of those who cannot now afford them. Such schemes are best viewed as attempts to lighten somewhat the cost burden on everyone attending college, not to change the higher education marketplace or alter the pattern of attendance. Of course, if institutions raise their tuitions to take advantage of across-the-board student subsidies—an obvious risk whether the subsidies are grants or tax credits—then the intended financial relief for students will vanish.

purchasing power. It also embodies, though in a most unsatisfactory way, a second principle in its half-cost ceiling: a federally aided student must pay some portion of his college costs himself, so that he remains aware of price differences among institutions instead of being entirely shielded from the marketplace. The program also establishes a direct relation between the federal government and the student: two similarly situated students are treated in exactly the same way even if they enroll in different institutions; and each student can readily ascertain in advance the amount of federal assistance for which he is eligible rather than have his aid subject to later decisions by campus officials.

Two major changes in the present basic grants program are required, however, if it is to be made more sensitive to differing college prices without inviting schools that now have low tuitions to raise them to the level of those with high tuitions. First, the resource level around which the program is built must be lifted well above the $1,800 authorized at present, and brought closer to the true cost of attending private, and out-of-state public, institutions. Second, however, the increase must be substantially greater for students attending those schools than for students enrolling in public colleges and universities in their own states. In effect, the program must be bifurcated into a two-tiered assistance scheme, so that a student favoring a higher-priced institution is entitled to a greater assured resource level than he would be if he chose a college heavily subsidized by the state.[22]

A Revised Basic Grants Program

I have not attempted to develop a revised basic grants program in detail; my purpose is simply to suggest a way of conceptualizing one such approach. Although the example deals only with outright grants, the federal subsidy could be provided through other means, such as federally financed student jobs. This program does not deal with loans or federal-state scholarships either, but, as will become apparent, the heavy self-help requirement it levies on recipients leaves ample room for such supplements, as well as for aid provided by the state alone, by colleges, and by other private sources. It seems preferable, however, to allow for

22. A similar proposal for a two-tiered assistance scheme, sometimes known as Super-BEOGs, was sketched out by John F. Hughes and Patricia Smith in "Policy Options for Federal Consideration" (American Council on Education, Policy Analysis Service, April 1976; processed), app. A.

other programs rather than to predicate the federal program on state or private action.[23]

Assume that the costs of two typical colleges—one public, one private—are the averages shown in table 3-1 for resident students in four-year institutions in 1977–78, and assume that the federal program adopts those averages to fix the "resource base" needed for a student to attend one or the other type of institution. College A—the public institution—thus costs about $2,900 a year to attend; private College B requires an outlay of $4,800.

Under the hypothetical two-tiered program, the federal government would assure a student 75 percent of his cost of attending College A (that is, $2,175), and that amount plus half the private college surcharge ($2,175 + 0.5 [$4,800 − $2,900] = $3,125) if he enrolled in College B. In each case, the student's family contribution is subtracted from his federal entitlement and, in each case, he also has a self-help requirement to complete his financing package.

With these assumptions, a very low income student with no family contribution would be entitled to the full $2,175 in federal assistance at College A, or $3,125 if he chose College B. His annual self-help obligation (cost of attendance minus [federal grant plus family contribution]) would total $725 or $1,675. This sum could come from a summer job, a loan, a state scholarship scheme, financial aid resources belonging to the college, or elsewhere. As the family contribution increased—that is, as income rose—the federal subsidy would taper off. The self-help requirement, however, would remain the same, for it is controlled by the cost of the college rather than by ability to pay.

If the student elected a public campus that cost less than College A, his entitlement would diminish, for it is limited to 75 percent of his actual costs. It would also diminish if he opted for a private institution costing less than College B, for in no case could he receive more than $2,175 plus half the difference between the actual cost of his college and $2,900. In both situations, however, his self-help obligation would also decline. By choosing a public institution with costs of $2,000, for example, he could save $225 (0.25 [$2,900 − $2,000]); by electing a private campus costing $4,000 he could reduce his self-help payment by $400. It is assumed that this ability to cut his own out-of-pocket expenses by seeking a lower-

23. Robert W. Hartman reached the opposite conclusion in "Federal Options for Student Aid," in Breneman and Finn, eds., *Public Policy and Private Higher Education.*

priced college would leave him sensitive to price differences, but that making him responsible for only a portion of those differences would cushion their effect on his range of choices. The amount he is responsible for could of course be varied. There is no magic in the 25 and 50 percent self-help ratios suggested here. And also, since his federal entitlement would be tied to the *average* cost of attending a particular college, he could lighten his self-help burden by living frugally, thus keeping the "controllable" portions of his actual costs below the average.

But he could not increase his federal entitlement by selecting a more expensive college within either the public or the private sector. The maximum grant would remain tied to average costs, meaning that the added cost of enrolling at a higher-than-average-priced institution would translate into a dollar-for-dollar increase in his self-help requirement, unless he were able to obtain more aid from other sources.

The one exception—and it is an important one—is that if he attended an out-of-state public institution and were required to pay a tuition surcharge, his federal aid entitlement would be calculated on the higher (that is, the private sector) resource base. Thus he could afford to enroll in college in another state if he wished to and could gain admission there. But since the self-help burden is heavier under the private sector schedule than under the public sector one, it would still be worth his while to take up residency in the new jurisdiction or otherwise qualify for home-state tuition rates as quickly as possible.

Program Variables

One key "controllable" variable of the program is the level of resources guaranteed to participants. Is it reasonable to make average attendance costs into resource bases for purposes of calculating federal aid? Doing so obviously penalizes the higher-priced institutions within each sector, for their students would have a larger un-aided (or self-help) obligation. At the same time, colleges priced below the average might decide to raise their charges in order to maximize their federal yield. Although neither outcome is desirable, at some point precision must give way to simplicity and certainty. At least the dual resource base would discourage public institutions from charging private college prices; and using an average as a limit should make higher-priced schools cautious about raising their tuitions still further. Moreover, regulations could be devised to keep lower-priced colleges from suddenly inflating their costs. The federal government could simply disallow costs from individual schools that rose faster than a certain rate. If 5 percent a year were the rate, for example, then a $2,000 college heading toward the $2,900 ceiling could not raise its prices—or more precisely, its estimated student costs of attendance—more than $100 in the first year.[24]

The program resource bases would also need to move, at least to keep up with inflation. Yet, while actual college prices provide a reasonable place to start the program, it would be undesirable to permit future increases in tuitions to control future levels of federal aid. The program should have a cost-of-living escalator of some sort, but one keyed to the economy as a whole or to an index of higher education costs, rather than one controlled by the combined pricing decisions of the nation's university trustees.

Note that in this program federal subsidies are not calculated as a percentage of tuition alone, or, as some have suggested, as a share of noninstructional costs, but rather as a portion of a student's entire cost of attendance.[25] It happens that the maximum subsidy for a state college student—$2,175 in this example—corresponds closely to the average total expenses *minus* tuition and fees of a resident student in a public or private institution in 1977–78. Thus another way of conceptualizing the program is to think of Washington as guaranteeing nearly all the nontuition costs of attendance for a public or a private college student, and approximately one-third of average private sector tuitions as well. Table 4-1 shows the relation of subsidies to costs, at five different types of institutions, for students qualifying for the maximum federal assistance.

Nevertheless, it is better to construe the federal subsidy as covering a portion of total costs rather than just nontuition costs. Otherwise an

---

24. The federal government would not fix prices. It would simply limit the amount for which federal student subsidies might be granted. In the example cited, the college might raise its tuition $200, but the student subsidy would rise only $75, that is, 75 percent of the permissible increase.

25. Several groups and individuals have recommended that helping students to meet noninstructional costs provides the best available rationale for basic grants, arguing that to do so would (a) leave states with the primary task of assisting with instructional costs, whether through subsidized tuition, student aid, or both; (b) sidestep much of the dispute between public and private institutions, since noninstructional costs are remarkably similar in both and since the arguments usually arise in connection with tuition; and (c) provide a readily calculated "index" for future program adjustments, one that is apt to track the consumer price index and to be relatively immune to institutional decisions. For a presentation of this view, see Lois D. Rice, "Federal Student Assistance: Title IV Revisited," in John F. Hughes and Olive Mills, eds., *Formulating Policy in Postsecondary Education* (American Council on Education, 1975), pp. 149–68.

Table 4-1. *Estimated Average Annual Costs at Public and Private Institutions of Higher Education, and Maximum Federal Subsidy, 1977–78*

Amounts in dollars

	Type of institution and student				
Item	*Public four-year, home-state, resident*[a]	*Public two-year, home-state, commuter*	*Public four-year, out-of-state resident*[a]	*Private four-year, resident*[a]	*Private four-year, commuter*
Tuition and fees	600	400	1,600	2,500	2,500
Nontuition costs	2,300	1,900	2,300	2,300	1,800
Total costs	2,900	2,300	3,900	4,800	4,300
Maximum Step 1 subsidy	2,175	1,725	2,175	2,175	2,175
Maximum Step 2 subsidy	...	...	500	950	700
Maximum total subsidy	2,175	1,725	2,675	3,125	2,875
Self-help	725	575	1,225	1,675	1,425
Total subsidy as percent of total costs	75	75	70	65	67
Self-help as percent of total costs	25	25	30	35	33
Step 1 subsidy as percent of nontuition costs	95	91	95	95	121
Step 2 subsidy as percent of tuition costs	...	...	31	38	28

Source: Author's estimates.
a. Resident refers to a student living in housing provided by the institution.

unwanted premium is put on low tuitions, particularly in the public sector. And elected officials have reason to ask why all their funds should go for living expenses rather than for the more obvious costs of higher education, those tied to instruction.

Is it fair, though, to base a major federal aid program on a crude division of all higher education into public and private sectors (grouping out-of-state public charges with the private) and to allow an average price differential to mask the wide variation in actual charges within each sector? Regrettably, the alternatives seem worse. If the entitlement were tied to private college prices—say, two-thirds of the first $4,800 in total attendance costs—states would be tempted to raise their public college tuitions. Any attempt to freeze the charges of colleges and universities would inexorably lead to a program with three thousand separate resource bases, each of them having to be recorded, policed, and periodically negotiated, an invitation to federal intrusion. But a limit pegged to public college prices would, as indicated earlier, do nothing to enhance student choice or the competitiveness of the private sector.

The other key "controllable" variable in these calculations is of course the student's "expected family contribution." Since the program is means tested, and the federal subsidy declines as income rises, a fundamental question is how fast does it decline, that is, how punishing is the effective tax on income. That will determine how successfully the program attains its multiple objectives, how many people are assisted by it, and how much it will cost. Whereas decisions about assured resource levels are issues for educational policymaking, it is in settling upon the means test that basic social policy is made about income redistribution, public and private spending priorities, and the nature of the nation's commitment to equal opportunity.

Many approaches are available to those designing a family contribution system, and trade-offs must be made among competing objectives. If targeting aid precisely on those who need it (and denying it to those who do not) is considered very important, for example, the preferred scheme will embody a number of variables and will be constructed to discriminate meticulously among individuals. If, on the contrary, a central purpose of the aid program is to expand enrollments, or to encourage people to enroll in college who might not otherwise do so, a simple allocation formula is more desirable.

The present basic grants program uses a relatively simple but demanding schedule for determining the contribution that can be expected of families at various income levels.[26] The major private need analysis systems are more intricate in design but financially less exacting.[27] If the

26. Various proposals made in early 1978 to extend basic grants to "middle income" students consisted, in the main, of relaxing that means test, thus assuming less by way of family contributions and rendering more people eligible for assistance. In fact, this could be accomplished without new legislation, for the existing law gives the commissioner of education great flexibility in designing each year's basic grants contribution schedule, although once it is constructed, he is required to submit it to Congress for review.

27. Recent studies show a large gap between what even the least demanding need analysis schemes suggest that families should be expected to contribute and what actual families are willing to spend. In a survey of 10,000 families expecting to make some contribution toward the college education of their children in 1977–78, the average sum "offered" by parents was $422, although the average amount they were expected to contribute was $762 (according to the "consensus methodology" used by the College Scholarship Service and others) or $1,293 (according to the family contribution schedule used by the federal basic grants program). See James E. Nelson, William D. Van Dusen, and Edmund C. Jacobson, "The Willingness of Parents to Contribute to Postsecondary Educational Expenses" (CEEB, March 1978; processed).

system of the College Scholarship Service (see table 3-4), for example, were applied to the grant program sketched above, not until a family attained a gross income of $9,375 would it be expected to contribute anything. With an income above $21,125, the expected contributions would exceed the $2,175 maximum grant available under the first tier of the aid program, which is to say that no subsidy would be forthcoming. When the family's income reached $24,375, its expected contribution would place it beyond eligibility for the second tier as well.[28]

This suggests that every family with income below $9,375 would be entitled to the maximum federal subsidy (assuming that college-going costs were large enough to warrant it), and no family with income above $24,375 would receive any assistance.[29] Parents with incomes between $21,125 and $24,375 would be eligible for assistance only if their son or daughter enrolled in a private (or out-of-state public) institution. And then the aid would be no more than $950.[30]

Effects of the Program

Different need analysis systems can readily be devised. That used by the College Scholarship Service is merely illustrative. This is an important variable, for the choice of a means test influences not only the efficacy of the program but also its costs. The variable that cannot readily be calculated or controlled is the number of new students an entitlement program of this sort would attract, and the changes in student behavior it might induce. Thus it is not possible to forecast accurately how much the program would cost.[31]

28. College Scholarship Service of the College Entrance Examination Board, *CSS Need Analysis: Theory and Computation Procedures for the 1977–78 PCS and FAF* (CEEB, 1976), table F. In practice, a need analysis system takes account of many variables, ranging from family size to extraordinary expenses of one sort or another. For simplicity I have taken a hypothetical family of four with one child in college and used the standard CSS estimate for "parents' contribution from total income before taxes."

29. Presumably the workings of any actual need analysis system would result in aid for some families above that line, such as those with many dependents or more than one child in college.

30. As income rises, and the family contribution nears the resource guarantee level, the amount of federal assistance to which the student is entitled shrinks. In order to avoid a large number of very small aid payments, many programs determine a minimum grant and provide no assistance unless the student's need justifies a grant of that size or larger. The present basic grants program, for example, has a minimum of $200.

31. In order to work properly from the student's standpoint, the program must function as an "entitlement," meaning that every eligible student must be assured

Had such a program been in effect in school year 1977–78, its gross costs would probably have been in the range of $4 billion to $5 billion.[32] But the net cost would depend in part on which of the extant federal student aid programs were replaced. Obviously, the current basic grants scheme would be subsumed within this one, as would supplemental grants. An argument might be made for retaining work-study to assist needy students with their self-help burden, and a less convincing one for the subsidized direct loans program. State student incentive grants could be retained as a stimulus to states to provide student assistance, and very likely some continuation of federally guaranteed (though not subsidized) loans would be desirable as well. But all these programs could also be phased out as the new grant scheme phased in, and if so, the net cost of the plan would be reduced considerably. Any "savings" from the shrinking GI bill, or from reducing or ending social security student benefits, would further ease the price tag.[33] Neither the executive branch nor the Congress, however, is organized to consider such interagency trade-offs, and it would therefore be a mistake to rely on them too heavily.

The results such a program would have are hard to predict; and some outcomes might not be universally applauded. The cost of higher education would not decline, though some would find it easier to pay the cost. Prices would remain uneven and irrational, though many would find the effect of these prices blunted. The states would not be treated with the sensitivity that their differences might warrant, although they would be treated uniformly. Some students would find themselves getting less aid than they might receive from the present programs, while others would get more. Some colleges would reap less benefit, even as others fared better. Some public funds would subsitute for private expenditures; other private outlays would supplant public costs. But no amount of analysis can accurately anticipate all the results, good or bad, of this (or

---

the assistance that the aid tables lead him to expect. If costs prove too high, subsidy levels may be reduced over time or family contribution expectations increased, but in any given year the program must deliver the stated aid to all who qualify. This is similar to keeping the present basic grants program "fully funded," but quite different from the practice in current campus-based programs, in which a fixed appropriation is simply stretched as far as it will go.

32. This rough estimate by the author is an extrapolation of a somewhat more precise calculation for the 1974–75 school year made by Dr. Alan Wagner, using data submitted to the College Entrance Examination Board's grant estimation model.

33. As noted earlier, because the social security benefits are trust fund expenditures, a more complex series of adjustments would have to be made to use savings there as an offset against the cost of a program that relies on appropriated funds.

any other) major alteration in the structure of federal student aid. People make their college decisions on many grounds, only some of them economic, and the variables apt to make a difference in the student marketplace are increasingly volatile. Thus the chief drawback to launching a new program may be the uncertainty. How many students will alter their behavior? Which colleges will get more applicants, and which less? How will state governments respond? How many additional people, if any, will enter the higher education marketplace? Not being sure of the answers, is a new program worth the risk?

The spokesmen for national associations of colleges and universities are likely to think it is not. Their mounting fears for the future have produced a conservative attitude toward federal student aid policy, in which the present programs, whatever their shortcomings, are known quantities and thus safer bets than new schemes with unforeseeable consequences. Against their understandable self-interest must be placed the nation's commitment to equal educational opportunity and the goal of providing assistance in ways that treat students equitably wherever they live and whatever school they wish to enroll in.

Myriad variations may be devised for the program sketched above, and a number of questions remain to be answered.[34] The main purpose of this lengthy scrutiny of student aid is to suggest that, for all its complexity and ambiguity, augmenting the purchasing power of students, which is likely to remain the principal mode of federal involvement in higher education, can be made to serve a quartet of worthy objectives: helping people go to college who could not do so without assistance; providing them with reasonable choice among the colleges that will accept them; strengthening the position of private colleges and universities without giving up the virtues of the marketplace or snaring Washington in a web of institutional subsidies; and reconstructing a major area of federal social policy so as to make it more rational, comprehensible, and equitable.

34. For example, how would independent students and older people be treated? Would graduate students be eligible as well as undergraduates? What about students pursuing technical training or other nondegree educational programs at the postsecondary level? What type of federally guaranteed loan program, if any, would be best suited to complement the direct grant scheme? Would the states be invited to participate in and augment the federal program, or left to run their own separate assistance plans if they are so inclined?

Chapter Five

Support for Institutions

The greatest unmet need in federal support for higher education is an institutional *support program through which flexible, predictable funds are made available to colleges and universities on a continuing basis.*

NATIONAL ASSOCIATION OF STATE UNIVERSITIES AND LAND-GRANT COLLEGES;
AMERICAN ASSOCIATION OF STATE COLLEGES AND UNIVERSITIES, 1969

Higher education has been deemed important to the government only to the extent that it has accomplished particular purposes that the government deemed important, and could accomplish them more effectively, faster, or cheaper, than someone else.

DANIEL P. MOYNIHAN, 1970

DIRECT federal support for colleges and universities comes close to being a contradiction in terms, since little of the money customarily entered under this heading had its origin in any express government intent to assist colleges and universities as institutions. It is nevertheless an important and expensive contradiction, amounting to $4.44 billion in fiscal 1977 (see table 1-1). These payments are made to the colleges themselves, in contrast to the two other modes of federal expenditure: payments to individual students, and reductions in federal revenues stemming from private transactions that enjoy tax benefits.[1]

Three attributes of federal funding of colleges and universities are important. First, though the total amount has grown, recently the money given to institutions has not kept pace with the growth of higher education or the expansion of federal student aid; in several key categories it has not even kept up with inflation. Second, the principal bene-

---

1. As noted in chapter 3, approximately one billion dollars in student aid monies —those appropriated for the campus-based programs—are channeled through the institutions, although their purpose is individual assistance. In addition, a wide range of federal graduate fellowship programs is administered on the government's behalf by the universities.

ficiaries are a small group of major universities; most institutions get little money. Third, with rare exceptions the federal officials authorizing and administering the programs do not regard support of colleges and universities as anything but an artifact of expenditures directed toward other national objectives; the universities supply services that the government wants, but the adequacy of the services, not the well-being of the providers, is the overriding consideration in Washington.[2]

To say that institutional payments were not meant to support the institutions needs several qualifications, however. First, federal programs often blur means and ends, sometimes framing a problem so that only a university can provide the solution. For example, the shortcomings of health care in the United States are often defined in terms of the supply of physicians and other medical workers; once that statement of the problem is accepted, the government has little choice but to give money to institutions capable of augmenting that supply. After several years of "capitation grants" for medical students, the universities have come to see these federal outlays as a form of general operating support and to regard them as their due.

Second, though a federal agency is generally involved with only part of a university, its actions affect the entire institution. A program officer in the Agricultural Extension Service may think that what he is doing is supporting the College of Agriculture (or its Department of Animal Husbandry or a single professor in that department) rather than Ohio State University, just as an official at the Department of Energy directs his attention to the Plasma Physics Laboratory at Princeton, not to the quality of undergraduate teaching there. But the proposition that all money is green applies when one turns from the perspective of Washington to that of the university president. Though his auditors can demonstrate that, for any given grant or contract, all the work being charged to the government's money is work being done on the government's behalf, the president knows there is more to it than that. If the College of Agriculture and the physics laboratory were suddenly to cease getting federal funds, either their activities would dwindle or—more likely—they would consume unrestricted university funds now being used for theology, library acquisitions, football scholarships, and the like. Not

2. This, obviously, is an impression, not an empirical finding, and others hold different views. One reader, for example, says that the point "is overstated, an expression of traditional bureaucratic cynicism based on a fear of being sentimental, a defense against budget reductions, a profitable myth to cover up a desired reality."

only is Washington supporting the parts of the university it thinks it is supporting, its funds also support the whole institution if only because they free some monies for other purposes.

Third, a few federal programs actually provide something close to unrestricted subsidies for entire institutions, although that fact is seldom acknowledged in the authorizing legislation. The land-grant payments to the big state universities have few strings attached, but they totaled just $11.5 million in fiscal 1978. The funds for "strengthening developing institutions"—$120 million in fiscal 1978—have elaborate application procedures in which the uses of the federal dollars must be specified, but in practice they underwrite routine expenses for their recipients, about half of which are "traditionally black" colleges. And, of course, there are some unique cases, such as the hefty annual subventions HEW gives Howard University and Gallaudet College.

But despite these qualifications, two observations are still justified: the federal government has never assumed responsibility for maintaining the generality of American colleges and universities, and the programs that do give something approaching unrestricted support to the institutions are small and benefit a limited number of schools. The average college gets only a tiny fraction of its income from Washington, and only by pledging to do something a federal agency wants done. It cannot rely on those funds from one year to the next, and it cannot openly treat them as unrestricted revenues.

One consequence of Washington's recent emphasis on student aid is that the funds directed to institutions have not grown rapidly. Table 1-2 indicates that five-sixths of the increase in federal higher education expenditures between 1968 and 1977 is attributable to student aid; table 5-1 shows the recent financial history of government obligations to the colleges and universities themselves since fiscal 1963, in current and constant (1972) dollars.

In current dollars the growth has been fairly steady, if slow. But in constant dollars backsliding is evident from the 1967 peak to the mid–1970s, even though the number of students increased from 7.4 million to 11.3 million between 1967 and 1975. It is not surprising, therefore, that since 1970 there has been a decline in the percentage of college and university income supplied by the federal government (see table 1-3).

In good years and bad, federal institutional funds have been concentrated in a small number of universities. In 1975 the 100 universities receiving the most money from the federal government got more than

Table 5-1. *Federal Obligations to Universities and Colleges, in Current and Constant (1972) Dollars, Selected Fiscal Years, 1963–76*

Millions of dollars

Fiscal year	Total obligations[a] (current dollars)	Total obligations (constant 1972 dollars)[b]
1963	1,413	1,949
1967	3,311	4,170
1970	3,227	3,550
1972	4,131	4,131
1974	4,463	3,963
1975	4,517	3,631
1976	5,399	4,047

Source: National Science Foundation, *Federal Support to Universities, Colleges, and Selected Nonprofit Institutions, Fiscal Year 1975* (GPO, 1977), p. 3; and *Federal Support to Universities, Colleges, and Selected Nonprofit Institutions, Fiscal Year 1976: Detailed Statistical Tables, Appendix B* (NSF, 1978), p. 1.

a. Although the National Science Foundation's annual tabulation of federal support for colleges and universities (measured as obligations) approximates in total dollars the "institutional support" figures compiled by the Office of Management and Budget (measured as outlays) and shown in tables 1-1 and 1-2, the elements are somewhat different. The NSF data have the advantages of a time series and of greater detail for purposes of analysis.

b. Constant dollars are derived by using the GNP implicit price deflator.

$11 million each, and accounted for 65 percent of the institutional monies. Of the remaining 2,900-odd colleges and universities, some 1,800 received less than $500,000 apiece and about 500 got nothing.[3]

Thus three basic policy questions emerge. Should the federal government persist with practices that allow or encourage the continued concentration of funds in a small number of universities, or should it spread resources more evenly? Should the revenues continue to be channeled through categorical programs, or should unrestricted funds be made available to sustain the essential activities of all institutions of higher education? Should the emphasis on student aid continue, even if it means a shrinkage of institutional programs, or should a conscious effort be made to direct more resources to the colleges and universities themselves, perhaps even by curbing the rate of increase in student aid expenditures?

Where the Money Comes From and What It Buys

Every dollar that the federal government channels into a college or university comes from the appropriation of one or another federal

3. National Science Foundation, *Federal Support to Universities, Colleges, and Selected Nonprofit Institutions, Fiscal Year 1975: Detailed Statistical Tables, Appendix B* (NSF, 1977), pp. 11–12, 49–123.

agency. Table 5-2 shows the distribution of these funds by agency for fiscal 1975 and selected earlier years. The table also shows both the growth and some of the fluctuations in government support, though it omits such new units as the arts and humanities endowments.[4] Note, for example, the modest declines in spending by the Pentagon and the National Aeronautics and Space Administration (NASA), the steady growth of the Department of Agriculture, the short life of the antipoverty agency, the mounting investment in energy and the environment, and the massive enlargement of HEW, which moved from 47 percent of the total in 1963 to 70 percent of a much larger total twelve years later.

Most of these monies sustain scientific research and development, and collateral activities keyed to the diverse missions of the federal agencies that supply them. The emphasis has changed considerably over time, however, as illustrated by the shifts shown in table 5-3 among the relative shares of the four major categories of support.

Until 1976 the largest share had consistently gone for research and development conducted on campus. Funds for "R&D plant"—essentially the construction and equipping of buildings used for scientific research —have shrunk, as has federal support of academic facilities generally.[5] "Other science activities" have also decreased since their peak in 1967, both in absolute dollars and as a percentage of the whole, primarily because large training programs run by HEW, the National Science Foundation, and other agencies have dwindled and, in some cases, have ended. Nonscience activities, on the other hand, have mushroomed, both in absolute dollars and as a percentage of the total, with two units within HEW—the Health Resources Administration and the Office of Education—deploying most of these monies for campus-based student aid and medical training programs.[6]

4. The National Science Foundation estimates that the agencies included in its annual tally account for 95 percent of all federal obligations to institutions of higher education, although individual campuses may receive substantial portions of their revenues from agencies not included here.

5. Although not separately examined in this book, the sharp erosion in funds for construction, maintenance, instrumentation, and other forms of capital investment and support services that undergird research has created grave problems. These are documented and analyzed, and their implications probed, in Bruce L. R. Smith and Joseph J. Karlesky, *The State of Academic Science: The Universities in the Nation's Research Effort* (Change Magazine Press, 1977), especially pp. 162–78.

6. As indicated in chapter 3, although the student aid funds included here are channeled through the colleges and universities—hence counted as federal obligations to the campuses—they are meant to assist individuals, not institutions.

Table 5-2. *Federal Obligations to Universities and Colleges, by Agency, Selected Fiscal Years, 1963–75*

Milloins of dollars

Agency	1963	1967	1970	1972	1974	1975
Department of Agriculture	104	145	182	239	261	291
Energy (Atomic Energy Commission, Energy Research and Development Administration, Nuclear Regulatory Commission)	76	110	115	95	99	124
Department of Commerce	2	8	5	26	30	26
Department of Defense	218	264	266	244	185	191
Office of Economic Opportunity	...	...	36	30	10	...
Environmental Protection Agency	...	...	...	23	31	39
Department of the Interior	4	27	28	24	24	29
National Aeronautics and Space Administration	87	132	131	119	99	108
National Science Foundation	256	395	387	459	450	491
Department of Transportation	...	...	10	16	13	21
Department of Health, Education, and Welfare[a]	665	2,231	2,051	2,828	3,234	3,178
Other (includes Departments of Labor and Housing and Urban Development, Agency for International Development)	...	...	17	28	30	20
Total	1,413	3,311	3,227	4,131	4,463	4,517

Source: National Science Foundation, *Federal Support to Universities, Colleges, and Selected Nonprofit Institutions, Fiscal Year 1975: Detailed Statistical Tables, Appendix B* (NSF, 1977), p. 1; figures are rounded.
a. The National Institutes of Health and the Office of Education each account for about one-third of HEW spending.

Table 5-3. *Federal Obligations to Universities and Colleges, by Category of Support, Selected Fiscal Years, 1963–76*

Amounts in millions of dollars

Item	Research and development	R&D plant	Other science activities	Nonscience activities	Total
1963					
Amount	830	106	393	85	1,413
As percent of total	59	7	28	6	100
1967					
Amount	1,301	111	911	987	3,311
As percent of total	39	3	28	30	100
1970					
Amount	1,447	45	696	1,039	3,227
As percent of total	45	1	22	32	100
1972					
Amount	1,853	37	709	1,532	4,131
As percent of total	45	1	17	37	100
1975					
Amount	2,223	45	522	1,727	4,517
As percent of total	49	1	12	38	100
1976					
Amount	2,419	24	513	2,443	5,399
As percent of total	45	<1	10	45	100

Source: National Science Foundation, *Federal Support to Universities, 1975: Detailed Statistical Tables*, pp. 1–2; and *Science Resources Studies Highlights* (NSF, May 1978); figures are rounded.

Research and Development

Scientific research and development is the heart of federal funds for universities, accounting for nearly half the total, but these monies go to relatively few institutions. Only 588 campuses received any R&D funds in fiscal 1975, with the top 100 getting 85 percent of the total in amounts ranging from $5.4 million at Florida State to $68.7 million at MIT.

Most colleges and universities, therefore, do not benefit—or benefit very little—from federal expenditures on research. But there is nothing very mysterious about this, let alone anything mischievous on Washington's part. Most colleges conduct little scientific research on the scale that federal agencies are wont to sponsor. Furthermore, nearly half the federal funds for research are supplied by the National Institutes of Health. Most colleges and universities without medical schools would not even apply for such funds, and there are only 120 medical schools in the United States.[7]

Federal research managers ordinarily seek out universities with the requisite facilities, academic strength, organizational capacity, and desire to undertake specific projects congruent with the agency's own needs and interests. This generally means large campuses with specialized faculties, a strong commitment to research and graduate training, and often a history of successful research projects for the government, possibly for the same unit within the same agency.

Federal officials look for more than speed and economy when they select universities for research purposes. They also seek quality of mind and performance. The R&D enterprise is the one area of federal higher education policy where old-fashioned meritocratic norms are still significant. Where is the ablest scholar or research team in the country that could undertake a particular inquiry? Which among ten applicants shows the greatest promise of making a valuable contribution to human knowledge in a stated field?

Agency officials do not rely wholly on their own judgment in these matters. If the research is sophisticated or arcane, they may not know enough about the subject and probably do not know who is doing the most promising work in the pertinent discipline. Moreover, when handing out large sums of tax dollars in accord with subjective criteria, a civil servant must be able to defend his decision if he is to resist the charge of favoritism. Scientists and universities may have friends in the executive branch and the Congress who wield much influence, and the career project officer in the middle level of an agency must be able to invoke more than his own judgment if he is to withstand the pressures that always build when many apply but few are chosen.[8]

Thus over the years most of the federal agencies that sponsor research and development, and particularly those that support basic scientific research, have devised variations of the "peer review" system, whereby expert (and ostensibly disinterested) judgment from outside the gov-

7. That figure represents the 1978 membership of the Association of American Medical Colleges. Of course some universities without medical schools do engage in biomedical research and may receive federal funds for that purpose.

8. The adroit agency official may also manipulate the "peer review" process, through the choice of reviewers, through the formulation of questions put to them, and of course through the use to which he puts their recommendations.

ernment is brought to bear on funding decisions the agency must make. The reviewers are told to apply qualitative standards, to invoke their own knowledge of the field and the prospective researchers, and to advise the government research managers whether a particular proposal should be approved, or which among several is worthiest.[9]

This complex of external advisers, meritocratic norms, and subjective appraisals is a surrogate for hard-edged gauges of institutional quality, which—if they existed—would assist government agencies in obtaining the best available work for their money. But there is some circularity to the process, as over time the presence of federal research funds bolsters the capacity of the universities receiving them to conduct the high quality research that will qualify those institutions to win further competitions in later years.

Universities outside this system understandably aspire to enter it, and every few years Capitol Hill erupts with charges by sympathetic congressmen that the peer review system is nothing more than an old boy network that helps the rich to get richer, invites logrolling among reviewers and grant applicants, and denies promising colleges and universities their chance for a piece of the federal action. Sometimes it is a state or region that is alleged to be getting starved, sometimes a particular class of institutions. Besides defending their procedures against such attacks, federal agencies have responded by trying to spread their funds more evenly. Between 1965 and 1972, for example, the National Science Foundation awarded $177 million in "science development" funds to thirty-one campuses in an attempt to move them into the front ranks of research universities and to ensure that more states had such universities within their borders.[10]

Some democratization has occurred, but not much. The top one hundred universities received 90 percent of all federal R&D obligations to colleges and universities in 1963, 85 percent in 1975. The top twenty slipped only from 50 percent of the total to 41 percent during the same period, and although there have been some changes within their ranks during that time, it is striking that the twenty institutions at the top in

9. Research universities are not the sole competitors for these funds. Although they dominate the field of federally sponsored basic research, in matters of applied research, development, or policy research, other nonprofit as well as profit-seeking organizations are also heavily involved.

10. National Board on Graduate Education, *Science Development, University Development, and the Federal Government* (NBGE, 1975), p. 7.

fiscal 1975 have, as a group, received 38 to 45 percent of the funds every year since 1963.[11]

Changing Patterns of Federal Support

The dominant feature of the federal research enterprise—in contrast to federal student aid—has been its ability to resist populist tendencies and to confine most of the funds to elite institutions by means of meritocratic practices. This may foster sound research, but it hardly makes for widespread popularity, and the unsteady course of federal support for scientific research in recent years may be explained in part by the small constituency for such activities.

As shown in table 5-3, federal R&D funds for colleges and universities rose from $830 million in fiscal 1963 to $2,419 million in 1976. In constant dollars, however, growth virtually ceased in 1966, and the amounts actually declined between 1969 and 1971, and again between 1974 and 1975. The increase in 1976 merely brought expenditures back to the 1972 level.[12] Particularly troubling to institutions of higher education was the decline in federal support for basic research, which, in constant dollars, fell by 15 percent between 1968 and 1976.[13]

This slack period affected far more than colleges and universities. The federal government's overall commitment to research and development, wherever performed, shrank in real terms during the decade after 1966, from $18.2 billion to $15.1 billion (amounts given in 1972 dollars). What kept the total national investment in research and development fairly steady during that period was the growth of nonfederal funding sources, especially private industry. But the economy moved faster still; whereas R&D expenditures from all sources represented 2.97 percent of the gross national product in 1964, they amounted to 2.25 percent in 1976. The federal share fell faster still, from 1.98 percent of GNP to 1.19 percent.[14]

This softening of the nation's commitment to research has implications far beyond the walls of academe and is a legitimate concern

---

11. Smith and Karlesky, *State of Academic Science*, p. 41; NSF, *Federal Support to Universities, Colleges, and Selected Nonprofit Institutions, Fiscal Year 1975* (GPO, 1977), p. 16.

12. NSF, *Federal Support to Universities*, p. 3.

13. Smith and Karlesky, *State of Academic Science*, p. 19.

14. National Science Board, *Science Indicators 1976* (GPO, 1978), pp. 207, 208.

in its own right. For present purposes, it is interesting to note that over the past decade universities have consumed a growing slice of the federal research pie, even as the pie itself was being nibbled away. In 1964 obligations to colleges and universities accounted for 7 percent of total federal R&D expenditures; ten years later, the corresponding figure was 11 percent. In the area of basic scientific research, where universities have traditionally been the heart of the entire national enterprise—and where federal funds sustain two-thirds of that enterprise—their share of total federal outlays rose from 48 percent to 56 percent during the same period.[15] From higher education's standpoint, then, the changing pattern of federal research support is worrisome but not acutely alarming.[16] Indeed, for the past several years there have been signs of a reassuring turnaround in the President's annual budget requests for scientific research generally and basic research in particular. For fiscal 1977, for example, the Ford administration proposed an 11 percent increase in funds for research and development. The following year the White House asked for an 8 percent increase, including a 3 percent real (that is, constant dollar) increase for basic research. For 1979 President Carter sought a 6 percent rise in total R&D funding and a 9 percent rise in basic research spending, and estimated that university-based research activities would receive an 8 percent increase.[17] Still, so significant was the previous slackening of federal support that (in constant dollars) the basic research figures for 1979 merely restore the federal investment level of 1967 and make no allowance for the expansion of the research enterprise—and the number of researchers—during that period. Moreover, Congress does not necessarily share the newfound enthusiasm of the executive branch. In cutting the National Science Foundation's 1978 appropriation $41 million below the President's request, the House Appropriations Committee chose to contrast federal research funding with the progress of the economy as a whole and observed—with no apparent basis in fact—that "the growth of federal support for academic research has exceeded that of the gross national product by a comfortable margin and has more than

15. The main loser has been industry, which received 61 percent of federal R&D funds in 1964, 49 percent in 1974. Industry's share of federal basic research funds shrank from 10 to 6 percent during the same period. National Science Foundation, *National Patterns of R&D Resources, 1953–1975* (GPO, 1975), pp. 18–21.

16. For a more detailed appraisal—and a gloomier conclusion—see Smith and Karlesky, *State of Academic Science.*

17. *Special Analyses, Budget of the United States Government, Fiscal Year 1977*, p. 276; *Fiscal Year 1978*, pp. 290–93; and *Fiscal Year 1979*, pp. 310, 313.

compensated for the effects of inflation at a time when other important federal programs were not so favored."[18]

A Problem of Dependency

The elite research universities are dependent to varying degrees on federal R&D agencies and are consequently vulnerable to fluctuations in funding levels, topical emphases, and management practices. Private universities tend to be affected the most, both because, relative to their size, they are more involved in research and because they lack the annual state appropriations of their public sector counterparts. Stanford and the University of California at Los Angeles, for example, received similar amounts of federal R&D money in 1975, but this constituted 21 percent of the private university's total current revenues that year, compared to 12 percent of the state institution's budget. The University of Michigan and Johns Hopkins also received kindred sums, but for the former this meant 10 percent of its revenues and for the latter, 18 percent.

Not surprisingly, the private research campuses have grown accustomed to receiving a larger portion of their income from Washington.[19] But public or private, the more successful a university has been in winning federal grants and contracts, and the more it has come to depend on them for a sizable share of its revenues, the more vulnerable it is. This takes four forms.

First, if government appropriations for campus-based R&D do not keep pace with rising university budgets, institutions that look to Washington for a large part of their income will be hard hit.

Second, any changes in the procedures by which government research monies are allocated among colleges and universities are apt to hurt the institutions that prospered from the previous procedures. If peer review were weakened, for example, or geographical distribution broadened, some major research universities would suffer.

Third, the "overhead" or indirect cost payments attached to research grants and contracts are large. Of the $63 million that Harvard University received from Washington in 1973–74, nearly $13 million was re-

18. Quoted in *Higher Education and National Affairs*, May 27, 1977, p. 2. In voting a smaller sum than the White House sought, the committee nevertheless increased the science foundation's appropriation by $68 million over the 1977 figure.

19. See Lyle H. Lanier, and Charles J. Andersen, *A Study of the Financial Condition of Colleges and Universities: 1972–75* (ACE, 1975), pp. 95, 98.

imbursement for indirect expenses.[20] Much has been written about this complex subject, but the essential point is straightforward: the government ordinarily balks at paying for campus activities that it feels the universities would have supported anyway, and for those not demonstrably related to the particular work the agency is procuring. The universities argue that their research libraries, their central administrations, their physical facilities, and a hundred other items in their budgets cannot be carved away without threatening their very existence as institutions capable of undertaking the kinds of work the government wants done, as well as the kinds they want to do themselves. This is a particularly sore point on private campuses, since their public sector counterparts could—and some do—obtain such revenues from their states as part of their general operating subsidies, whereas the private universities plausibly claim that they have nowhere else to turn except to student tuition and fees. Thus every time the federal auditors and research managers try to curb the overhead rate or narrow the "base" on which universities are allowed to calculate their indirect costs, the anxiety level rises especially high on private campuses.[21]

Fourth, shifts in federal spending priorities within the R&D domain naturally mean the greatest dislocations for the institutions that most depend on research funds. Larger appropriations for biomedical research cannot instantly or easily replace shrinking funds for aerospace engineering. A university that for ten years supported most of its physics department on a large grant from the Atomic Energy Commission cannot readily switch over to the National Endowment for the Humanities just because federal priorities have changed.

These fluctuations are especially disturbing within the category of basic research, for it is here that the universities have had the greatest control over the work they undertake for Washington and here that the federal funds come closest to supporting the kind of scholarly inquiry the university deems central to its own mission. Changes in disciplinary emphasis in basic research are most keenly felt during a time when the total expenditures are shrinking, such as between 1968 and 1974. Table 5-4 shows what this has meant for selected fields of study on the campuses.

20. *Financial Report to the Board of Overseers of Harvard College, Fiscal Year 1973–1974* (Harvard University, 1974), p. 15.

21. The issue of indirect costs is also probed more deeply in Smith and Karlesky, *State of Academic Science*, pp. 200–07.

Table 5-4. *Estimated Federal Basic Research Expenditures in Selected Fields at Universities and Colleges, Selected Years, 1968–76*

Millions of constant (1972) dollars

Category	1968	1970	1972	1974	1976
Total, all fields	2,084	1,929	1,974	1,752	1,753
Engineering	189	197	185	161	178
Physical sciences	725	645	625	519	493
Environmental sciences	241	280	291	275	267
Life sciences	701	606	668	633	656
Mathematics	81	63	63	42	46
Psychology	67	61	54	42	38

Source: National Science Board, *Science Indicators 1976*, p. 229. Columns do not add to totals because some disciplines are omitted.

Each university must judge whether it has the capacity and desire to reorganize its academic program to conform to evanescent federal priorities. Generally speaking, the broader the institution's range of interest and the more diverse its sources of support, the more easily it can make some adjustments without sacrificing its own sense of sovereignty and stability, whereas a school deeply committed to a single field of inquiry or reliant on a single federal agency finds such accommodations more taxing. But in the short run, it is never easy, even for the strongest universities and most adroit practitioners of federal grantsmanship. Academic institutions are ponderous and slow-moving creatures with many tenured staff members, long "start up" and "phase out" periods, and a durable commitment to scholarly inquiry in many fields. Gyrating government research priorities can throw a university off course and, in the long run, ill serve the government as well. "The fluctuations in federal funding of basic research which we have seen recently are extremely damaging," Jerome B. Wiesner, president of MIT, said in 1976. "The upswing to 1968 and the precipitate decrease since then have led to serious imbalances between fields; to an apparent lack of opportunity in some fields which drives good young people away, only to present us with 'shortages' in the future; to the destruction of many research teams carefully assembled over many years of effort; to the under-utilization of important facilities and in some cases to their premature demise."[22] Moreover, the understandable desire of federal research managers to obtain the greatest returns for each year's appropriation leads

22. Quoted in National Science Board, *Science at the Bicentennial* (GPO, 1976), p. 38.

them to procurement practices that tend to exploit the university's ac-
cumulated intellectual capital rather than to underwrite the less utilitarian activities that would replenish and augment it.[23] This is the natural
outgrowth of Washington's emphasis on individual projects rather
than on institutional support, and is exacerbated by a shift in the funding
balance away from basic research and toward its applications.[24]

Yet it would be misleading to characterize the federal research investment as harmful to the universities that receive it. Even though the
pattern of research support is uneven among universities and among
disciplines, the conclusion drawn by Harold Orlans in 1962 remains
true today: "On the whole the effects have been decidedly beneficial."[25]
Certainly, without federal R&D funds it is inconceivable that the major
research universities could exist in anything resembling their present
form. The most helpful things Washington could do for those universities would be to increase its appropriations for research and development, particularly for basic research; to avoid sudden changes in the
disciplines that qualify for support; to acknowledge a responsibility to
underwrite the full costs of projects undertaken at its behest; and to
maintain its reliance on qualitative judgments as the chief criteria for
apportioning that support among the universities.

Nonresearch Support

Federal obligations to colleges and universities in fiscal 1976 for purposes other than the support of research and development (and R&D
plant) totaled $2,956 million.[26] One-sixth of that money sustained
science-related activities; the balance went for other endeavors such as
campus-based student aid and professional training. Because many col-

23. For an eloquent elaboration of this point, see Edward Shils, "Government
and University," in Sidney Hook, Paul Kurtz, and Miro Todorovich, eds., *The University and the State: What Role for Government in Higher Education?* (Prometheus Books, 1978).

24. For the background and nature of this change from basic to applied research,
see Smith and Karlesky, *State of Academic Science*, pp. 32–37.

25. *The Effects of Federal Programs on Higher Education* (Brookings Institution, 1962), p. 133. See also Charles V. Kidd, *American Universities and Federal
Research* (Harvard University Press, 1959), for a somewhat dated but still percep-
tive appraisal.

26. The figures and classifications used here are those of the National Science
Foundation in *Federal Support to Universities, Colleges, and Selected Nonprofit
Institutions, Fiscal Year 1976: Detailed Statistical Tables, Appendix B* (NSF, 1978).

leges and universities participate in such programs, the distribution of funds is broader than in the research field. In 1976, 2,526 institutions received funds for "nonscience activities," the 100 leading research universities accounting for slightly less than one-third of this money.

Because undergraduate and graduate student support makes up such a large part of the resources tallied under nonresearch support, it is misleading to depict those funds as true institutional subsidies (although they may indirectly have that effect by relieving pressure on a college's unrestricted funds). Along with student aid, however, there is a dizzying array of categorical programs, most of them small but many important to both the campuses that partake of them and the agencies that administer them.

These programs have little in common with one another. In some cases, such as the grants for curricular and pedagogical innovation made by the Fund for the Improvement of Postsecondary Education, it is fair to say that the colleges and their students are the principal beneficiaries of the program. But in other instances, such as regional media centers for the deaf, or civil rights technical assistance institutes, the college or university is more accurately viewed as assisting a federal agency to achieve an objective unrelated to the school's own central activities. Most programs fall somewhere in between, mutually beneficial if not entirely amiable undertakings whereby the college receives funds for a purpose it values while the cognizant Washington agency is helped to carry out its own mission as well.

So long as the purpose of a program is compatible with the college's self-concept, the distinction is unimportant. Nevertheless, categorical programs differ from general institutional support in several essentials, the most important being that colleges and universities cannot count on the funds. Instead, they must apply for them, agreeing in their proposal to do whatever it is that Washington wants done, be it teacher training, remedial instruction for disadvantaged students, or the development of a new sophomore year humanities curriculum. Agency officials evaluate these applications, accepting some, denying some, and negotiating changes in others. Once a grant or contract is approved, funds may flow for one year or several years, but only in a few cases, such as the annual land-grant payments, are they regular and predictable.[27] This

27. And these are predictable only because Congress has consistently restored them to presidential budget submissions that omitted them. Small categorical programs in higher education are frequent targets for Office of Management and Budget examiners.

makes categorical payments a valid and effective means of attaining limited objectives, be they the government's or the college's. But the programs are usually complicated and cumbersome to administer, and their proliferation invites increased federal regulation of higher education. Moreover, they confer uneven fiscal benefits on individual colleges and universities, and these differences may be wholly unrelated to the academic quality, competitive position, or economic condition of the recipients.

The Quest for Unrestricted Aid

In the years following the passage of the Higher Education Act of 1965, the foremost goal of the Washington-based spokesmen for higher education was to secure some form of unrestricted institutional aid from the federal government. "The principal unfinished business of the Federal Government in the field of higher education," proclaimed the American Council on Education in 1969, "is the necessity to provide support for general institutional purposes."[28] Citing the 1862 Morrill Act as precedent, the ACE and its sister associations forcefully argued for legislation that would aid every accredited college or university through a grant of unrestricted federal funds. Research and development and the myriad categorical programs that Washington supported did not go far enough: they were too uneven and unpredictable to assure the generality of colleges and universities the regular income they sought, particularly in a period of fiscal crisis. Student aid was welcome, but so long as it was confined to discrete categories of persons, it did not much avail the ordinary student or the institution that enrolled him. Furthermore, a heavy stress on student aid was an open invitation to high tuitions.

Even worse, the associations argued, categorical programs often ended up costing the university money, subsidizing the government instead of the other way around. If the "overhead" or indirect cost payment tied to a federally funded program did not meet the campus's full cost of conducting that program, the net effect on the institution's balance sheet would be negative. Similarly, a student aid program, even if it supplied the full tuition charge, would not pay the true cost of edu-

28. *Federal Programs for Higher Education: Needed Next Steps* (ACE, February 1969), p. 17.

cating the federally assisted students, since tuitions never equal costs.[29] Hence enrolling a federally assisted student was arguably also a net loss to the institution.

As a bookkeeping matter, these claims could be supported. As a political argument, the reasoning was a bit disingenuous, for it implied that the university was reluctantly but patriotically selling its services to the federal government rather than avidly searching out the projects and the students. A faculty member whose salary must be paid costs the institution even more if no government money helps underwrite him, and a wealthy student who signs a personal check for the entire tuition also creates a dollar loss for the university.[30] One skeptical congressman commented privately that the spectacle of colleges chasing after additional students while arguing that every matriculant cost them more money than he brought in was reminiscent of the haberdasher who said he lost five dollars on every shirt he sold and was therefore trying to make it up in volume.[31]

The idea of unrestricted federal funds for colleges was not new. Land-grant support was a century old. President Truman's Commission on Higher Education had recommended in 1947 that Washington undertake a massive program of "general support of institutions of higher education," although the program then envisioned would have channeled the federal funds to the states "on an equalization basis," and would have limited the recipient colleges to "institutions under public control."[32] Babbidge and Rosenzweig had articulated the standard rationale for federal institutional aid in 1962, stating that the federal interest in higher education would—and should—subsume a growing share of the *national* interest in higher education, which "consists in developing to the fullest the capacity of institutions of higher education to preserve, enlarge, and transmit the culture of man." They had, how-

29. This view is largely based on the fallacious equation of marginal and average costs. For discussion, see Susan Nelson, "Financial Trends and Issues," in Breneman and Finn, eds., *Public Policy and Private Higher Education.*

30. Again, this assumes (a) that tuition levels are set lower than average cost levels and (b) that the costs for a given student are properly construed as the average rather than the marginal figures.

31. Of course, if the federally aided students require more expensive educational services, such as remedial instruction, than those who might otherwise have enrolled, a case can be made that the economic burden on the college is heavier, assuming the extra services are actually provided and assuming also that people not requiring such services were prepared to enroll.

32. President's Commission on Higher Education, *Higher Education for American Democracy*, vol. 5, *Financing Higher Education* (GPO, 1947), pp. 54–63.

ever, also cautioned that "it is time to drop the idea that the Government will make large grants of money to institutions to use in any way they see fit."[33]

It is easy to quibble over the question of when money is unrestricted and when it is categorical. Clearly the goal of higher education spokesmen in the late sixties and early seventies was to secure federal funds for their institutions with as few strings as possible. The simplest justification was the best: the existence of colleges and universities is, a priori, in the national interest and, by extension, it is also in the interest of the national government. Washington was free to procure specific services from the academy, but the most important thing it could procure was the survival and health of the institutions without which there would be no academy. John F. Morse of the American Council on Education analogized this to "a national endowment, with annual payments assured to all accredited institutions to be used exactly as if it were endowment. . . . Such a program could undergird the various categorical programs we have been discussing. It could provide funds indirectly for institutional programs that are not likely to win direct Federal support. It could enable institutions to resist the explosive pressure to increase their charges to students. It could help the weaker institutions improve the quality of their work, while at the same time enabling the strong institutions to move toward even greater excellence."[34]

Two issues presented themselves, one constitutional, the other practical. Though it was reasonably clear that the federal government could contract with sectarian institutions to perform specified, nonsectarian functions on its behalf—church-affiliated universities had been among the leading recipients of federal research funds for years—it was less clear that Washington could give them money to use as they wished. The education legislation of the Great Society had sidestepped the church-state problem but not resolved it and, with one out of four colleges and universities affiliated with a religious body, any generalized institutional aid plan had to reckon with the possibility of being thrown out by the courts.[35]

33. Homer D. Babbidge, Jr., and Robert M. Rosenzweig, *The Federal Interest in Higher Education* (McGraw-Hill, 1962), p. 185.

34. Quoted in Laura C. Ford, "Institutional Aid," *Journal of Law and Education*, vol. 1 (October 1972), p. 557.

35. Truman's 1947 commission, chaired by George Zook, president of ACE, had insisted that, while general educational support would go only to public institutions, student aid and categorical programs would be open to public, private nonsectarian, and church-related colleges alike.

The practical question was how to parcel out the funds. Whatever formula was chosen, it had to be evenhanded and nondiscretionary, for to allow a federal agency to pick and choose among colleges was to invite federal control and political meddling. But it was patently ridiculous to suggest that a tiny college and a vast university should receive the same amount, so in backing away from subjective criteria the evangelists of institutional aid moved toward what the Carnegie Commission termed the "quantitative dimension."[36] A school's allotment would depend in some measure on its size.

A great amount of effort went into designing specific formulas, and the higher education associations had trouble agreeing among themselves, for it was apparent that every formulation could be said to favor some kinds of institutions over others.[37] The universities would benefit if extra weight were given to graduate enrollments, while the colleges would fare better with a strict "head count." The private sector would benefit from a stress on smallness (such as more money for each of the first one thousand students than for the rest). The public sector would benefit from an emphasis on largeness, or "lower division" (that is, freshman and sophomore) enrollments. And so it went, as the various factions tried to tilt the formula toward their own interests.

What brought them back together was a shared political problem that grew more acute as the legislative battles of 1970–72 heated up. Even though the spokesmen for institutional aid were careful to voice their commitment to equal opportunity for students, they could not ignore the possibility that money for institutions might become an alternative to student aid. Federal funds would never be sufficient to accomplish all desirable purposes, even within higher education; hence an investment in the colleges might mean less money for helping needy students to enroll in them. The Carnegie Commission on Higher Education was troubled by this, observing in 1972 that "new forms of direct aid to institutions may be gained at the expense of present programs of aid to institutions and students."[38]

Nor are institutional aid and student aid interchangeable means to the same ends. In 1969 Rivlin and Weiss reiterated a point that analysts had long understood: if the social policy objective is to equalize educational

36. Carnegie Commission on Higher Education, *Institutional Aid* (McGraw-Hill, 1972), p. 17.

37. For a good general discussion, see ibid., especially app. F.

38. Ibid., p. 93.

opportunity by drawing low-income people into college, then the most effective vehicle is need-based student aid. Subsidizing institutions, thereby scattering funds across everyone enrolled in them, is wasteful and ineffectual by comparison. If, on the contrary, the purpose is to curb tuition levels, to raise expenditures per student, or simply to equip the colleges with added revenues, the most direct way is to assist the institutions.[39]

In the deliberations over the Education Amendments of 1972, these divergent goals and the different funding mechanisms linked to them fueled a historic confrontation on Capitol Hill. Favoring institutional aid, and the middle-class student most likely to benefit from it, were Congresswoman Edith Green (Democrat from Oregon), chairman of the House Special Subcommittee on Education, and all the major higher education associations. Defending need-based student aid was an unusual alliance that included Senator Claiborne Pell (Democrat of Rhode Island), chairman of the Senate Education Subcommittee, Congressmen John Brademas (Democrat from Indiana) and Albert Quie (Republican from Minnesota), and the Nixon administration.[40]

As with most higher education legislation in recent years, the debate cut across party alignments. A moderate Republican administration, a medley of economists and study groups, and a number of liberal legislators from both parties found themselves favoring a progressive allocation of public subsidies to the neediest students, while the colleges and their allies (also from both parties) preferred an approach more immediately beneficial to the institutions and to their predominantly middle- and upper-class clienteles. Congresswoman Green, whose bill became the chosen instrument of the higher education associations, pro-

39. Alice M. Rivlin and Jeffrey H. Weiss, "Social Goals and Federal Support of Higher Education—The Implications of Various Strategies," in *The Economics and Financing of Higher Education in the United States,* a compendium of papers submitted to the Joint Economic Committee, 91:1 (GPO, 1969), pp. 543–55. See also *Higher Education Amendments of 1970,* Hearings before the Senate Labor and Public Welfare Committee, 91:1 (GPO, 1971), pp. 344–437. Much the same point was made by the National Commission on the Financing of Postsecondary Education in its report, *Financing Postsecondary Education in the United States* (GPO, 1973), especially pp. 103–18.

40. See, generally, Lawrence E. Gladieux and Thomas R. Wolanin, *Congress and the Colleges* (D. C. Heath, 1976). For an account of the Nixon administration's education policy development in 1969–70, see Chester E. Finn, Jr., *Education and the Presidency* (D. C. Heath, 1977). As an example of the forces prodding government officials to emphasize student aid rather than institutional aid, see Frank Newman and others, *Report on Higher Education* (GPO, 1971).

posed to retain certain student aid programs but also to add a major program of enrollment-based institutional grants for colleges and universities. The Pell forces put their emphasis on a thorough overhaul of student aid policies that would create a need-based "entitlement" for impoverished students. Although the debate was colored by many side issues, in a large sense it came to be seen as a choice between helping colleges and helping students.

In their attempts to persuade Congress, the higher education associations reinforced this dichotomy, though the student remained the nominal object of their concern. A panel of association representatives testified in 1971:

It would be cruel indeed if the hopes of young people for post-secondary education were raised by promises which cannot be kept. . . . An additional student . . . is no financial boon to a college; instead, he represents an additional cost which, somehow, must be met. . . . Institutions are stretched to the breaking point. What is needed now from the federal government is support to institutions to be used to meet their day-to-day operating costs. . . ."[41]

But between the poles of student aid and institutional aid lay a zone where compromise was possible. It was the concept known as cost-of-education (or cost-of-instruction) allowances, payments to institutions that are piggybacked on payments to students. A federally aided student would come to the college bursar's office bearing not only his own tuition, which the government was helping him to pay, but also an additional sum that the college would receive directly by virtue of his enrolling there.

This too was an old idea. The original GI bill incorporated one version of it. Many fellowship programs for graduate students employed it. Some of the staunchest advocates of need-based student aid, such as the Carnegie Commission and the Rivlin task force in HEW, had endorsed it. The rationale for cost-of-education allowances had three key elements: that because tuition did not cover the college's average cost of educating a student, if the federal government wanted to encourage postsecondary study for certain groups of people it should compensate the institutions for the costs of enrolling them; that teaching disadvantaged students was more expensive than educating other kinds of students and thus the government should pay a premium to the colleges they attended; and that the church-state barrier could be surmounted by linking the institutional payments to a well-accepted federal interest. Implicit in these justifications was a touch of extortion. Since no college

41. Quoted in Ford, "Institutional Aid," p. 573.

was obliged to admit a single federally aided student, and since the government had nowhere else to turn to obtain postsecondary education for those it sought to help, Washington had reason to make it worth the colleges' while to teach them.

A fractious Senate-House conference yielded a clear victory for the advocates of need-based student aid, but the cost-of-education allowance survived in the legislation that President Nixon signed in June 1972. An extremely complicated formula held out the promise of federal payments to the colleges of $100 to $500 for each student aid recipient they enrolled. It was not outright institutional support, for a school that had no federally assisted students would not get any, but neither was it orthodox student aid, for the money would go straight to the college.

The promise turned out to be empty, however, for the cost-of-education scheme has never had a penny appropriated.[42] Favoring outright aid to students from the beginning, the executive branch has not budgeted any money for the program, and despite its habit of heavily amending presidential education budgets, Congress has declined to touch this provision, although higher education leaders have annually beseeched it to do so.

The university lobbyists had been bruised in the authorization battle, both because of their identification with the losing side and because of the unfortunate—and partly undeserved—impression that they cared more for their own institutional balance sheets than for the access of the poor to higher education. Certainly the cause of unrestricted aid for colleges and universities took a beating in part because of their single-minded advocacy of it. Congressman Brademas charged: "We turned to the citadels of reason. We said, 'Tell us what you need,' and they answered 'We need $150 per student because that's what we've been able to agree on.' "[43]

The government's disinclination to fund the cost-of-education provision was not simple petulance or retribution. The formula was complex and the program expensive. The law had been written as an "entitlement," and would have cost about $670 million a year to fund,[44] at a time when the student aid programs authorized in 1972 promised to take up a growing share of the federal education budget. The delicately

42. A similar, but smaller, program supplying allowances to colleges enrolling veterans is a going concern, and other federal programs embodying cost-of-education allowances, such as graduate fellowships, also continue.

43. Quoted in Gladieux and Wolanin, *Congress and the Colleges*, p. 242.

44. Estimated in "Payments to Institutions of Higher Education" (College Entrance Examination Board, June 1974; processed).

balanced compromises among provisions sought by high- and low-priced colleges had been achieved primarily by retaining extant student aid programs even as new ones were created. Although the executive branch tried to persuade Congress to cease funding some of the programs it thought superfluous, that effort failed, and the result is a costly array of somewhat redundant programs. Given a choice between continuing to supply these funds for millions of students or directing resources into a new program of benefit chiefly to a few thousand colleges and universities, neither the White House nor the appropriations committees had any difficulty deciding which they preferred.

The Next Round

Higher education's desire for federal cost-of-education allowances or other forms of institutional support did not wane after the President signed the 1972 amendments into law. But the following year the issue grew more complex when several respected study commissions assaulted the bulwark of low tuition—the doctrine on which all public colleges and universities are founded—and with it the principal rationale for institutional subsidies of every kind. Although this attack did not directly involve federal policy, it had significant implications for any future federal support for higher education.

An inevitable consequence of the low-tuition doctrine is that some people are provided with a subsidized higher education who do not "need" the subsidies, because they have the private resources to pay the full costs themselves. Those who regard higher education as a public good have no quarrel with that outcome. But those more concerned about the equitable allocation of public subsidies object. "Why," asked Milton Friedman, "should the families in Watts pay taxes to subsidize the families in Beverly Hills who send their children to U.C.L.A.?" Or, he might have added, to Stanford.[45]

45. "The Higher Schooling in America," *The Public Interest*, no. 11 (Spring 1968), p. 108. The redistributional effects of higher education subsidies are hotly debated. Marc Nerlove has contended that "even with progressive general taxation . . . it is clear that public support of low- or zero-tuition public institutions redistributes income primarily from low- and very high-income groups to middle-income groups." "On Tuition and the Costs of Higher Education: Prolegomena to a Conceptual Framework," *Journal of Political Economy*, vol. 80, (May–June 1972), pt. 2, p. S192. For additional discussion, see *The Economics and Financing of Higher Education in the United States*, a compendium of papers submitted to the Joint Economic Committee, 91:1 (GPO, 1969).

When resources are scarce, and other legitimate public services lay claim to them, Friedman's query becomes more disturbing, particularly since the bulk of college students are from middle- and upper-income families. Moreover, when the limited public funds for higher education are spent to hold down tuitions for all, less remains to help the impoverished meet the sizable nontuition costs of college.

Thus for some scholars and other people concerned about the efficiency of the higher education market and the equity of public subsidies, it appears more sensible to let prices at all institutions rise close to the true costs of the product being provided and to use tax-generated subsidies to help students unable to pay those prices. That course of action has several attractions: it would reduce total public expenditure for higher education,[46] narrow the tuition gap between public and private campuses, concentrate subsidies on the poor, and direct them into the marketplace in ways that let colleges compete for students on a fairer basis. If the student aid subsidies were financed with revenues generated by the higher tuitions in state colleges and universities, then the higher education system would itself redistribute income in a progressive manner. Families in Beverly Hills would pay more to send their children to UCLA, in part so that families in Watts would be able to pay less.

Such reasoning yielded a series of proposals in 1973 for states to drive up the tuitions charged by their public postsecondary institutions and to redirect resources into need-based aid programs for students who could then use their subsidies to attend either public or private colleges.[47]

46. If "need" were generously enough defined and individuals generously enough assisted, it is possible that eventually the expenditure would not be less.

47. The best-known of these proposals were made by the Carnegie Commission on Higher Education, in *Higher Education: Who Pays? Who Benefits? Who Should Pay?* (McGraw-Hill, 1973), and by the Committee for Economic Development, in *The Management and Financing of Colleges* (CED, 1973). Although the "Second Newman Report" did not explicitly urge increases in public sector tuitions, it stressed the importance of channeling higher education subsidies through students rather than institutions wherever possible, leaving the clear implication that tuitions should rise. See Frank Newman and others, *The Second Newman Report: National Policy and Higher Education* (MIT Press, 1973). Finally, the National Commission on the Financing of Postsecondary Education, while also refraining from any direct advocacy of higher tuitions, made clear that access to higher education is best fostered through need-based aid to students rather than institutional subsidies. See its report, *Financing Postsecondary Education in the United States* (GPO, 1974). For a summary and critique of all four studies, see Howard R. Bowen, "Financing Higher Education: The Current State of the Debate," in Kenneth E. Young, ed., *Exploring the Case for Low Tuition in Public Higher Education* (Iowa City: Amer-

Although the idea of escalating public tuitions did not directly concern the federal government, which has no control over institutional charges, the advocates of that idea assumed that Washington would bear much of the student aid burden that would have to be shouldered if college were to remain within reach of low- and middle-income people. The Committee for Economic Development saw this as a redirection of existing federal subsidies away from (unspecified) programs of institutional support and into student assistance, whereas the Carnegie Commission envisioned a rise in Washington's share of total higher education costs.

Despite its considerable logical appeal, the idea of full-cost pricing, or the more limited versions actually advanced by Carnegie, CED, and other groups, fell on barren soil in the nation's capital. The timing was dreadful. Lobbyists for the universities, congressmen, and administration officials were still weary from the lengthy examination of higher education policy that led to the 1972 amendments. With the new legislation not due to expire for several years, there was no incentive to take up a different scheme that would draw the federal government into a controversial area—the setting of actual or "posted" tuition rates—where it had no experience and little leverage.

But the main objection to higher public tuitions was doctrinal rather than practical, for the whole idea clashed with the first tenet of public higher education: the belief that colleges and universities *should be* available to all comers without charge. Although public college tuition levels have tended to rise—in percentage terms they have mounted somewhat faster since 1970 than their private sector counterparts—they remain a sensitive issue. To boost tuitions on the theory that middle- and

---

ican College Testing Program, 1974), pp. 11–31. For a more recent commentary, see Carol Van Alstyne, "Rationales for Setting Tuition Levels at Public Institutions," *Educational Record*, vol. 58 (Winter 1977), pp. 66–82.

For a description of the theoretical underpinnings of these proposals, see W. Lee Hansen and Burton A. Weisbrod, "A New Approach to Higher Education Finance," in M. D. Orwig, ed., *Financing Higher Education: Alternatives for the Federal Government* (American College Testing Program, 1971), pp. 117–42. A more recent variant is John Silber's voucher plan. See John R. Silber, "Paying the Bill for College," *The Atlantic*, vol. 235 (May 1975). It should be remembered that actual educational costs vary a good deal among colleges, and that private institutions generally spend more per student than do public. Thus full-cost pricing would not homogenize tuitions. It would simply remove the "artificial" subsidy of public sector tuitions and bring college prices into more of a true marketplace, where rules of supply and demand prevail.

high-income students *should* pay a larger share of their education costs, or because doing so would indirectly strengthen the competitive position and institutional health of rival private colleges, was—and remains —anathema to most leaders of public higher education.[48]

For their part, private college leaders were surprisingly apathetic toward the idea of full-cost pricing. Although they had seemingly been handed a golden opportunity—respected advisory groups invoking progressive ideas about income distribution and subsidy structures in ways that would benefit private higher education—and although their widely publicized financial problems had cleared the way for such a proposition, the idea never became a part of their policy agenda.[49]

Most college leaders, private as well as public, believe that student charges should be low. Economists may demonstrate again and again that full-cost pricing is the most rational point from which to seek equity in the allocation of public subsidies, but educators remain convinced that the benefits of higher education accrue to the society and society should therefore bear their costs, preferably through institutional subsidies to public and private colleges alike, and that any remaining tuition gap should be dealt with by expanding aid to students in higher-priced institutions.

The controversial high tuition proposals of 1973 thus afforded the American Council on Education a chance to advance a new agenda around which public and private colleges could unite, and it accordingly stated that "private education should support low public tuition and

48. For other arguments against high tuition, see Young, ed., *Exploring the Case for Low Tuition.*

49. There was a brief flirtation. In October 1973 *Newsweek* reported "some support . . . by representatives of the nation's private colleges, who hope that higher tuitions at public schools would make their own look less formidable." And a task force of the National Council of Independent Colleges and Universities, struggling with solutions to financial dilemmas of private colleges, entertained in its early drafts the possibility of presenting higher public tuition as one option. But the final version of that report mentioned nothing of the sort, and the Board of Directors of the Association of American Colleges (with which NCICU was affiliated) announced that it viewed "with grave concern the threat presented to all of higher education by the divisive effect of current arguments about tuition charges in publicly-controlled institutions. . . . This Board is convinced that it is illusory to believe . . . that an effort to assist private institutions by increasing tuitions in public institutions, however well intentioned, can be effective." "AAC Statement on Tuition Policy" in Young, ed., *Exploring the Case for Low Tuition,* p. 167. For the final text of the task force report, see *A National Policy for Private Higher Education,* Report of a Task Force of the National Council of Independent Colleges and Universities (Association of American Colleges, 1974).

that public education should encourage the use of public funds for the assistance of private education."[50]

All such a plan needed was money. Whereas the high-tuition idea would reduce government subsidies to public institutions, the alternative of "tuition offsets" that began to emerge in 1974 and 1975 would retain those subsidies and give new ones to private colleges and universities. Instead of prosperous public sector students having to pay more tuition, students in private institutions would also enjoy a bargain price courtesy of the taxpayer.

Confidence verging on hubris was required, but the higher education community was not found wanting. The social benefits of learning and scholarship, whatever they may be, are not confined to public institutions, so it stands to reason that a society willing to underwrite them in the one group of colleges might properly be asked to sustain them in the other as well. The fact that some states had already begun new forms of aid to private higher education lent credence to such faith. Explicit programs based upon it were tendered in 1975 by the Carnegie Council on Policy Studies in Higher Education and by the National Council of Independent Colleges and Universities, each of which urged that tuition offsets for private colleges and universities be financed by a mixture of federal and state resources.[51]

Tuition offsets are, so to speak, the programmatic opposite of full-cost pricing. And they are, of course, commensurately more expensive for the taxpayer. But they do not threaten the low-tuition doctrine—to

50. "ACE Statement on Tuition Policy," in Young, ed., *Exploring the Case for Low Tuition,* pp. 165–66.

51. In the space of two years, the Carnegie Commission on Higher Education and its successor, the Carnegie Council on Policy Studies in Higher Education, seemingly executed a 180-degree turn. In 1973 the commission was one of the two most prominent sources of the idea of higher public sector tuitions linked to increased student aid. This was proposed in large part as a solution to problems of private higher education. See Carnegie, *Higher Education: Who Pays?* Two months later, in a "supplemental statement," the staff of the Carnegie commission, while not explicitly withdrawing these recommendations, took such pains to qualify, limit, and put them into context that the second document was widely regarded as a policy reversal and many observers assumed it had been so intended. See *Tuition* (Carnegie Commission on Higher Education, 1974). In March 1975 the new Carnegie Council, staffed largely by the same people, released its recommendations in *The Federal Role in Postsecondary Education* (Jossey-Bass, 1975), urging a new program of "tuition equalization grants" for private colleges and universities. As noted in the text, such tuition offsets are the exact opposite of higher public tuitions coupled with increased student aid.

the contrary—and therefore offer a basis for public-private compromise so long as the presumption of sufficient funds remains inviolate.

Unfortunately for the advocates of tuition offsets, though several more states enacted similar programs, Washington was not receptive to the idea. Instead, as Congress reexamined the student aid programs in 1975 and 1976, the nascent split between public and private colleges opened wide. With neither the House nor the Senate evincing any interest in tuition offsets or other schemes targeted solely on the private sector, with little likelihood of across-the-board institutional subsidies getting funded, and with well-publicized prophecies that enrollments would soon decline and competition among colleges intensify, the details of existing student aid programs become more important and contentious.[52]

Tension mounted within the higher education community in 1975–76. Several public college associations joined with labor, religious, civil rights, and student groups in an alliance called the National Coalition for Lower Tuition in Higher Education. In the fall of 1975, the American Association of State Colleges and Universities resolved: "No federal or state aid program to the private . . . sector should be at the expense of public college students, either in terms of reduced appropriations for the public sector or increased tuition and student charges at public colleges."[53]

The private colleges had never had a satisfactory national organization of their own. The institution-based associations that attempted to look after the interests of the private sector were less than fully representative of it or were constrained because they had public members, too. In early 1976 private college leaders moved to correct that situation, creating out of the old Association of American Colleges (and its state-based affiliate, the National Council of Independent Colleges and Universities) a new organization consisting solely of private institutions: the National Association of Independent Colleges and Universities.

While uniting in many other endeavors, such as in their efforts to reduce federal regulation, public sector and private sector spokesmen continued to exchange heated comments about financing arrangements. "While I am a strong supporter of our dual system of higher education,"

52. For an examination of those details, see chapter 3.
53. "Public Aid to Private and Proprietary Institutions," policy statement adopted at the 15th annual meeting, November 1975, Boston, Mass. (AASCU; processed).

Allan W. Ostar, a leader of AASCU, observed, "I also believe that private institutions must not be permitted to attempt to resolve their financial difficulties at the expense of the public sector." Terry Sanford, president of Duke University, retorted that he found it "appalling" that "the principal proponents of starving the private colleges off the land should be many of [those] who lead public colleges."[54]

The short, troubled life of the high-tuition proposals of 1973, the ill-fated tuition-offset proposals that succeeded them, and the increased bickering between public and private college leaders served to draw the higher education community away from the common quest for federal institutional aid that had ranked so high on its policy agendas a few years earlier. In any case, that quest had brought no tangible results, only an unfunded authorization on the statute books, and by 1977 the major Washington higher education associations had seemingly suspended hope for it.[55] Instead, they chose to concentrate their energies on several other provisions that promised institutional payments for somewhat better disguised and more narrowly defined purposes. The 1976 amendments had authorized "administrative allowances" of $10 per recipient to colleges and universities enrolling basic grants and guaranteed loans recipients.[56] Funding those provisions—which required their own appropriations—would have cost $30 million in fiscal 1978, not an enormous sum, but money the institutions wanted badly. The 1976 amendments also included a complex "trigger" provision whereby after student aid appropriations reached a certain amount ($2.8 billion in fiscal 1978), for every two additional dollars appropriated for student aid one dollar must be appropriated for a trio of categorical programs especially popular with the institutions.[57]

54. Quoted in Malcolm G. Scully, "Public, Private Colleges in Open Conflict over Support," Chronicle of Higher Education, November 22, 1976, pp. 1, 6.

55. See, for example, its omission from the American Council on Education's fiscal 1978 budget recommendations: Memorandum from Charles B. Saunders, Jr., to Allan Jackson and Leonard Spearman (October 22, 1976; processed); and from the statement of eight higher education associations to the Senate Appropriations Committee (April 6, 1977; processed).

56. For some years institutions receiving allocations for the three campus-based student aid programs had been permitted to retain 3 percent of the funds for administrative expenses—further reason for the popularity of campus-based aid among college and university spokesmen. The 1976 amendments also increased this to 4 percent.

57. These were Title X (Community Colleges), Title I (Community Services), and Title VII-C (Facilities Loans) of the Higher Education Act as amended. Funds appropriated to these three programs through the "trigger" mechanism were limited to $215 million.

Though neither the administrative allowances nor the programs affected by the "trigger" were equivalent, in flexibility or scale, to the
cost-of-education allowances authorized in 1972, and though neither
came close to unrestricted support for all postsecondary institutions,
these new provisions struck association leaders as a good way to obtain
the type of federal funds they sought. But for a time at least, it seemed
that they were again guilty of wishful thinking, as the Carter administration included no funds for administrative allowances in its budget for
1978 and sought to repeal the "trigger" provision. In neither case did
Congress appear disposed to take the institutions' side against the administration, if doing so meant less money for student assistance. The President's budget request for 1979 did, however, contain some funds for the
administrative allowances.

For the Future

Despite the proliferation of federal higher education programs, the
idea of unrestricted aid to colleges and universities has made little head-
way in Washington. Even when formulated in less ambitious terms and
tied to popular programs of student aid, measures for institutional subsidy have been enacted only with difficulty and have then gone without
funds more often than not.

Should institutional aid therefore be judged a dead issue? Is it fundamentally a good idea whose time has not yet come, or does it rest on a
flawed conception of the federal role in higher education? The answer
depends on one's objectives. If one believes that the federal government
should support the ordinary activities of institutions of higher education,
the most direct means to that end is to devise a simple formula for the
allocation of federal funds. Assuming its uses are genuinely unrestricted,
such aid has the further virtue of minimizing government controls and
requirements of the type associated with categorical funding. Once the
formula is determined, and a college renders itself eligible, the money
flows smoothly from the federal Treasury into the institution's coffers.

Today, the national government subsidizes a remarkable assortment
of institutions and organizations, ranging from hospitals to steamship
companies to airplane manufacturers. Sometimes these subsidies are
categorical, money paid to do something in particular that a government agency wants done and that the recipient may or may not do
without the federal payment. Sometimes they are unrestricted, money

transferred from Washington to the recipient simply to sustain its ordinary activities.

Is it reasonable to impose on federal policy toward colleges and universities a discipline that the government so often dismisses when other interests—and interest groups—are at stake? Assuredly the colleges do not think so, nor ought they be expected to. Their proper concern is with their own welfare, and if they sometimes clothe their pleas in rhetorical trappings of the "general welfare," so do many others.

Elected officials do not always think so, either. Congresswoman Edith Green chided HEW Secretary Elliot Richardson in 1971 for what she saw as the administration's double standard, its willingness to seek emergency assistance for Lockheed and the Penn Central while denying financial help to institutions of higher education. Despite his demonstrated enthusiasm for student aid, John Brademas interrupted the colloquy to say "Right on!"[58]

Without passing judgment on the wisdom of other federal subsidies, however, several likely consequences of unrestricted institutional aid for colleges and universities should be considered.

First, in subsidizing producers rather than—or even in addition to—consumers of higher education, Washington could easily find itself sustaining institutions for which there is little real demand, cushioning them against marketplace pressures, and discouraging enterprise and innovation.[59]

Second, however they are formulated, institutional payments serve to subsidize the education of all students, rich as well as poor. To be sure, the states already do this in their public campuses, and Washington does it, too, with categorical programs that support university libraries, medical schools, or whatever. But if equalizing educational opportunity is a leading federal objective, underwriting the instruction of those who could pay for it themselves is inefficient and wasteful.

Third, an institutional support program will inevitably compete for money with student assistance programs. If funds are ample, this may not be a problem. But if appropriations for the institutional programs mean inadequate funding for need-based student aid, the result is worse than simple inefficiency: many people may be denied access to higher education even while colleges and universities are nourished.

58. *Higher Education Amendments of 1971*, Hearings before the House Education and Labor Committee, 92:1 (GPO, 1971), p. 128.

59. Linking the subsidy to enrollment mitigates this risk. A college with no students would presumably get no money.

Fourth, since institutional payments are apt to give every college the same amount of money per student, they will not correct existing distortions in higher education finance, narrow the tuition gap, or improve the competitive position of weak institutions. Schools that now enjoy large public subsidies will enjoy larger ones; alternatively, their sponsoring jurisdictions will reap a fiscal windfall as new federal payments allow them to reduce their own outlays.

Fifth, though unrestricted grants do not have all the "strings" of categorical payments, they will tend to make educational institutions even more dependent on government. The threat of control may be subtler, but it is no less real. For all the complexity of administering categorical programs, their limitations impose some self-discipline on Washington and the campus alike. Unrestricted support for the ordinary activities of colleges could bind those activities more tightly to the political process.

Finally, the church-state issue would have to be joined again. It is doubtful, in the light of recent decisions, that the courts would look kindly upon direct federal subsidies for the ordinary instructional activities of church-related educational institutions.

Even less judicious are emergency rescue operations. The statutes already contain one small but disturbing example, the decision by Congress to grant struggling Eisenhower College a percentage of the profits from the minting of silver dollars bearing the likeness of its namesake.[60] A generous and fitting gesture perhaps, but also an instance of private legislation in a public policy domain. A far larger and more worrisome example of the same concern was seen in the Education Amendments of 1972, which authorized a substantial sum to be set aside for "emergency assistance" to higher education "institutions which are determined . . . to be in serious financial distress," and which left to the commissioner of education wide discretion to decide which colleges and universities were worthy of such aid. Never funded, this provision expired in 1974 and has fortunately not been repeated.[61]

The proposal for publicly financed tuition offsets for private colleges and universities also appears, at least from the standpoint of federal policy, to be a misguided solution to a genuine problem. Though the states naturally remain free to subsidize their private institutions in any way they see fit—indeed even to erase the distinction between public

60. 88 Stat. 1262; see also Gordon F. Sander, "Eisenhower College: From Riches to Rags—and Back?" *Change*, vol. 7 (November 1975), pp. 13–16.
61. 86 Stat. 245-47.

and private—the federal government can more effectively deploy its resources to help all needy students afford the colleges of their choice, rather than to isolate one type of institution and underwrite the education of all who attend it.[62]

On balance, it would appear that none of the major alternatives to the present set of federal financing arrangements has advantages that outweigh its drawbacks.[63] Although it is normal and proper for college and university leaders to continue their quest for institutional subsidies, it is also proper for federal policymakers to resist them. To say this is not to argue that the present programs are well tailored to the many different contours of American higher education, however. Each program should be carefully scrutinized every few years to ensure that its effects on colleges and universities are largely beneficial. Changes in higher education's environment, particularly changes associated with shrinking enrollments, will probably warrant a series of adjustments in the major institutional programs as well as in student aid. But since these programs originate in so many different agencies and are nominally attached to so many different federal missions, it would be desirable from the colleges' standpoint if Washington had a greater capacity for appraising their composite effect on higher education and its various subdivisions. Chapter 7 contains further analysis of this issue and recommendations for change. But first it is necessary to examine an increasingly controversial aspect of federal higher education policy, the issue of regulation.

62. Federal (and state) programs tailored to assist private colleges and their students are discussed at length in Breneman and Finn, eds., *Public Policy and Private Higher Education.*

63. Other alternatives have not been examined here because they do not appear to be practical possibilities. One could, for example, conceive of an American equivalent to the "university grants committees" (or commissions) that are commonplace in England and some other parts of the British Commonwealth. That would be a way of allocating federal funds to colleges and universities without all the difficulties found in formula aid and political decisions. But, in practice, the Congress is reluctant to give so much discretion to autonomous boards, and the American higher education enterprise is so large and diverse that it is doubtful that its leaders would welcome the suggestion that they, in effect, divide up the federal pie among their own jealous factions. At least that was their response in 1970 when President Nixon proposed a scaled-down version of this idea, known as the "National Foundation for Higher Education."

Chapter Six

Exploring the Regulatory Swamp

Direct federal control would in the end produce uniformity, mediocrity, and compliance. Verve, initiative, and originality would disappear. Institutions would act as Congress wills. This must not be. There must be no such control. We know of no one who advocates this central control. But those who advocate the extension of federal financial support are treading down this path.

COMMISSION ON FINANCING HIGHER EDUCATION, 1952

In connection with Federal assistance, the more Federal assistance you get, of course, the more Federal control of your institutions there is, because there is a great deal of truth in the old adage "He who pays the piper calls the tune."

CLAIBORNE PELL, CHAIRMAN, SENATE SUBCOMMITTEE ON EDUCATION, 1974

Use of the leverage of the government dollar to accomplish objectives which have nothing to do with the purposes for which the dollar is given has become dangerously fashionable. . . . It might be called the "now that I have bought the button, I have a right to design the coat" approach.

KINGMAN BREWSTER, PRESIDENT, YALE UNIVERSITY, 1975

THE PRIMORDIAL FEAR of educators and others weighing the costs and benefits of federal aid to colleges and universities was that money from Washington would bring control. When the Senate Labor and Public Welfare Committee favorably reported the National Defense Education Act, Barry Goldwater recalled the "old Arabian proverb" about the camel's nose. "If adopted," the senator prophesied, "the legislation will mark the inception of aid, supervision, and ultimately control of education in this country by Federal authorities."[1] Though few dromedaries have been sighted on American campuses in recent years, in the main he and the university leaders who shared those apprehensions

---

1. Quoted in "Minority Views of Senators Barry Goldwater and John G. Tower," *National Defense Education Act Amendment of 1961*, S. Rept. 652, 87:1 (GPO, 1961), p. 117.

were right.[2] Money has brought even more varied and pervasive controls than they anticipated. But many of the constraints that colleges and universities find most offensive no longer have much to do with federal money; even if the financial spigot were shut off tomorrow, the regulations would remain and the protests would continue.

How could this have happened? Have not the basic national education statutes included, since the 1950s, a stern prohibition barring "any department, agency, officer or employee of the United States" from exercising "any direction, supervision or control" over the educational process in schools and colleges?[3] In a word, federal control is illegal. Yet the possibility that mounting government regulations are smothering the educational process in ways that cannot readily be distinguished from such "control" is probably the single most controversial element of higher education policy in the late 1970s, surpassing in intensity the fractious disputes over financial assistance to students and institutions. More than anything else, it reveals—and deepens—the erosion of the barrier between what Martin Trow terms the "public and private lives" of higher education, and in so doing threatens to turn the campus into a pedagogical equivalent of the electric company. So, at least, many educators fear.[4]

In pursuit of a multitude of laudable goals, the federal government has been empowered in recent years to monitor and shape aspects of personal and institutional behavior that not long ago were left to private decisions or to state and local governments. In almost every instance, the federal sentries have acquired their own constituencies: individuals and groups whose devotion to the goals of particular regulations leads them to "watch the watchdog," to insist on vigorous enforcement, and

2. Groups such as the United States Chamber of Commerce, the National Association of Manufacturers, and others dedicated to restraining the growth of government also routinely invoked the threat of federal control in explaining their unyielding opposition to aid for schools and colleges.

3. 20 USC, 1232a.

4. Martin Trow, "The Public and Private Lives of Higher Education," *Daedalus*, vol. 2 (Winter 1975), pp. 113–27. For a "sampler" of complaints about and commentaries on federal regulation, see the articles reprinted in *Regulations for the Education Amendments of 1976*, Hearing before the House Education and Labor Committee, 94:2 (GPO, 1977), pp. 23–89.

It may be noted that another regulatory phenomenon, symbolized by the word "busing," is surely the most controversial aspect of federal policy toward elementary and secondary schools.

to avail themselves of the courts whenever, in their view, the executive fails to carry out the spirit and details of the pertinent legislation with sufficient fervor.[5]

This is the first point to emphasize in any discussion of federal regulation of higher education: every single one of those regulations, procedures, forms, and lawsuits can be traced to a law (or executive order) that was enacted in response to constituent pressure, and those constituencies now monitor the performance of the government enforcers with fierce dedication and single-minded enthusiasm. The bureaucrats are not to be blamed, except perhaps for occasional excess or whimsy in interpreting the law. It is the lawmakers who are responsible, but they acted in order to help or appease groups that sought changes. Hence anyone who seeks to mitigate the effects of government regulation on colleges and universities had best recognize at the outset that it is not a struggle between the academy and the bureaucracy, but between parts of the society that want change and parts that resist changing.

It is not surprising that colleges and universities have been affected by such pervasive developments in American society. The question is whether higher education warrants special attention, or whether its regulatory distress is equivalent to that of auto manufacturers, banks, and purveyors of children's nightwear. Some in the academic world subscribe to the doctrine that universities are unique and fragile institutions that should receive extraordinary treatment.[6] Others, more often found in government, hold to the view that laws and regulations must apply equally to all.[7] Some add that if educators want greater autonomy they should stop taking money from Washington and lobbying for an activist federal government.[8]

5. For a particularly erudite appraisal of the utilitarian and constituency-serving aspects of government regulation, see Herbert Kaufman, *Red Tape: Its Origins, Uses, and Abuses* (Brookings Institution, 1977).

6. For strong statements of this view, see Edward Shils, "Government and University," in Sidney Hook, Paul Kurtz, and Miro Todorovich, eds., *The University and the State: What Role for Government in Higher Education?* (Prometheus Books, 1978), and Estelle A. Fishbein, "The Academic Industry—A Dangerous Premise," in Walter C. Hobbs, ed., *Government Regulation of Higher Education* (Ballinger, 1978).

7. See, for example, Ernest Gellhorn and Barry B. Boyer, "The Academy as a Regulated Industry," in Hobbs, ed., *Government Regulation of Higher Education*.

8. See, for example, Robert H. Bork, "A Taste of Their Own Medicine," *The Alternative*, vol. 10 (April 1977), pp. 20–22.

Nuisances and Principles

For present purposes "regulation" may be defined as actions by the federal government that compel a college or university to do something it would not otherwise have done, that make it worth the institution's while to do so, or that make it painful to refrain from doing it.[9] But what are the "somethings," and what is the basis for the anxiety they cause? Sometimes the problem is inconvenience or expense. Doing what Washington asks may cost money, involve elaborate and time-consuming procedures, or disrupt long-established practices. Sometimes, however, compliance with federal requirements may infringe on cherished rights and violate ancient doctrines.

When a college is obliged to pay the minimum wage to the grounds crews that rake the campus lawn, plainly that costs more than compensating them at lower rates. When a university is told to improve the sprinkler system in its chemistry labs to comply with safety standards, another expense is incurred. When a classroom building must have ramps installed for the physically handicapped, still more money must be spent. It would be hard to fault any of these on grounds of principle, for each would seem a humane and desirable thing to do. But paying for them is another question. Washington levies the requirements, but it seldom furnishes the funds; therefore, colleges and universities must either pass the costs on to their consumers and patrons or reduce their outlays for other activities.[10]

These costs defy calculation, however, for they take many forms, and it is hard to know which of them are properly blamed on Washington, which are expenses the school would have incurred anyway, and

9. I do not suggest that the federal government is unique in this regard. State governments have a heavy and diversified regulatory presence, particularly on public campuses. And institutions of higher education must also reckon with their local governments in many matters, ranging from such mundane issues as the respective jurisdictions of town and campus police officers to such intricate intrusions as the recent effort by the city government of Cambridge, Massachusetts, to prescribe the types of genetic research that may be conducted by Harvard University and MIT.

10. I would suppose that roughly three-quarters of the academy's protests about government regulation might be ended by the simple (if costly) expedient of Washington's agreeing to supply all the funds necessary to comply with its requirements. But then, of course, one would have to ask whether higher education was "selling out."

which are outgrowths of desirable actions that may cost more because of government standards.[11]

"Inconveniences" include federal paperwork,[12] burdensome reporting requirements, time-consuming litigation, and the nuisance of having to deal with multiple federal agencies on the same issues. Drawing on his experience as president of Columbia University, William J. McGill pointed out in December 1976 that "one of the first tasks to which the new administration should address itself if it intends to limit the almost cancerous growth of regulatory initiatives by government, ought to be the maze of bureaucratic conflicts and overlapping jurisdictions that have developed around the important social legislation of the last two decades."[13]

At the opposite pole are objections to government requirements that appear to threaten academic freedom and to infringe institutional sovereignty in areas where the academy is accustomed to regulating itself. These are matters such as faculty hiring, student admissions, curriculum, and research that Harvard's Derek Bok rightly terms "the principal academic functions of higher education."[14] The most celebrated example is "affirmative action," a maze of laws, presidential directives, and agency regulations that circumscribes the historic right of the college to employ whomever it likes to teach its students. Controls on research involving human and animal subjects, rules and court decisions

11. One small but systematic effort to gather data on the dollar costs of federal regulation is Carol Van Alstyne and Sharon L. Coldren, *The Costs of Implementing Federally Mandated Social Programs at Colleges and Universities* (American Council on Education, 1976). The study sample contained just six campuses, however, and even these proved resistant to comparisons. Individual institutions sometimes attempt to add up their costs of federal regulation too. See, for example, the self-study by George Washington University in Charles M. Chambers, "An Institutional View of the Costs of Government Regulation," in Hook and others, eds., *The University and the State.*

12. See "Education," A Report of the Commission on Federal Paperwork (April 29, 1977; processed).

13. William J. McGill, "Government Regulation and Academic Freedom," in Hook and others, eds., *The University and the State.* It should be noted that this often-voiced complaint may be exaggerated, at least in the eyes of the regulators. A federal interagency task force on "higher education burden reduction" found in 1976, for example, that with respect to civil rights "regulations and instructions . . . there is no significant redundancy in recordkeeping and reporting requirements." "Report of the Interagency Task Force on Higher Education Burden Reduction" (Office of the Secretary, HEW, December 1976; processed).

14. Derek C. Bok, "The President's Report, 1974–1975," *Harvard Today*, vol. 18 (Winter 1976), p. 10.

affecting student admissions, and strictures on the privacy of student records are also primarily opposed on principle.[15]

Much government regulation blends expense, inconvenience, and wounded convictions. The onset of faculty collective bargaining, for example, supervised by the National Labor Relations Board, will disturb some college leaders because it adds to the personnel budget, others because it formalizes and prolongs decisions that once were subjective and quick, and still others because it seems to erode the collegial spirit of the academic enterprise.

Modes of Government Regulation

For all its varied detail, federal activity of a regulatory nature can be put into three categories—allocation of funds, use of funds, and social regulations—each worth a brief examination from the government's standpoint as well as the campus's. My purpose is not to appraise individual regulations but, rather, to suggest a rough typology that may help to clarify the broader issues.

Allocation of Funds

When federal funds are made available for certain activities but not for others, they have an effect on the campus that is politely described as an "incentive," informally characterized as a "carrot," and criticized as a "bribe." When a college or university pursues such funds, it may end up doing something different from what it would have done had it eschewed the money or had the money been available for unrestricted purposes. This is an old lament, but not an obsolete one.

Although it is not regulation in any formal sense—the college can avoid the problem by declining to seek the money—this alternative is ever less practical, both because campuses need the income and because government programs have become so pervasive that *not* to partake of them may also distort the institution's agenda. Refusing all federal funds could, for example, mean denying admission to students the college

15. For an excellent case study of federal civil rights enforcement efforts at the college level, see Crystal C. Lloyd, "*Adams* v. *Califano:* A Case Study in the Politics of Regulation" (Sloan Commission on Government and Higher Education, January 1978; processed).

would otherwise welcome, simply because they have government stipends. A few staunchly independent colleges have made a point of spurning federal funds, but even they have difficulty refusing federally assisted students. For most institutions the programs are there to be tapped, and the distortions that may result are a predictable if unwelcome consequence.

From the federal government's point of view, however, there are no distortions. Every year Congress appropriates funds to the various agencies of the executive branch for the purpose of carrying out their legislative mandates. Whether the mission is the improvement of solar energy technology, the production of more dentists, or the vocational readiness of low-income people, insofar as the higher education industry is suited to help achieve a specified goal, the cognizant agency will make funds available in ways that encourage colleges and universities to partake of them and, in so doing, to subscribe to the purposes for which they were intended. What may look to the campus like a "bribe" sure to distort the institution's own program and erode its self-determination is nothing more nor less than a "procurement" of the desired service, activity, or product. If the higher education industry were disposed to serve Washington's purposes without the inducement of federal funds, the money might better be reserved for situations in which a financial incentive *would* make a difference.

Use of Funds

It follows from the categorical nature of most federal programs that funds obtained for one purpose may be used only for that purpose and that the recipient institution will be held accountable for the uses it makes of public monies. With a few exceptions, each consignment of funds from Washington must be sequestered and accounted for in ways that will satisfy the auditors that the college spent it solely for the activities agreed to when the grant or contract was approved.

That would seem reasonable enough, but in practice it is burdensome to the colleges. Most federal agencies want evidence not only that the funds were spent as intended but also that they accomplished the purposes intended. What did the researchers actually learn? How many students were aided? What effect did the new economics curriculum have? Did the veterans enroll in the prescribed number of courses and complete those they enrolled in? Thus a superstructure of program evaluation and reporting requirements rises on top of the strictly financial recordkeeping, and the more federal programs the college taps, the more quarterly reports it must file and evaluations it must endure.[16]

The purely financial accounting is not as routine as one might expect, either. Universities resist certain kinds of record-keeping and analysis that ease the auditor's task but fit poorly into the academic enterprise. "The government would like to see us get into some very specific kinds of accounting," a Stanford University official observes, "but you just can't put time-clocks on faculty members and expect them to be productive." Disputes often arise. In early 1976, for example, Defense Department auditors recommended that Stanford repay the government some $155,000 because faculty members supported on federal research funds had spent too much of their time on outside consulting. At any one time the National Institutes of Health are engaged in negotiations with fifteen to twenty universities for the return of money that government auditors believe to have been misspent. The HEW inspector general reports that of $1.2 billion in research contracts audited by the agency during fiscal 1977, more than one-third of the money was inadequately accounted for. And in fiscal 1976, according to an estimate by the General Accounting Office, the Veterans Administration disbursed $823 million in unwarranted GI bill benefits to ineligible persons, chiefly because the recipients and their schools failed to notify the VA promptly of changes in the status of individual students.[17]

Most such controversies stem from sloppy record-keeping, not from attempts to defraud the government, but they also hint at divergent conceptions of what federal funds are meant to pay for. When Washington procures a service from a university, has it any responsibility to help underwrite the ongoing activities without which there would be no university worth procuring services from? It costs less to pay only for the specified service, but academic institutions must replenish their in-

16. A reader adds that in his experience "one other result of federal reporting and auditing requirements has been a shift in influence from academic administrators with teaching credentials to lawyers and bookkeepers who master the new requirements." For additional discussion, from the university president's standpoint, of the effects of these changes upon traditional patterns of academic government, see Robert L. Ketter, "By Hemp or by Silk, the Outcome Is the Same," in Hobbs, ed., *Government Regulation and Higher Education.*

17. *Chronicle of Higher Education,* April 19, 1976, pp. 1 and 10; ibid., May 24, 1976, p. 11; *Higher Education Daily,* October 26, 1976, p. 2; *New York Times,* January 8, 1978.

tellectual capital, too, or their value to the nation—and to the govern-ment—will decline.[18]

Government officials, on the other hand, believe that once there is agreement that a certain sum will be allocated to a college (or student) for a set purpose, they are obliged to see that the money is used only for that purpose. Because the head of a program or agency wants to stretch his appropriation as far as possible and be able to demonstrate that it was well spent, he has an incentive to haggle about overhead rates, to insist on progress reports, to watch the recipients carefully lest they use his money for other activities, and to terminate the relationship as soon as the objectives have been attained or the attempt proves fruitless.[19] In other areas of federal activity where successfully transferring resources from Washington to their designated recipient is accomplishment enough, officials need only guard against egregious abuse or demon-strable folly. But because federal support for higher education has de-veloped through a lengthening list of categorical programs rather than through a pattern of unrestricted subsidies, the agencies allotting the funds have good reason for a vigilance that may strike their beneficiaries as regulation.

Social Regulations

For colleges and universities the problems associated with obtaining and accounting for government funds date back to the earliest days of federal grants and contracts. They may find that burden heavy, but it is not unfamiliar. What is newer and more onerous is the need to comply with a growing list of "social" regulations, for which the institutions are rarely compensated. These range from the equal treatment of male and female students to safety requirements in campus laboratories, from standards for employee pensions to procedures for ensuring the con-fidentiality of student records, from controls on certain forms of sci-

18. See the discussion of indirect cost payments in chapter 5.

19. For a description of some of the quandaries faced by administrative agencies in the development of regulations to carry out program legislation, see Theodore Sky, "Rulemaking in the Office of Education," *Administrative Law Review*, vol. 26 (Spring 1974), pp. 129–40. For a series of examples of "policy implementation" processes and problems in executive branch agencies, see *Policy Sciences*, vol. 7 (December 1976), passim.

entific experimentation to changes in the composition of medical residencies in university-affiliated teaching hospitals.

It is important to be clear about the links between federal funding and social regulation. In many instances money has virtually nothing to do with government regulation. As corporate entities, employers, users of energy, tax-exempt organizations, land owners, emitters of air- and water-borne effluents, producers and consumers of copyrighted material, healers of the sick, temporary domiciles of foreign nationals, and in numerous other organizational capacities, colleges and universities find themselves subject to laws and regulations that would bind them even if they successfully divested themselves of every single federal dollar.

But other regulations are attached to the receipt of federal money, and the withdrawal of government money is often the sanction for noncompliance, even if there is no clear link between the purposes for which the money was given and the nature of the particular regulation. Nor does compliance with that regulation strengthen Washington's chances of getting its money's worth from institutions that participate in a given program. Instead, secondary and tertiary—some would say higher-order—goals have been placed on top of ordinary funding programs. And rarely does the money offset the costs of complying with such regulations.

No two institutions would draw up quite the same list of regulations they object to, nor would all parts of a single campus.[20] Each has its favorite grievances, its biggest irritants, and its chosen example of "the last straw." The health manpower codicils that enrage medical school deans have little in common with the Title IX regulations that mandate equal treatment of men and women students. The affirmative action "goals" that plague the faculty of arts and sciences share few traits with the occupational safety standards that mean massive expenses for the college of engineering. Because these complaints are so diverse, and because in examining any of them, even on a single campus, it quickly develops that one person's most hated intrusion is another's noblest cause, "federal regulation" tends to be discussed either as a generic problem or as quarrels over the wording of isolated paragraphs. Only the boldest of educational leaders dares to assert that the social objective behind a

20. A number of specific examples are cited, along with a thoughtful analysis and good bibliography, in Louis W. Bender, *Federal Regulation and Higher Education*, ERIC/Higher Education Research Report no. 1 (American Association for Higher Education, 1977).

particular law or regulation is undesirable or that colleges should be exempt from it. And when one does utter such a sentiment in public, he is apt to be disputed by colleagues who believe in the objective, whose institutions have already complied with the regulation, whose schools are unaffected by it, or who want the money and have convinced themselves that the compliance burden is tolerable.

Viewed from the banks of the Potomac, higher education is not a "regulated industry" like airlines, meat packers, or stock exchanges. No historic act of Congress brought higher education under federal scrutiny, and no government agency has as its mission the regulation and supervision of the academy.[21] What the colleges see as controls and intrusions are, by and large, the results of normal behavior by diverse federal agencies going about their appointed rounds. That higher education may feel itself singularly oppressed by the ways in which these functions are carried out is quite another matter. In fact, it is simply being treated much like other sectors of the society.

When a piece of "social" legislation is passed, or an executive order issued, one or more agencies are empowered to enforce it with the compliance tools given them. These take many shapes: standards to be met; activities that are forbidden; pledges to be obtained; targets to be aimed at; a complaint or grievance to be investigated; a process to be supervised. The federal enforcers see themselves as merely carrying out the law. With this dutifulness come potential hazards—overzealousness, single-mindedness, unevenness, unreasonableness, inattentiveness, capriciousness, sluggishness—but these are endemic to the regulatory mode. In the main, officials charged with enforcement of a particular requirement evidence no more interest in the effects of compliance on the affected institutions' health and happiness than internal revenue agents display toward the effects of paying taxes on the vacation budget of families, or than customs inspectors show toward the privacy and comfort of arriving travelers. One may reasonably expect them to be courteous in a businesslike way, but not to lie awake nights worrying about the general welfare of those with whom they deal. In this sense, *not* being a "regulated industry" with a federal agency all its own may actually make life harder for higher education, which must instead contend with multiple agencies and overlapping requirements. Here, as in

21. At the state level, however, it is normal to find a coordinating board, board of higher education, or board of regents that resembles a regulatory commission for colleges and universities.

its financial relations, the decentralized and piecemeal nature of the academy's dealings with the federal government has drawbacks as well as advantages.

For their part, government officials from the mid-ranks of the civil service to the barons of Congress generally subscribe to the idea that Washington's money should foster Washington's purposes, that those receiving it should be held accountable for what they do with it, that "social" regulations, whether desirable or not, are made to be obeyed, and that the academy has no distinctive claim to special treatment. They never have to deal with the question of whether higher education should be "regulated" or not, for that issue does not reach their desks. Higher education must simply accept the terms attached to the money and heed the requirements that everyone else is expected to comply with. Capricious or unreasonable enforcement is another matter. That kind of complaint can be dealt with, but always within the context of a specific regulatory process, not as a question of whether the provision itself is well-conceived or whether colleges and universities should be subject to it.

Limits, Excesses, and Accommodations

No concordat exists between the federal government and the academic community. No body of mutually accepted principles fixes a boundary between them, the consequences of crossing it, or the circumstances in which incursions may be warranted. Despite wide acceptance of the general concept of "academic freedom," the phrase has no operational definition that could guide lawmakers even were they disposed to be so guided. Instead of having durable behavioral benchmarks, the university president and the government official must contend with each situation on its own terms. Yet higher education is not putty in the hands of government. Indeed, it is increasingly evident that higher education, when it gets itself organized for the purpose, is capable of altering the course of federal regulatory policy. Four recent examples may be cited.[22] Although none resulted in a clear-cut victory for the academy, all offer hope to those who believe that the shrewdest tactic for

22. Earlier examples include the notorious "disclaimer affidavit" battle precipitated by the National Defense Education Act of 1958. As originally passed, the NDEA required that before any person could receive financial assistance—loans, grants, fellowships, and so on—under it he must first execute an oath of allegiance

survival in an increasingly regulated society is to scream loudly when hurt, and—when possible—to find others in similar pain and yell along with them.

1. The "Buckley amendment"—properly the Family Educational Rights and Privacy Act—was brought up on the Senate floor, without benefit of committee hearings, by Senator James L. Buckley of New York, and became law in early 1974. It provided that federal education funds would be withheld from any school or college that "has a policy of denying, or which effectively prevents, the parents of students . . . the right to inspect and review any and all official records, files and data directly related to their children."[23]

This benign-sounding requirement was chiefly aimed at primary and secondary schools, in the aftermath of widespread publicity about students whose later careers were impaired by school files—which they were never allowed to inspect—containing hearsay, falsehoods, and negative comments by biased teachers.

From the colleges' standpoint, this legislation created serious problems. "There is a perfectly reasonable bill that can be written on students' rights but this bill has not been well thought out," said John Kemeny, president of Dartmouth College.[24] As enacted, it provided for the disclosure to students and parents of recommendation letters already in the files that had been solicited and written on the presumption of confidentiality. It opened the possibility that students would have access to their parents' income tax information contained on confidential financial aid applications. It failed to differentiate between academic records and medical, psychiatric, and guidance files of a sort customarily covered by professional privilege and doctor-patient relations.

The Washington higher education lobbyists were caught off guard

---

to the United States and also an affidavit affirming that he was not a member of and did not support any organizations advocating the overthrow of the United States government.

Although a similar provision in the earlier National Science Foundation fellowship program had elicited little controversy, in 1958 the McCarthy era was still fresh in academic memories and 105 universities elected to protest the new affidavit requirement. Twenty-two of them—including Amherst, Harvard, Yale, and other well-known institutions—felt so strongly that they declined to participate in the program. Presidents Eisenhower and Kennedy both called for its repeal. Civil rights and educational associations lobbied against it. And in 1961 Congress agreed to drop the affidavit, although it retained the oath and also made it a crime for an individual belonging to a subversive organization to receive funds under the program.

23. 88 Stat. 572.
24. Quoted in *New York Times*, November 17, 1974.

by the suddenness with which this bill was brought up and enacted.[25] Thereupon they mobilized to seek amendments needed to forestall massive administrative confusion and to clarify the most sensitive issues. With assistance from Senator Claiborne Pell, they prevailed, and amendments passed late in 1974 accommodated their main concerns. Although universities are still required to disclose many kinds of information to students and parents that they had previously been allowed to seclude in file drawers, and although professors wanting to make candid comments about their students' suitability for graduate school and the like may now pick up the phone rather than sit down at the typewriter, nonetheless few in the academy would contend that the law as finally amended either gives serious inconvenience or violates important principles.

2. In late 1976 Congress revised the health manpower legislation to require that universities receiving capitation grants for their medical schools must thereafter conduct themselves in specific ways. Protracted negotiations between academic leaders and congressmen softened some of the proposed requirements the medical deans found most worrisome, but the version signed into law by President Ford kept one provision deemed so offensive that several prestigious universities announced that they would forgo the capitation funds rather than obey it. Briefly stated, this provision required that, for a period of three years after enactment, any medical school desiring such grants (or whose students sought federal loans) must participate in a national program through which American citizens studying medicine overseas would be allowed entry into the third-year class of stateside medical schools. The secretary of HEW was empowered to "equitably apportion a number of positions adequate to fill the needs of [these] students . . . among the schools of medicine in the States.[26] The legislative language and the accompanying conference committee report implied that the secretary would determine which institution was to enroll which student, as well as the total number of transfers each school would have to accommodate. Moreover, in evaluating the papers of students covered by this provision, the medical schools were forbidden to apply "requirements related to academic qualifications." Congress thus appeared to be thrusting the federal government into one of the academy's holiest rites, the process

25. When Buckley had first introduced the measure as a separate bill, the Washington-based associations had cautioned Claiborne Pell, chairman of the Senate Subcommittee on Education, that it could cause them problems. It was the hasty floor action that surprised them.

26. 90 Stat. 2294.

by which each university's admissions office determines which candidates meet its entrance standards and which do not.

The congressional motive was apparently benevolent: to help some of the six thousand or so Americans then studying medicine abroad to complete their professional training in American universities. Reasoning logically, if somewhat simplistically, that the most direct means of bringing about this goal was to coerce medical schools into accepting such students as transfers, Congress made doing so a precondition for future capitation grants.[27] These amount to approximately $2,000 per student a year, or about $800,000 annually in the case of a medical school the size of Stanford's.

The reaction in many parts of the academic community was to eschew these funds rather than submit to this particularly ugly form of regulation. By November 1977 fourteen universities had decided to forfeit $11 million in fiscal 1978 capitation grants rather than comply with it.[28] But by that time, in response to intense lobbying by medical school and university leaders, Congress was on the way to modifying the requirements and reaffirming the medical schools' authority to accept or reject individual students. Adopting a floor amendment introduced by Senator Charles Mathias, Jr., the Senate voted to do away with the entire provision. The House preferred to modify the law to require that for two years the medical schools must expand their third-year classes to make room for more students drawn from a pool of eligibles consisting almost entirely of Americans studying medicine overseas. In conference, the House approach prevailed, but only for a single year's increase of 5 percent in third-year enrollments. This provision may be objectionable, but it is far less onerous from the university's standpoint than the original three-year requirement and the ban on the use of academic standards.

Most colleges and universities lack medical schools and are thus unaffected, and one might judge that the entire dispute was escalated beyond reasonable proportions. Yet it illustrates two aspects of the present situation: first, the willingness of the federal government to engage in what Scalia calls "regulation by munificence,"[29] turning funds meant as a carrot to encourage one purpose into a stick intended to foster another, with the universities' hunger for resources being ex-

27. For an account of the origins and background of this legislation, see Antonin Scalia, "Guadalajara! A Case Study in Regulation by Munificence," *Regulation*, vol. 2 (March–April 1978), pp. 23–29.

28. *New York Times,* November 29, 1977.

29. See "Guadalajara!"

ploited to persuade them to accept a federally mandated result they could scorn if no money were involved.

Second, however, the episode demonstrates the academic community's sensitivity to the means adopted by Washington to secure federal ends; the willingness of some universities to set important principles ahead of pocketbook considerations; the ability of those universities to muster considerable political force behind those principles; and Congress' receptivity to strongly stated pleas that particular provisions of law be changed in the interest of academic freedom as defined by the academic community.[30]

3. In late 1977, as Congress was considering sharp increases in the payroll tax intended to put the social security system on a sounder financial footing, higher education joined with state and local governments and other nonprofit organizations in support of Senator John Danforth's proposal to apply separate, lower payroll tax rates to such institutions. It was argued that the benefit of being a "tax exempt" organization diminishes as a growing percentage of federal revenues is raised through payroll taxes, from which such organizations are not exempt; that businesses can deduct the employer's share of the payroll tax from their federal income taxes, while for nonprofit organizations every dollar in social security taxes costs 100 cents; and that special treatment was therefore justified.

This view prevailed on the Senate floor, after a debate marked by discussion of the economic burdens that this particular form of "social" regulation would otherwise impose on colleges and universities. Although the House adopted no comparable provision, and the Senate version was deleted in conference, the half-victory attests once again to the growing ability of the higher education community, here joined by a wide range of organizations with similar interests, to obtain favored treatment in the course of developing broad-gauged federal legislation that would otherwise apply uniformly to colleges and universities along with all other institutions.

4. In late 1977 Congress also took up the issue of age discrimination:

30. Congressmen and their staff members are also capable of striking back. In its report on the 1977 amendments, the House Committee on Interstate and Foreign Commerce, even as it expressed a willingness "to respond to the objections of some schools of medicine that existing law infringes on their academic freedom," also noted that "the announcement by some schools that they would forgo capitation support unless the conditions for receipt were altered raises a significant question as to the need for continuation of this type of support." *Health Professions Education Amendments of 1977*, H. Rept. 95-707, 95:1 (GPO, 1977), pp. 4-5.

the main concern was compulsory retirement, and the main objective of those seeking legislative change was to lift from sixty-five to seventy the age limit eligible for federal protection. The House bill provided no exemptions, but the Senate version contained two, both the result of intense lobbying by organizations that believed they would be hurt or inconvenienced if included in this change. One provision allowed colleges and universities to continue requiring tenured professors to retire at age sixty-five. (The other exempted high-salaried business executives.) The Senate was influenced by the strong pleas of university administrators that to raise the age of faculty retirement to seventy would be costly for the institutions and—given the prospect of stable or diminishing enrollments and consequent institutional shrinkage—would further reduce the already limited opportunities for appointing young scholars (including minority group members and women) to the professoriate.

Once again, senators treated one another to oratory about the importance of safeguarding and strengthening institutions of higher education, the hazards of treating them just like other institutions, and the consequent need to spare them from an otherwise laudable social reform. Once again, this line of reasoning prevailed in that body. And once again, the bill emerging from the House of Representatives contained no comparable provision. This time, however, the Senate conferees refused to yield entirely, despite mounting pressure from teachers' unions and professors' associations to give faculty members the same rights as everybody else. The conference was deadlocked for a long time. Finally, in March 1978 it was agreed to allow the university exemption but only for a few years, thus making it more of a "transition period" in which the colleges can adjust to retirement at age seventy than a lasting exclusion from the law. A modest victory, to be sure, particularly if one does not believe that Washington has any business regulating the age of faculty retirement in the first place. Still, it is a further sign of the academic community's real if still limited ability to mold regulatory legislation to its institutional contours.

Self-Regulation: A Vanishing Dream?

Those who spontaneously do what Washington wants have little to fear from government regulation, except perhaps the chore of documenting their compliance. The paperwork burden is not to be dismissed, but the main discomfort of being regulated is the friction that results when what one wants to do conflicts with what the government requires.

To a remarkable extent, higher education has enjoyed the ability to regulate itself on Washington's behalf in certain areas important to both the academy and the government.[31] That ability now appears to be eroding, not so much by conscious design as by mutual insensitivity to its benefits and some reluctance on both sides to change with the times. Cracks have appeared in various "understandings" by which higher education for a quarter century clung to the freedom to make important decisions for—or in close cooperation with—the government. Three examples will suffice: Washington's reliance on the "accreditation" system as a principal means of determining which colleges may participate in certain federal programs; the delegation to private "need analysis" systems of decisions as to which students should receive financial aid and in what amounts; and the use of "peer review" in its many variations as a key mechanism by which the government allots research funds among scholars and universities.

Each of these understandings dates back to the 1950s. Each sprang from Washington's need to farm out onerous tasks it was ill-equipped to handle directly and from the academy's determination to maintain the greatest possible control over decisions affecting it. And each is now threatened, on the one hand by increasing federal demands, and on the other by the higher education community's spotty record in strengthening and modernizing its own governance. It is by appraising the value of self-regulation in examples such as these that one can grasp both the potential of this major alternative to government controls and the slender prospects for its realization.[32]

31. The following discussion was first published, in somewhat different form, as "Federalism and the Universities: The Balance Shifts," in *Change*, vol. 7 (December–January 1975–76), pp. 24–29, 63.

32. A further instance of inadequate self-regulation by the higher education community is, of course, its failure to achieve "equal opportunity" in campus employment, particularly in professorial positions, during the many decades when the government showed little interest in the issue. Perhaps it goes without saying that much contemporary anguish over affirmative action, and the difficulties inevitably created when arbitrary goals result in clumsy formulations, such as the need to hire "three-fifths of a female associate professor in the Department of Animal Husbandry," could have been avoided if universities had spontaneously paid more attention to equity in filling their ranks.

Accreditation

A decision by Washington to underwrite any higher education activity has a definitional problem: what is a college, and which institutions styling themselves colleges shall be eligible for funds? Rather than evaluate thousands of separate schools, many federal agencies have relied on the private and voluntary mechanisms through which the academy defines its own institutional membership.[33]

The Korean War GI bill, passed in 1952, required the commissioner of education to develop and maintain a list of accrediting agencies that "he determines to be reliable authority as to the quality of training offered by an educational institution." The list was not binding, but the law nonetheless marked a notable event: acknowledgment by Congress that accreditation by a private agency was enough to make an educational institution eligible for federal funds.

The accrediting process received another infusion of delegated power in 1958 when the National Defense Education Act specified that one of the definitions of an "institution of higher education," for purposes of participation in NDEA programs, was that it be "accredited by a nationally recognized accrediting agency or association." It was again left to the commissioner to "recognize" the accrediting bodies.

This approach has prevailed in many other federal higher education programs. Being "accredited," a status conferred by nongovernment organizations, is one of the ways—for most institutions the simplest way—of gaining access to many government programs and the money funneled through them.

As programs multiplied and appropriations soared, more and more students and schools wanted the benefits of participation. Postsecondary education had come to include more than the traditional nonprofit colleges and universities; associations of correspondence schools, of cosmetology schools, and of other newcomers—many of them schools run to make a profit for their owners—now began to apply to the commissioner for recognition. As the number and variety of accrediting bodies increased, the Office of Education tried to set standards and monitor

33. This subject is exhaustively reviewed by Harold Orlans and others in "Private Accreditation and Public Eligibility," 2 vols. (Washington, D.C., October 1974; processed). See also David A. Trivett, *Accreditation and Institutional Eligibility*, ERIC/Higher Education Research Report no. 9 (American Association for Higher Education, 1976).

their behavior.[34] Seeking to protect their private character, the accrediting bodies fought such attempts, but the government persisted, for it did not want to evaluate every single school and saw no alternative but to shore up the accrediting system.

On one level, regulation of private accrediting associations has even less justification than direct supervision of the colleges that belong to them, for the associations themselves are not federal clients and generally receive no money from Washington. The accreditation process is the education community's own "admissions office," run by organizations that screen schools and colleges seeking to join the community and that periodically check to see if they warrant continued membership. Educational quality and comparability are the main concerns.[35]

On another level, however, educational accrediting bodies, like bar associations and medical societies, have assumed certain responsibilities of public stewardship. In regulating their membership according to the norms of the profession, they endow the schools that gain membership with certification that outsiders, whether individual consumers or government agencies, can use as a mark of reliability.

If accreditation did not exist, the federal government would have had to invent a substitute for it, and, indeed, some agencies and programs have done just that, relying on state licensure or their own criteria for judging institutional eligibility. Agencies such as the Office of Education that rely heavily on private accreditation may set other requirements and may also offer an alternate method by which schools not fully accredited can become eligible. But the existence of the private accreditation system has given inestimable help to lawmakers and program administrators seeking a clear-cut basis for judging which schools and colleges deserve serious consideration among the thousands seeking funds. The federal government's willingness to make use of private accreditation buttressed the academy's ability to govern itself and curbed

34. This process took what Orlans and his associates described as a "quantum jump" in 1968 when Commissioner of Education Harold Howe II established an accreditation and institutional eligibility staff within the Office of Education. At its first meeting the new advisory committee to that staff determined that not only did the Office of Education have a responsibility to "recognize" accrediting bodies but it must also require them to reapply for recognition and to reexamine them from time to time. Orlans and others, "Private Accreditation," pp. 119–97.

35. See "Accreditation: The Quality of Institutions," a discussion by F. Taylor Jones, William K. Selden, David Riesman, and Owen B. Kiernan, in Seymour E. Harris and Alan Levensohn, eds., *Education and Public Policy* (McCutchan, 1965), pp. 147–66.

the amount of federal regulation to which colleges would otherwise have been subject.

This happy arrangement might have continued if every accredited institution had handled its federal funds in unimpeachable fashion or if accrediting associations had withdrawn their seal of approval from schools that did not. But the associations, though willing to let Washington use their approval of a college as a surrogate for its own investigation, have resisted efforts to make them alter their criteria and police their membership in order to satisfy the government's needs. "Accreditation can and does perform a common welfare purpose," argued Frank G. Dickey, executive director of the National Commission on Accrediting, in 1974, but it "cannot, philosophically, procedurally or financially serve the general welfare purpose of formulae making for the reallocation of public tax dollars for educational purposes." If "policing and fiscal accounting" for federal funds must be done, Dickey added, "only governmental machinery can effect such monitoring," and the private accreditation system ought not be burdened with this public function.[36]

A growing problem burst into the headlines in the early 1970s, when the number of students defaulting on federally guaranteed loans rose rapidly and when it was alleged that the accrediting system could be held partly responsible. "For Thousands Accreditation Has Spelled Deception" trumpeted an article in the *Washington Post* on June 26, 1974. Some students said they were defaulting because the school or college in which they had enrolled had failed to provide the educational program it had promised. In a number of instances, the students claimed, the school had lured them with the prospect of a federally insured loan, which it was able to do because, being accredited, it was eligible to participate in the loan program. Once the student had signed over his borrowed funds to the school in the form of tuition, the institution had its money and did not care if the student paid off the loan—if he didn't the government would.

Washington plainly needed a better way of policing the schools, both to look after the interests of students as consumers and to protect its own monies. The accreditation system was not the only possible mechanism, but there was much to be said for delegating this task to it and expecting the associations to take some responsibility for the financial probity of institutions they accredited. "Because of the vast sums

36. *Federal Higher Education Programs: Institutional Eligibility*, pt. 1, Hearings before the House Education and Labor Committee, 93:2 (GPO, 1974), pp. 88–89.

of Federal money which ultimately flow through reliance upon the accrediting mechanisms," officials of the executive branch advised Congress, "the Office [of Education] has deemed it only prudent to establish, and gradually intensify, Federal oversight of the operations of those accrediting agencies recognized by the Commissioner."[37] The government's only clear alternative was to monitor all the schools and colleges that participated in its programs, a course of action that obviously would enlarge the domain of direct federal regulation and erode the academy's ability to regulate itself. "The question," an administration official reminded Senator Pell, "is one whether or not we want the Office of Education to become a regulatory agency," substituting its own appraisal of an individual school's organizational stability, educational quality, and fiscal reliability for that of the private accreditors; the school's future eligibility for funds would therefore depend on a government procedure rather than on the approval of the accrediting body.[38] Accrediting spokesmen in effect answered yes. "Accreditation," Dickey warned, "cannot be a surrogate ministry of education."[39]

The administration and the associations jousted with each other throughout 1974 and 1975. Neither wanted full responsibility for the touchy task of stripping schools of eligibility for participation in federal programs. Senate and House committees held hearings on the subject, for the loan default scandal loomed too large for Congress to ignore, and it was apparent that someone would have to be forced to take on the assignment of policing the schools and colleges.

By 1976 Congress had made up its mind, and that year's education amendments placed the burden squarely on the commissioner of education. Accreditation would continue as a criterion for initial eligibility, but the Office of Education was given guidelines as well and, most important, the commissioner was made responsible for monitoring the fiscal and managerial behavior of participating institutions and suspending individual schools from the programs.

In time, this tightening up of the federal programs will curb some of the abuses, and that is good. But there is a price, and it will be paid in the form of increased direct federal regulation of colleges and universities:

37. *Federal Higher Education Programs*, Hearings, p. 28.
38. Testimony of S. W. Herrell, Acting Deputy Commissioner for Postsecondary Education, in *Accreditation of Postsecondary Educational Institutions, 1974*, Hearings before the Senate Labor and Public Welfare Committee, 93:2 (GPO, 1974), p. 105.
39. Ibid., p. 240.

more reports to file, more audits to endure, more rules to obey, and more administrative procedures to follow. A college president may not much care whether his watchdog is a public agency or a private association. But from the perspective of the academy as a whole, the decision to place more of this responsibility on federal officials represents a further loss of autonomy and self-rule, a loss that could probably have been averted if the higher education community had shown more willingness to regulate itself.[40]

Student Aid Need Analysis

The first decision about a student aid program is which colleges may participate. The second is which students qualify and how much money each may receive. As explained in chapter 3, need analysis has evolved into an intricate and controversial procedure. Though it displays the trappings of objectivity, the tables and calculations at its heart are highly judgmental in their construction. Someone must decide how much a family earning $14,000 a year *should be able* to contribute toward the education of one of its children at a particular college. On that decision and others like it rests a multibillion-dollar income redistribution system, largely financed with federal tax dollars, by which some students get subsidies and others do not.

Each college makes many of these determinations in its own way, but the essential normative judgments that underlie most financial aid decisions on most campuses, including decisions governing the flow of hundreds of millions of "campus-based" federal dollars, can be traced to the calculations and convictions of two large voluntary organizations, the College Scholarship Service (CSS) and the American College Testing Program (ACT).[41]

This arrangement also dates back to the National Defense Education Act, and was not accidental at the time. One veteran participant recalls the "dictum" of Homer Babbidge, an assistant commissioner of education in the early days of NDEA, that "the government should not, could not, and would not devise its own system of measuring need. That was

40. The new Council on Postsecondary Accreditation represents a serious attempt by higher education leaders to monitor and regularize the actions of dozens of private accrediting bodies, as well as to represent them in their dealings with the federal government.

41. Recently these two organizations have agreed to a common set of family contribution schedules, known as the "uniform methodology."

a job for the private sector. How could the bureaucracy devise a system better than the one that had been developed with such care as the CSS system?"[42] Washington was thus able to sidestep the task of evaluating hundreds of thousands of students, and the private need analysis systems flourished in part as a result of the general understanding that a college employing their procedures was conforming to federal requirements. As also noted in chapter 3, however, the Education Amendments of 1972 marked a change in these amiable arrangements, at least with respect to the new basic grants program. National in scope, it is administered directly by the Office of Education, which devises its own need analysis tables based on general criteria set out by Congress. The Senate Labor and Public Welfare Committee had been explicit: "The commissioner is not to adopt the schedule of either the College Scholarship Service or the American College Testing Student Need Analysis Service. He must develop his own schedule."[43]

But the campus-based programs continued much as before, with college financial aid officers handing out federal money on the basis of tables devised by the CSS and the ACT, or their own variants of them. The 1972 amendments did not end private control of these public programs.

In 1975, however, the CSS and ACT announced sweeping revisions of their tables. The changes had the effect of reducing the contribution that would be expected from families at most income levels.[44] Justified by their authors as an overdue response to the pressures of inflation and recession on the disposable income of the American family, these revisions resulted in making many middle-income students eligible for assistance, in raising the amount of aid due virtually every student, in encouraging individual colleges to spread their scholarship resources more widely, and in applying pressure on Washington to increase its student aid outlays to meet the larger aggregate "need" that the new tables generated.

A clash was inevitable. The revisions, Commissioner of Education Terrell H. Bell testified, "produced such a great additional drop in expected parental contributions that we considered them a violation of

42. John F. Morse, "How We Got Here from There," in Lois D. Rice, ed., *Student Loans: Problems and Policy Alternatives* (College Entrance Examination Board, 1977), p. 7.

43. *Education Amendments of 1971*, S. Rept. 92-346, 92:1 (GPO, 1971), p. 35.

44. For an explanation of the new norms, see James L. Bowman, *A Uniform Methodology for Measuring Ability to Pay: The CSS National Standard* (CEEB, June 1975).

the implicit understandings according to which CSS had been recognized as an approved need analysis system for purposes of Federal programs of student financial aid." The essential problem, the commissioner observed, was one of "allowing private organizations to have unfettered discretion in establishing eligibility for the receipt of Federal funds." So long as the contribution curves had undergone modest, incremental changes, the issue of control did not arise. But when the private organizations amended their tables in ways that federal officials saw as challenging the "fundamental premise of student aid," there was reason to attach some fetters.[45]

The Office of Education therefore proposed to institute an annual review of any need analysis system intended for use in parceling out federal student aid monies and to limit the amount by which family contributions might be changed from one year to the next in need analysis systems seeking federal sanction. A set of private decisions heretofore largely free of government supervision would, under the new procedures, now be regulated. But spokesmen for the need analysis services insisted on remaining free to make whatever assumptions they saw fit as to a family's ability to "contribute" to higher education. They also demanded to be allowed to measure a student's need in their own way, regardless of whether the participating colleges or the federal government was able to supply all the funds implied by those measurements.

James O'Hara of Michigan, chairman of the House Postsecondary Education Subcommittee, sought to mediate this dispute through public hearings and private negotiations, and in time the principals reached a clumsy compromise. The commissioner of education gained the right to review the private need analysis systems in the future, but agreed to include among his considerations some of the economic factors the CSS and the ACT thought important. For their part, the need analysis services agreed to modifications of their tables that rendered them more acceptable to the Office of Education and also agreed to publish the commissioner's own preferred gauges as an "option" for colleges wishing to use them. Since then the services and the Office of Education have taken pains to consult each other in advance so as to ensure that the privately generated tables would meet the government's requirements, and have finally agreed to employ a "common form" for individual student aid requests.

These accommodations appear to allow the Office of Education and

45. *Student Need Analysis (Budgetary Concerns or Ability to Pay?)*, Hearing before the House Education and Labor Committee, 94:1 (GPO, 1975), p. 25.

the private need analysis services to coexist in harmony again, and the entire incident could be dismissed as a brief disruption of a durable relation. Yet something more important was involved. When a private organization gains responsibility for a system by which public monies are meted out in pursuit of public objectives, it also assumes certain obligations. It agrees, in effect, to keep the public objectives clearly in focus and to conduct itself much as the cognizant federal agency would if the task had not been delegated. When it violates that understanding, however valid its reason for doing so, it risks having the informal made formal and its future discretion cramped. Particularly when large sums of government money hang in the balance, and when the access of many people and institutions to that money depends on a pattern of private decisions, it is irresponsible of public officials *not* to react warily to sharp changes in the accustomed pattern. That the incident ended as amicably as it did suggests that both parties still favor the basic arrangement, but it is certain that the Office of Education will hereafter keep a shorter rein on need analysis than was thought necessary before, and that the academy's ability to regulate itself in dealings with the federal government will be correspondingly reduced.

Peer Review

The third large power entrusted to the academy over the past two decades has been that of helping the bureaucracy decide which research projects merit federal support. The details differ among agencies, programs, and disciplines, and peer review is not really a "system" at all, nor does it formally empower private organizations to make decisions on behalf of the government in the manner of accrediting bodies and need analysis services. Still, as recounted in chapter 5, a sizable portion of federal payments to universities for research and development goes to support projects that have been favorably judged by outside scholars called in to advise the government. In particular, most grants made by the National Institutes of Health and the National Science Foundation— agencies that account for two-thirds of total federal R&D expenditures in colleges and universities—fund proposals that have survived scrutiny by teams of reviewers assembled from among the ranks of leading American researchers.

Not everyone likes peer review, or the panels of readers, advisory committees, and consultants that serve much the same purpose. A common complaint is that peer review has led to scientific inbreeding and logrolling and to the concentration of federal research dollars in the relatively few universities that supply many of the reviewers.

It is never easy to apply meritocratic norms to the allocation of public monies in a democracy, and peer review has been the inevitable prey of its own success. A process that has helped create a few score outstanding research campuses in the United States, in part by shielding government officials from the political consequences of such resource concentration, has itself come under fire from institutions that want to enter that privileged company—or at least to gain a share of its riches.

The two- and four-year colleges and lesser universities periodically mount assaults on the peer review process, seldom uttering an unkind word about the principle of merit but conveying their intent through populist appeals—every state or every campus should receive its share— and straightforward attempts to get portions of the money withdrawn from competition and set aside for institutions such as their own.

The community colleges have been exceptionally forthright. Testifying before a Senate Appropriations Subcommittee reviewing fiscal 1976 funding for the National Science Foundation, the vice president of the American Association of Community and Junior Colleges (AACJC) observed that the use by federal science agencies of "outside readers and peer reviewers . . . is fine if you are a member of a small fraternity of university peers, but very difficult to break if you are not in the select fraternity." "Try as they may," he continued, "community and junior colleges seem to get no further than a polite (very polite) refusal notice on their grant applications. We fear that the root of the problem may rest with NSF's own perception of community and junior colleges as not deserving of serious consideration in competitive grant awards situations. In short, community and junior colleges have tried from every conceivable angle to break the NSF funding barrier. At this point we feel that a setaside [of funds] is the only answer."[46]

Applying this position to all federal higher education programs, the AACJC in 1975 recommended that "Congress give serious consideration to an overall policy of providing setasides for two-year colleges in programs directed to institutions of higher education." Acknowledging that "it may be unfortunate that minimum percentages must be mandated to

46. *Department of Housing and Urban Development, and Certain Independent Agencies Appropriations, Fiscal Year 1976*, pt. 2, Hearings before the Senate Appropriations Committee, 94:1 (GPO, 1975), pp. 1237-38.

ensure that federal programs reach all those for whom they are intended," the AACJC policy statement nonetheless asserted that "it is one of the facts of life" and that therefore "equity is better achieved through the formula grant approach directly to institutions, under which any applicant meeting the established criteria is eligible for support and the judgment factor is reduced to a minimum."[47]

Some members of Congress are usually willing to support such appeals. In 1974–75 Senator William Proxmire of Wisconsin energetically joined in a foray against the concentration of research funds in what he termed the "academic oligarchy of large universities."[48] In the House, Congressman John B. Conlan of Arizona described peer review procedures as "incestuous," "an old boys' system," and "monopoly grantsmanship."[49] Their chief concern was whether funds were widely enough distributed and whether the peer review process impedes wider distribution. But that concern became entangled with a familiar issue: the accusation that federal research agencies, in spite of or because of their review procedures, pump tax dollars into frivolous, offensive, or absurd projects. Proxmire's office periodically announces a "Golden Fleece Award" for some grant or contract that appears to waste the taxpayer's money. And in 1975 Conlan and Congressman Robert E. Bauman of Maryland denounced a social studies curriculum project funded by the National Science Foundation: they found its content unseemly and its promotion under federal auspices a threat to local control of the schools.[50] Paradoxically, in this instance Conlan charged the foundation with abusing its own peer review process by not paying attention to one reviewer's misgivings about the proposed project.[51] But the remedy the House adopted would have had a chilling effect on the foundation's autonomy, including its ability to fund peer-approved projects. In the "Bauman amendment" to the NSF authorization bill, the House voted to require the foundation to submit lists of all its proposed grants to Congress, which would then have thirty days to veto individual projects.

47. "Toward Universal Opportunity," Recommendations approved by the Board of Directors of the American Association of Community and Junior Colleges (April 1975; processed).

48. Press release, Office of Senator William Proxmire, March 2, 1975.

49. Quoted in *Higher Education Daily*, July 23, 1975, p. 3.

50. Deborah Shapely, "Congress: House Votes Veto Power on All NSF Research Grants," *Science*, April 25, 1975, pp. 338–41.

51. John Walsh, "NSF and Its Critics in Congress: New Pressure on Peer Review," *Science*, June 6, 1975, pp. 999–1001.

This idea got nowhere in the Senate—even Proxmire admitted that burdening Congress with review of every NSF grant was not a suitable remedy—and died in conference. But the point had been made and, it appears, was heard in the executive branch. Philip Handler, president of the National Academy of Sciences, said that the Bauman amendment was "tantamount to book-burning," warned that "the intrusion of political considerations in the award of grants . . . is unacceptable," and charged that Proxmire's "seemingly capricious behavior . . . combined with the action taken by the House constitutes the wedge of a powerful threat to the operation of the peer-review system of decision making."[52] H. Guyford Stever, then director of NSF, said that the House amendment was a "signal which all scientists should heed," even if it was not part of the law.[53]

Congressional dislike of particular research projects is not, of course, the same thing as community colleges' unhappiness with the modest fraction of federal monies they receive. But both kinds of criticism can serve only to erode established grant-making practices in government agencies, pushing them instead toward more evenhanded distribution of funds and more cautious activities. No federal agency can confidently proceed on its accustomed course after its director receives a letter from the chairman of the House Appropriations Committee announcing that he is "sick and tired of responding to correspondence from citizens who are blaming Congress for some of the idiotic things done by a few unstable people in the executive branch" and warning that "if I discover 'damn fool' projects which have been approved by the National Science Foundation, I am going to try to cut millions of dollars out of your budget."[54]

Some form of peer review will doubtless endure. It is sensible and strategic, the more so when political scrutiny is intense, for the more recondite the research the less likely is a civil servant to trust—or to be able to defend—his own judgment of the merits of competing proposals. He has little recourse but to retain some system in which knowledgeable persons share in his decision and support him once it is made.

Because peer review is inseparable from the idea of merit, and because

52. Quoted in Phillip M. Boffey, "Outlook for Science: 'Clouds on the Horizon,'" *Chronicle of Higher Education*, May 5, 1975, p. 7.

53. Quoted in *Science*, April 25, 1975, p. 339.

54. Letter from Congressman George H. Mahon to NSF Director H. Guyford Stever, quoted in Philip M. Boffey, "NSF Funds Threatened," *Chronicle of Higher Education*, May 27, 1975, p. 6.

scholarly quality is not evenly distributed among the nation's three thousand campuses, it is unreasonable to fault the peer review process for contributing to the uneven distribution of federal research funds. Thus the National Science Foundation responded to its critics in 1975 in straightforward terms:

We select those projects which, in our judgment, will do most to advance scientific knowledge, and select knowledgeable advisors to help us to choose the most scientifically meritorious opportunities for the investment of research support funds. Other things being about equal, we give preference to those advisors and projects which will give us a broad distribution of institutions and locations, but there is no doubt that research capability tends to concentrate. We cannot, however, control either the faculty job opportunities or the choices individuals make among job offers. It is rather common for individuals who prove themselves to be highly competent to move to more prestigious institutions. It cannot be surprising that, when the most capable individuals are disproportionately found in a small number of institutions, the same institutions are found disproportionately listed among our advisors and grantees.[55]

Moreover, though federal research funds do remain concentrated in a relatively small number of universities (see chapter 5), the degree of that concentration has been diminishing, not rising.[56]

Yet traditional peer review practices will come under mounting pressure as the financial and political stakes both increase, particularly if federal research funding priorities continue to shift from the support of many separate scholars to the support of a smaller number of large projects that are more "applied" than "basic." "When competition is among individual scientists," Smith and Karlesky observe, "awards are based on the capability of the individual and the scientific merit of the proposal; this award process is almost completely nonpolitical. In the case of very large awards, however, the process tends to contain greater political elements, since the stakes are high for both the competing universities and the communities involved."[57]

55. "Peer Review and Proposal Evaluation: Staff Study" (National Science Foundation, June 1975; proceessed), app. 1, p. 2.
56. "Geographical Distribution of Federal Science Funds to Colleges and Universities," Report of the Comptroller General of the United States (General Accounting Office, April 16, 1976; processed). See also *An Analysis of the Geographical Distribution of NSF Awards as Compared with Other Selected Indicators* (National Science Foundation, Directorate for Administration, July 1975). And for a general discussion of institutional and geographic concentration, see Bruce L. R. Smith and Joseph J. Karlesky, *The State of Academic Science: The Universities in the Nation's Research Effort* (Change Magazine Press, 1977), pp. 40–45.
57. *State of Academic Science*, p. 245.

The higher education community's own ambivalence toward the distributional effects of merit-based and peer-reviewed federal funding decisions is not a recent development. In the early sixties Homer Babbidge warned of "a polarization of the haves and the have-nots of higher education," in which "humanists and smaller institutions seek by political action to improve their lot" while "scientists and large universities seem better satisfied with the status quo." He anticipated that piecemeal federal funding policies would worsen the factionalism of the academy and counseled that "the ad hoc, opportunistic coloration of higher education's posture must be modified in the direction of longer-term and more rational policies."[58]

The political dynamics of which he wrote have not changed greatly in sixteen years, nor are "more rational" policies much closer to realization. But the have-nots have massively increased their numbers and their influence. When the American Association of Community and Junior Colleges protests the consequences of discretionary programs and asks for set-asides and greater emphasis on formula funding, it does not escape notice on Capitol Hill that every state, and each of 426 House districts, has one or more community colleges, or that community colleges now enroll 36 percent of all students, whereas the elite research universities are far fewer in number, are concentrated in a few jurisdictions, and account for a relatively small number (and diminishing percentage) of students.

It is not necessary to change the nature of peer review itself to curb its impact. Much the same result obtains when federal funds are directed into student aid and institutional programs where their allocation is governed by formula or where principles other than merit are involved. Thus some college leaders pursue their institutional interests quite subtly, not taking on the idea of peer review itself but arguing, for example, for a reallocation of science funds so that a larger portion of them will flow into "science education" rather than into basic research.[59] Two consequences of such a shift would naturally be a broader distribution of federal money among postsecondary institutions and a reduction in the amount given out according to the peer review process.

58. Homer D. Babbidge, Jr., "Scientist Affluent, Humanist Militant: Faction in Higher Education," *Graduate Journal*, vol. 5 (1962 Supplement), pp. 153–62.

59. See, for example, the testimony of Thomas Wenzlau, on behalf of the Associated Colleges of the Midwest, in *Department of Housing and Urban Development*, pt. 2, Hearings, pp. 1266–89.

The divisions within the higher education community can only encourage members of Congress and senior administration officials to supervise the allocation of federal science monies more closely. Even if pressures for set-asides and other noncompetitive funding processes are resisted, broader participation, greater intellectual caution, enhanced political wariness, and a larger and more diversified list of beneficiaries can be anticipated. Such democratization will probably make the funding process slower and more laden with appeals, reviews, and litigation. The accustomed delegation of governmental authority to the traditional academic and scientific elite will be less generous, and its processes and outcomes subject to more scrutiny and reversal.

Summary

It may be argued that none of the above three "systems" was meant to discharge the functions it is now being accused of not carrying out. Accreditation was a private club competent to pass on its own candidates for membership but scarcely equipped to police their handling of the government's money and certainly not designed to regulate profit-seeking schools that abjure traditional academic norms. Need analysis, as developed on the campuses and in their associations, was intended to help college administrators gauge the resources and needs of students seeking assistance, not to implement the government's policy priorities or its ideas about income distribution. Peer review was a form of scientific quality control, not a way to distribute federal funds among three thousand institutions or to tailor project contents to congressional tastes. All three arrangements arose in a time when the academic world was smaller and more homogeneous, when federal funds for higher education were scarcer and the government's purposes more clear-cut. All three were informal, grounded in tacit understandings, and workable only so long as they served Washington's needs as well as the academy's. That they have endured at all attests to their adaptability and their continued usefulness, despite the evolution of higher education into a vast, unruly assortment of disparate elements and competing interests. Perhaps it was inevitable that the complex requirements and high costs of present-day funding programs would oblige public officials to supervise the recipients more closely. But, at least in a few areas, the academy might have reduced such regulation by anticipating Washington's needs and devising better ways of disciplining itself. For the future, it would be well to heed the observation by Charles Saunders, vice president for governmental relations at the American Council on Education: "The challenge facing American universities is not merely to learn how to cope with federal regulation, but to develop new mechanisms for self-regulation so that the higher-education community as a whole can better fend off the continuing encroachment of government controls."[60]

The Challenge for the Future

The persistence of Washington's categorical approach to funding higher education means that colleges wanting federal money will continue to risk having their institutional priorities distorted and their accounting systems strained. A shift to general support would lighten those burdens, but the academy finds it no easier to convert government officials to that approach than to persuade them that universities should be exempt from regulation. The two notions are complementary to a degree: if universities deserve federal support for their ordinary activities, it is presumably because those activities have value and ought not to be disrupted, whether by financial starvation or external controls. Conversely, an institution that merely provides a service has no basis for being treated differently from vendors of other goods and services bought by federal agencies.

College leaders will undoubtedly persist in their dual quest for unrestricted federal funds and freedom from federal controls. It is normal, rational, self-interested behavior for any government client. But increasingly those objectives will be set forth, with all the trappings of eloquence and principled argumentation that the academy can muster, more for strategic purposes than as goals to be achieved.

When it comes time to negotiate with congressional committees and executive branch agencies, higher education's Washington representatives have begun to display a more pragmatic attitude. Some of the early fruits of their adroit lobbying and political compromise have already been described. For the future, Saunders warns his colleagues that "we

60. Charles B. Saunders, Jr., "Federal Regulation vs. More Self-Regulation," *Princeton Alumni Weekly*, September 12, 1977, p. 26. For a less optimistic appraisal of the prospects for self-regulation, particularly in the realm of equal opportunity, see Sheila Tobias, "Government Regulation, Institutional Self-Regulation, and Access to Academic Employment," in Hobbs, ed., *Government Regulation and Higher Education*.

need a moratorium on indignant rhetoric and vague laments that government will be the death of us. As both Congress and executive agencies become more alert to the problems of regulatory burden, the search for solutions will place a premium on hard facts and precise proposals. If the campus contributes only anecdotal complaints and expressions of outrage, there is a danger that it may lose a real opportunity for major reforms to ease the federal regulatory burden."[61]

Surely this is shrewd tactical advice. But it will be hard to follow. On the whole, academics are far more prone to the liberal ideologies and activist constructions of the federal role that give rise to increased regulation than is the electorate as a whole.[62] Moreover, many factions within the campus community—women and members of minority groups come first to mind—see their own interests advanced by vigorous government regulation of colleges and universities and accordingly fight proposals to constrain it.[63] With divisions apparently as deep within the academic community as between it and the federal government, it will be more prudent to seek livable compromises on particular issues than to try for agreement on general principles.[64]

Yet that sensible tactic may not constitute a sufficient strategy for dealing with the multiheaded creature known as federal regulation. The continuing lack of a basic statement of principles to guide the relations between the federal government and the colleges means that particularized negotiations have no philosophical anchor and that the negotiators have few standards and little perspective. Hence Louis Bender calls—rather grandly—for development of a "Magna Carta for Higher Educa-

61. Charles B. Saunders, Jr., "Easing the Burden of Federal Regulation: The Next Move Is Ours," *Educational Record*, vol. 57 (Fall 1976), pp. 217–24.

62. For an exhaustive documentation of this phenomenon—and some of the ambiguities it creates on campus—see Everett Carll Ladd, Jr., and Seymour Martin Lipset, *The Divided Academy* (McGraw-Hill, 1975).

63. At a 1976 conference on federal regulation of higher education, and kindred issues, Dr. Kenneth S. Tollett of Howard University said, "We are very much disturbed by those who seem to be disturbed by what the Federal Government is doing in higher education. We're not sure [whether] they are upset by the red tape or disturbed by the support and advancement that the Federal Government has brought for blacks in higher education." Quoted in the *New York Times*, December 13, 1976. See also Kenneth S. Tollett, "What Is All the Shouting About?" in Hook and others, eds., *The University and the State*.

64. The perspective, stature, and customary pragmatism of college and university trustees might usefully mediate some of these disputes and also strengthen the lobbying abilities of educational institutions. For a constructive attempt to involve trustees more heavily in regulatory matters, see "A Call to College and University Trustees" (New York: Peat, Marwick, Mitchell and Co., March 1978; processed).

tion."[65] But even if there is no such sweeping resolution of the dilemmas of regulation, there are several avenues for improvement. Washington could lighten the reporting and compliance burden on colleges by reducing parallel, overlapping, and duplicative requirements imposed by multiple agencies. It could consolidate some responsibilities in fewer units and delegate some from one agency to another.[66] Certain steps are already being taken, both in response to careful studies, such as that by the Federal Paperwork Commission, and through organizational changes to improve governmental efficiency, such as President Carter's recent proposal to consolidate most federal fair employment enforcement activities within the Equal Employment Opportunity Commission.

Many agencies could also apply a stricter test of necessity to the regulations promulgated to carry out legislative mandates, although, as Saunders points out, "this will require some discipline on our part, because many of the detailed instructions written into current regulations were placed there at our request, so that we might know more precisely what the government required of us."[67] Senior federal officials might also join with higher education leaders in an attempt to develop a usable set of

65. *Federal Regulation and Higher Education*, pp. 69–70. In October 1977 the Alfred P. Sloan Foundation announced the formation of a blue-ribbon commission on government and higher education, chaired by Louis W. Cabot. The commission staff is currently at work under the direction of Dr. Carl Kaysen, its vice chairman and director of research. Its efforts could yield the necessary analytic base for such a statement. For earlier efforts, see Committee on Government and Higher Education, *The Efficiency of Freedom* (Johns Hopkins Press, 1959), and Commission on Financing Higher Education, *Nature and Needs of Higher Education* (Columbia University Press, 1952).

66. There is precedent for this. For example, on delegation from the Department of Labor, HEW's Office for Civil Rights has responsibility for monitoring the civil rights part of federal contract compliance when the contractors involved are schools and colleges. Similarly, when a university receives grants and contracts from several agencies, the Office of Management and Budget has devised a procedure whereby one of those agencies (usually HEW) is designated to negotiate the university's overhead rate, which is then applied to its dealings with the other agencies. The Education Amendments of 1976 included another provision, intended to "eliminate excessive detail and unnecessary or redundant information requests," whereby the data requirements of several units within HEW must be better coordinated than has been the practice. Though it may seem strange that Congress found it necessary to legislate something that the secretary of HEW could presumably have done administratively, the purpose is nonetheless laudable. 90 Stat. 2231.

67. Charles B. Saunders, Jr., "Getting Our Act Together (or, How to Keep the Government from Playing the Featured Role)" (address to the National Assembly of the National Center for Higher Education Management Systems, November 8, 1977; processed).

general principles or guidelines that embody the concept of academic freedom in terms that members of Congress and civil servants can understand. The evolution of this ancient concept has been much studied,[68] but it is little understood by the public, and for the federal government it remains, at most, part of the common law, whereas practices that may threaten it are written into the statute books.[69]

If higher education hopes to vouchsafe its sovereignty, it must demonstrate its willingness to regulate itself in some areas and to comply spontaneously with societal norms and expectations in other areas. It will have to strengthen its capacity to produce accurate and timely data and to develop serviceable indexes of its own performance. It should increase its ability—and its willingness—to negotiate directly with public officials and to enlist the aid of others who can influence government actions. And it must edit, simplify, invigorate, and, where possible, document the arguments it uses to persuade others that in the central university functions of teaching and research, academic freedom, when sensibly defined and responsibly applied, will confer greater benefits on society than will any alternative yet devised.

68. For a scholarly account—inevitably from the perspective of two faculty members—see Richard Hofstadter and Walter P. Metzger, *The Development of Academic Freedom in the United States* (Columbia University Press, 1955).

69. Proposing in 1977 to rectify this situation, Congressman James G. Martin of North Carolina introduced a bill called The Academic Freedom Act of 1977, intended to "preserve the academic freedom and the autonomy of institutions of higher education and to condition the authority of officials of the United States to issue rules, regulations, or orders with respect to institutions of higher education." (H.R. 8547, 95:1.) Others, however, reasoning that statutes can always be changed, doubt that this would place academic freedom on a firm enough foundation. Estelle A. Fishbein suggests that the time may have come for a constitutional amendment to establish the sovereignty of colleges and universities. "The Academic Industry," in Hobbs, ed., *Government Regulation of Higher Education*.

Chapter Seven

Policy and Structure

BECAUSE higher education plays a supporting role in so many federal policy dramas, because its own well-being is ancillary to myriad other governmental missions, and because the effect on it of a decision made in Washington ordinarily holds limited interest for the persons making the decision, it is not surprising that responsibility for programs and policies of considerable importance to colleges and universities is strewn across many units of the federal government. Insofar as higher education has been deemed a means to other ends, and inasmuch as government structures are generally designed around primary governmental objectives rather than around the mechanisms for achieving those objectives, it would follow that federal decisionmaking structures and organizational units will be poorly suited to foster a concern with higher education as a whole or to develop a coherent federal policy toward it. In this chapter I test that supposition, weigh some suggestions for altering the present arrangements, and sketch some recommendations of my own.

The Present Condition

The central structural problem for higher education in Washington is symbolized, though not explained, by the fact that dilemmas and proposals such as those described in the previous chapters have no one apparent audience anywhere in the federal establishment. "As a federal function," Rufus Miles, a former top HEW administrator, asserts, "education . . . is now leaderless. No person in the federal government has the combination of prestige, staff resources, time, and assignment of responsibility to be the leader of the government's education programs. No person has the opportunity to look holistically at the educational institutions and systems of the Nation and the education programs of the federal government with the purpose of trying to develop a coherent and consistent philosophy of relationships between the federal government and the educational systems."[1]

Programs for higher education overlap and are scattered among many multifunction agencies. Policymaking by agency officials and congressional leaders is fragmented, spasmodic, and issue specific. Problems that cut across program lines and agency boundaries find no person or group in a position to consider what, if anything, the federal government might do about them.

Executive Branch Agencies

The four hundred-odd separate programs through which Washington channeled money into higher education in 1974 were administered by twenty-five separate federal agencies and more than fifty major organizational units within those agencies, ranging from the Bureau of Mines to the National Institutes of Health.[2] But five agencies account for 90 percent of total federal outlays, although only two of these—the National Science Foundation and the Department of Health, Education, and Welfare—have higher education among their foremost concerns, and in the former that link is tenuous. The other three are the Veterans Administration and the Defense and Labor departments.[3]

VETERANS ADMINISTRATION. The VA, which administers the largest single federal higher education program (the GI bill), has never conceded an interest in higher education itself, and is opposed to meshing its activities with those of other agencies even where they may overlap or clash. Instead, it simply does Congress' bidding with respect to veterans and shows greater sensitivity to the manpower considerations of

1. Rufus E. Miles, Jr., *A Cabinet Department of Education* (American Council on Education, 1976), p. 36. It should be noted that Miles is referring here to all education, not just higher education.

2. These programs are grouped by agency and purpose in Pamela Christoffel and Lois Rice, *Federal Policy Issues and Data Needs in Postsecondary Education: Final Report to the National Center for Education Statistics* (GPO, 1975), apps. A and B. The listing by agency (and major organizational units within agencies) is reproduced in Carnegie Council on Policy Studies in Higher Education, *Federal Reorganization: Education and Scholarship* (Carnegie Foundation for the Advancement of Teaching, 1977), app. These inclusive typologies attempt to embrace all "postsecondary education," not just the traditional institutions of "higher education."

3. The 90 percent estimate is that of the National Commission on the Financing of Postsecondary Education. See *Financing Postsecondary Education in the United States* (GPO, 1974), pp. 106-07.

the Defense Department than to the student aid priorities of the Office of Education. That it disburses billions of dollars in education benefits is seemingly a matter of marginal interest to the agency: the discussion of that huge undertaking took up 3 out of 122 pages in the administrator's 1974 annual report.[4]

The VA also engages university medical centers in various health care, research, and training programs, but neither it nor its patron congressional committees have shown much concern about the effect of their actions on higher education. Their primary concern has been directed to the efficacy and integrity of their programs, and to that end they have not been reluctant to develop funding formulas and to prescribe regulatory measures that colleges regard as unhelpful or even detrimental to themselves.

Lately, the congressional attitude has softened somewhat, particularly in the Senate Committee on Veterans' Affairs since Senator Alan Cranston assumed the chairmanship.[5] And the Veterans Administration has had to address itself to some of the concerns of higher education institutions, at least insofar as its own regulations, intended to tighten program administration and prevent abuses by schools and individuals, have elicited protests, lawsuits, and political pressure for legislative relief from inconvenienced colleges and universities.[6] But it is important to

4. Administrator of Veterans' Affairs, *Annual Report, 1974* (GPO, 1974).

5. In 1977, for example, the committee reported a bill (S. 457, 95:1) that, for the first time since 1952, would have tailored GI bill payments to varying college tuition levels by allowing recipients to "accelerate" a portion of their entitlements and thereby increase the sums available for use in a given month. While avoiding any suggestion that this change might serve the recruitment and enrollment interests of some colleges and universities, the committee did conclude that "an accelerated program . . . is needed to aid those veterans . . . enrolled in or desirous of enrolling in a high-cost program of education." The House of Representatives, however, remained firmly opposed to any such break with a quarter century of practice, and the version that emerged from conference was a faint shadow of what the Senate had approved. *GI Bill Improvement Act of 1977*, S. Rept. 95-468, 95:1 (GPO, 1977); quotation from p. 42.

6. The regulatory issues arose with a vengeance in the aftermath of 1976 GI bill amendments, requiring, among other things, that colleges and universities take specific steps to monitor (and report to Washington) the academic progress of individual veterans, and defining more narrowly the courses of study for which veterans may use their GI benefits. For background on the congressional action, see *Veterans' Education and Employment Assistance Act of 1976*, S. Rept. 94-1243, 94:2 (GPO, 1976), especially pp. 45–62. For a summary of the main objections by the higher education associations, see "Problems with VA Law (PL 94-502) and Regulations Encountered by Colleges and Universities" (American Council on Education, June 9, 1977; processed).

note that the main source of these controversies is the continuing insensitivity of the Veterans Administration and the committees that draft its legislation to the traditions and desires of educational institutions.[7]

DEPARTMENT OF DEFENSE. Aside from ROTC,[8] the service academies, and the support of officers studying at other universities, the Defense Department's place in federal higher education policy centers on its sizable outlays for research and development, about one-tenth of its huge budget. The bulk of Pentagon-financed R&D expenditures support intramural or industry-based activity, but much of the basic and some of the applied research monies are awarded to postsecondary institutions.[9] Thus in fiscal 1976 the Defense Department obligated some $291 million in research monies to universities and millions more in manpower training and other activities. But the Pentagon's role in education policy

7. The lack of appreciation of the GI bill's importance within the federal higher education enterprise extends to the top of the executive branch. When in May 1975 the Ford administration proposed to terminate the entire Vietnam-era GI bill program, neither the President's brief letter of transmittal nor the fuller justifications submitted by the administrator of veterans' affairs indicated any awareness that this program made up a large percentage of federal postsecondary outlays, that it had any standing as an education program, or even—a plausible argument—that with the advent of various student aid schemes needy veterans could get financial help from other federal sources. The principal rationale advanced by the executive branch was simply that "the educational assistance programs for World War II and Korean veterans, as well as for those eligible under current law, have all been readjustment programs designed to help veterans to adjust from military to civilian life by affording them monetary aid to obtain an educational status they might normally have aspired to and obtained had they not served their country in wartime or national emergency. It was not contemplated that educational assistance was to be a continuing benefit." Letter from Richard L. Roudebush, Administrator of Veterans' Affairs, to Vance Hartke, chairman of the Senate Veterans' Affairs Committee, September 29, 1975; reprinted in *Veterans' Education and Employment Assistance Act of 1976*, pp. 226–31. See also the letter from President Gerald R. Ford to Nelson A. Rockefeller, President of the Senate, May 7, 1975, reprinted in ibid., p. 272. As noted in chapter 3, Congress did agree to phase out the Vietnam-era GI bill, but replaced it with a new contributory program of educational assistance for people entering the armed forces.

8. ROTC can create controversies of its own, as was evident on a number of campuses in the mid-1960s, not only because it has a military tie but also because it involves the undergraduate curriculum, traditionally an area where the faculty is very sensitive to government interference.

9. The Defense Department played a larger role in the funding of campus-based research and development before 1970, when the "Mansfield amendment" to that year's Military Procurement Authorization Act forbade the use of Pentagon funds "to carry out any research project or study unless such project or study has a direct and apparent relationship to a specific military function or operation." 83 Stat. 206.

is both modest and diffuse. As if to underscore the point, of the nearly $1 billion that the Office of Management and Budget attributed to Defense in the government-wide education budget totals that year, none fit under "national education goals"; the whole amount went under "education support for other basic purposes."[10] The Pentagon typifies the "mission-oriented agency" that makes daily decisions of great consequence to higher education but seldom makes them with higher education in mind. Its senior education policy official is a special assistant to an assistant secretary.

DEPARTMENT OF LABOR. Estimates of the expenditures by the Labor Department for higher education may range from virtually nothing to nearly $1 billion a year, depending on how the tally is made. Except for a few modest research and training programs and some public employment titles from which colleges may benefit, most DOL expenditures are for employment training. Under the program reforms that took effect in fiscal 1975, these funds are parceled out to state and local "prime sponsors," which may or may not direct some of them into programs run by colleges and universities. So thorough has been the delegation of authority that no one in the Labor Department can say how much of this money—outlays of slightly more than $3 billion in fiscal 1976—may be going to postsecondary institutions. In any case, the secretary of labor has little control over the impact of that money on higher education.

NATIONAL SCIENCE FOUNDATION. Created to foster scientific research, the interests of the NSF naturally converge with those of the academic community. Eighty-three percent of the foundation's 1975 budget went for research and development, and 78 percent of those funds flowed to colleges and universities.[11]

The foundation's mission, however, is the support of science, not higher education, and most of its programs are conceived and run with science in mind. Although two- and four-year colleges have succeeded in garnering some NSF monies, the lion's share of foundation outlays remains concentrated in the small number of institutions most deeply committed to scientific research. In fiscal 1975, for example, one hun-

10. *Special Analyses, Budget of the United States Government, Fiscal Year 1978*, p. 172. Figures include elementary and secondary education and omit research and development.

11. National Science Foundation, *Federal Funds for Research, Development, and Other Scientific Activities: Fiscal Years 1973, 1974, and 1975*, (NSF, 1974), p. 18.

dred universities absorbed nearly 89 percent of NSF obligations to post-secondary institutions.[12]

The academic and scientific elite that receives the bulk of NSF appropriations also has much to say about the foundation's policies and projects. The National Science Board, consisting of prominent scientists appointed by the President, sets agency policy. And, as described in chapter 5, review panels that counsel program officers on which research proposals to approve generally represent kindred elements of higher education. Thus the National Science Foundation, the most important government science agency, is at once deeply enmeshed in national post-secondary policies and peripheral to much of the higher education industry.

DEPARTMENT OF HEALTH, EDUCATION, AND WELFARE. HEW is the only federal agency with education in its name; nevertheless, of the $3.2 billion that it obligated to colleges and universities in fiscal 1975, less than one-third came from the Office of Education.[13] Of course the same officials also gave out billions more in student assistance funds, but the point stands: even within HEW, policies and programs of great moment to higher education are scattered about.

The Education Division is a new (1972) bureaucratic structure superimposed on the old (1867) Office of Education and several lesser units. The assistant secretary who heads the division is nominally the ranking education official of the executive branch, but little real authority attaches to the position, since control over virtually all the division's programs and funds is still vested by law in subordinate officials, primarily the U.S. commissioner of education, who heads the Office of Education.

The commissioner's domain, in turn, covers numerous bureaus. Until 1977 one of these was devoted to postsecondary education and was headed by a deputy commissioner. In the organizational reforms announced early in the Carter administration by HEW Secretary Califano and Commissioner of Education Ernest L. Boyer, this unit was reconstituted as the Bureau of Higher and Continuing Education, and the major student aid programs were transferred to the new Bureau of Student Financial Assistance. Consequently, there are now two deputy commis-

12. National Science Foundation, *Federal Support to Universities, Colleges, and Selected Nonprofit Institutions, Fiscal Year 1975, Detailed Statistical Tables* (NSF, 1977), pp. 11–12.

13. Ibid., p. 3.

sioners with primary duties in the field of higher education. They report, however, not to the commissioner, but to one of his senior deputies, which means that they are now four steps removed from the secretary of HEW.[14]

Although the outlays of these two bureaus make up just part of the departmental and government-wide dollar totals, their programs are highly visible, are much debated, and come closer than most other federal activities to being directed at higher education in its own right. They include the six core student aid programs established under Title IV of the 1972 amendments to the Higher Education Act, a trio of special educational services for disadvantaged students, several shrunken programs of graduate fellowships and the like, the land grants, what little remains of college facilities grants and loans (but not dormitory construction, still a responsibility of Housing and Urban Development), and the program of assistance to "developing institutions."

If one adds up all the postsecondary expenditures of the Office of Education, whether to institutions, students, states, banks, or whatever, the sum is not inconsiderable. The fiscal 1977 appropriation totaled $2.9 billion for student assistance alone. Other programs fitting loosely into the category of postsecondary education raised the total to about $3.2 billion.[15]

But even these figures must be kept in perspective. In 1977 all the Office of Education postsecondary programs combined were smaller than the GI bill alone, and accounted for no more than one-fourth of aggregate federal higher education outlays. Moreover, as most of the money goes to students through formula-based assistance schemes, the responsible officials have little control over its effect on particular colleges and universities.

The major health and welfare units of HEW also heavily fund higher education. The Social Security Administration runs a large student aid program (see chapter 3). On the health side, outlays by HEW to col-

14. It may be noted, however, that Commissioner Boyer was formerly chancellor of the State University of New York, and Mary Berry, the assistant secretary for education, was chancellor of the University of Colorado. President Carter's break with the tradition of naming an elementary and secondary education specialist to at least one of the top education posts, while upsetting to some school and teacher organizations, does mean that two persons with considerable experience on the "receiving end" of federal higher education policy are now situated where they can influence such policy. But the structural problem endures.

15. *Higher Education Daily*, April 22, 1977, p. 1.

leges and universities totaled nearly $2 billion in fiscal 1975, most of it channeled through the National Institutes of Health. But NIH, like the National Science Foundation, concentrates on the campuses that share its specialized research and training interests. Thus, even though Yale's receipts from the Education Division barely exceed Princeton's, Yale, because it has a major medical center, gets nearly ten times more money from HEW as a whole than Princeton does.[16]

It goes without saying that neither the commissioner of social security nor the assistant secretary for health "reports" to the assistant secretary for education, let alone to a pair of deputy commissioners tucked away in the Office of Education. Although the secretary of HEW and his senior aides have the opportunity of examining policy issues that cut across jurisdictional lines within the department, the health and welfare agencies are themselves organized around their primary pursuits.

The department also contains a number of regulatory units that police diverse aspects of campus activity but that are not housed within the Education Division. From the academy's point of view, the most powerful of these is the Office for Civil Rights, the head of which answers directly to the secretary, though three-quarters of its activity is directed toward educational institutions.[17] Other regulatory offices fall within the health area and, if one accepts the proposition that Social Security is the costliest of all federal "social programs" that impinge on higher education, then it could be argued that the social security offices in Baltimore also house a particularly burdensome sort of regulation.[18]

Between and above the Agencies

Since 1964 education issues engaging more than one department have had a forum in the Federal Interagency Committee on Education (FICE), created by President Johnson as a mechanism for coordinating education policy on a continuous basis. The assistant secretary for education now serves as chairman of this body and in that capacity has

16. This is a fiscal 1973 comparison taken from U.S. Department of Health, Education, and Welfare, *DHEW Obligations to Institutions of Higher Education, Fiscal Year—1973*, vol. 2 (Office of the Assistant Secretary for Health, 1974), pp. 4, 7.

17. Miles, *Cabinet Department of Education*, p. 90.

18. See Carol Van Alstyne and Sharon L. Coldren, *The Costs of Implementing Federally Mandated Social Programs at Colleges and Universities* (American Council on Education, 1976), especially pp. 24–25.

nominal primacy in executive branch deliberations about education. FICE draws members from all the principal agencies involved with education—not only from those discussed above but also from NASA, the departments of State and Agriculture, and others—and over the years its small staff has prepared some useful reports. But the record of the committee has been disappointing, a classic case of a group with vast responsibility and no authority; it lacks a legislative charter and is hamstrung by the standard limitation on interagency groups: "Nothing in this order shall be construed as subjecting any Federal agency . . . to the authority of any other Federal Agency."[19]

Most top government officials are too busy to attend meetings of impotent committees. Consequently, to borrow a phrase from William Carey, FICE has been a "bottom heavy" body that attracts career administrators to its sessions and that takes no effective action.[20] In practice, FICE makes no education policy, and chairing it is a hollow honor.

The weakness of FICE attests to the failure of the executive branch to order its many education programs and agencies in ways that permit policy coordination, let alone direction. That tax, health, science, manpower, veterans', and social security policies, to name only the more obvious, all have an effect on higher education is clear; that their combined effect far outweighs that of the "postsecondary" programs run by HEW's Education Division is also apparent. But in the absence of a mechanism for appraising these scattered activities from a unified higher education perspective, that task goes by default to the Executive Office of the President. There, the Office of Management and Budget, which annually prepares a "special budget analysis" listing the education-linked expenditures of the various agencies, does keep an eye on the totals. Beyond that accounting function, however, even the OMB is limited, since its internal structure generally reflects the organization of the executive branch it oversees, leaving the program, policy, and budget review of higher education activities split among several staff units. This does not preclude policy coordination—more takes place in the OMB than elsewhere—but it is not easy or automatic.

The recently revived Office of Science and Technology Policy watches over one large—but limited—set of government activities that

19. Executive Order 11185; 29 Fed. Reg. 14399.

20. Carey applied this description to the Interdepartmental Committee on Scientific Research and Development in 1947; quoted in Milton Lomask, *A Minor Miracle* (National Science Foundation, 1976), p. 94.

interests higher education and that cuts across agency lines. And the President's domestic policy staff would seem to have the inherent ability to assay the totality of higher education policy if it were told to do so. This has not happened, however, nor is it reasonable to expect a White House unit charged with all of domestic policy to function as a regular arbiter of issues that, however complex and interesting, occupy only a narrow part of that spectrum.[21]

Congress

If one measure of adequacy in the federal machinery that handles higher education policy is its ability to cut across agency and program lines in order to address large issues in a coherent manner, Congress scores no higher than the executive branch it so often chides. Indeed, federal higher education policy illustrates Seidman's observation that "congressional organization and executive branch organization . . . constitute two halves of a single system."[22]

Neither the Senate nor the House has a standing committee devoted exclusively to education, let alone higher education, although each body does have a committee—Education and Labor in the House, Human Resources in the Senate—with education as one of its chief responsibilities. Yet neither of those units comes close to embracing the full range of program and agency jurisdictions that bear on higher education.

The Senate panel has the broader sweep, overseeing not only all HEW education programs, but also manpower, medical research and health professions, the National Science Foundation, and the Arts and Humanities endowments. Its single education subcommittee handles programs geared to every educational level from preschool to graduate school.

The corresponding House committee lacks jurisdiction over two agencies important to higher education: the health manpower and research programs of the National Institutes of Health (House Interstate and Foreign Commerce Committee), and the activities of the National Science Foundation (House Science and Technology Committee). Its education functions, moreover, are split among several subcommittees.

21. See Chester E. Finn, Jr., *Education and the Presidency* (D. C. Heath, 1977).
22. Harold Seidman, *Politics, Position, and Power: The Dynamics of Federal Organization,* 2d ed. (Oxford University Press, 1975), p. 38.

Although one—the Subcommittee on Postsecondary Education—has become expert at understanding the intricacies of the Office of Education postsecondary programs, its direct authority extends no further than that. Still, it has some ability to cast a wider policy net, using the "special oversight" authority that its parent Education and Labor Committee was granted in 1975 as the basis for hearings on higher education programs under the jurisdiction of other committees. In 1977, led by its new chairman, William D. Ford of Michigan, the subcommittee held six days of oversight hearings on all forms of federal student financial assistance, including the GI bill program of the Veterans Administration.[23]

Oversight hearings are a far cry from legislative "mark-ups," however, and in the Senate and House alike, many agencies and programs of great importance to higher education are the responsibility not of the committees with primary jurisdiction over education policy but of units that may have little interest in the subject and that are driven primarily by missions and constituencies quite different from higher education.[24] Tax matters—including such topical and fractious issues as tuition tax credits and such durable ones as the charitable deduction—belong to the House Ways and Means Committee and the Senate Finance Committee, as does the large student aid program embedded in the social security system. Research programs housed in agencies such as the Department of Defense, NASA, the Department of Energy, and the Environmental Protection Agency are handled by the committees with primary jurisdiction. The agricultural extension and research programs, important to many state universities, belong to the two agriculture committees. Dormitory construction goes to housing. GI bill education benefits fall

23. *Oversight Hearings on All Forms of Federal Student Financial Assistance*, Hearings before the House Education and Labor Committee, 95:1 (GPO, 1977).

24. When Chairman Ford criticized the Veterans' Affairs Committee for "not talking to the education community" and for its failure to be "more cooperative . . . in dealing with the problems of higher education for veterans," he elicited an intemperate response from Chairman Olin Teague of the Veterans' Education and Training Subcommittee. "I would remind the distinguished gentleman," Teague said, "that the Committee on Veterans' Affairs has exclusive legislative jurisdiction over veterans' readjustment benefits, including educational benefits. Mr. Ford's Subcommittee . . . has no authority to clean up 'messes' in the veterans' education program even if he were able to smell them out . . . his nose for inept education programs is suspect, however, if he is unable to scent the one in his own quarters. . . ." *Congressional Record* (daily edition), November 3, 1977, p. H 12149; and ibid., November 11, 1977, p. E 6983.

under the purview of the Veterans' Affairs committees. Funding levels for all of these programs are the concern of sundry appropriations sub-committees, with spending targets now fixed by the two budget com-mittees. And proposals to reorganize the executive branch to deal more satisfactorily with education are referred to the government operations committees. In all, during the Ninety-fourth Congress jurisdiction over programs affecting higher education was split among eighteen (of twenty-two) standing committees in the House, sixteen (of eighteen) in the Senate, one joint committee (Atomic Energy), and at least seventy subcommittees.[25]

In view of such divided jurisdiction, it is not surprising that of 1,151 "education bills" (as defined by Congressional Research Service staff members) introduced in the House during the Ninety-third Congress, only 419 of them went to the Education and Labor Committee. Of 193 education bills filed in the Senate during the same period, 89 were re-ferred to Labor and Public Welfare, as the principal education com-mittee was then called.[26]

In the mid-1970s both House and Senate reexamined their committee structures and related procedures, and each chamber adopted some constructive reforms. But in neither one did education emerge as a pow-erful organizing principle. Jurisdiction over programs affecting it still remains scattered. It is significant, for example, that in the new budget procedures through which Congress attempts to aggregate myriad pro-grams into large functional categories for purposes of analysis and fund-ing, less than one-fourth of the federal monies going to higher education are included in budget category 502, the "higher education subfunc-tion."[27] The remainder is accounted for under numerous other cate-gories defined by their primary purposes. Thus not even when it sets about to make bedrock decisions about priorities for allocating govern-ment funds does Congress have a comprehensive grasp of the implica-tions of its actions for higher education as a whole.

25. Robert C. Andringa, "The View from the Hill," in Institute for Educational Leadership, *Federalism at the Crossroads* (George Washington University, 1977), pp. 74–75. It should be noted that committee reforms adopted by the Senate in early 1977 slightly reduce this proliferation.

26. Memorandum from David C. Huckabee, Congressional Research Service (January 30, 1975; processed).

27. Fiscal 1977 estimates from Congressional Budget Office, *Postsecondary Education: The Current Federal Role and Alternative Approaches* (CBO, 1977), p. 3.

The Objectivity Gap

Despite a vast number of data compilations, program evaluations, and policy studies of every sort, government officials who deal with higher education often lack reliable information upon which to base their decisions. Kindred studies come to opposite conclusions. The data needed to foresee the consequence of a given choice are unavailable, dated, or flawed. Few analysts can agree on the gauges and criteria to be used. Recommendations invite skepticism because their authors are thought to have a stake in the outcome.

Actually there are four related problems:

1. The "experts" in the field of higher education are not accorded—and may not always deserve—the presumption of disinterestedness. When government officials look for informed advice about a complex policy arena, they customarily turn to universities and other groupings of scholars. Under most circumstances that is a reasonable stratagem, for even when one set of advisers is entangled with the customs and interests of a particular profession—as when the medical school dean is asked to do a paper on the health care delivery system—it is not difficult to recruit others with different points of view—in this case, economists, sociologists, or political scientists who have studied the health industry. But since almost everyone considered an expert on higher education policy works in an institution whose well-being depends in some measure on that policy, even the findings of scrupulous scholars can be branded as self-interested by those who disagree with them.

2. Executive branch agencies and congressional committees lack the capacity to generate sound analyses of higher education and the government policies affecting it. And when a policy study or evaluation is produced by one government agency, it is often greeted with derision or disbelief by other federal units. Though part of this problem has been alleviated in the past decade by the creation of analytic units such as the Congressional Budget Office and the Office of Technology Assessment and by the expanded scope of older units such as the Congressional Research Service and the General Accounting Office, in another sense the difficulties have been compounded by the proliferation of these offices and the ensuing rivalries among them.

3. Government agencies wanting policy studies conducted in the field of higher education frequently commission the higher education lobbying organizations to do them. The National Science Foundation may

turn to the Association of American Universities, the Office of Education to the American Council on Education or the College Board, and so forth. Generally speaking, the federal agencies are behaving rationally, since these private organizations understand the issues, have access to information, employ competent analysts, and are delighted to be asked (and to receive the funds that usually accompany such requests). Often the result is a careful and timely study. But regardless of their quality, such efforts invite conflict-of-interest charges. Organizations of colleges and universities are supposed to press for government policies that benefit their members. That is the main reason they have Washington offices. Though their views deserve a hearing by policymakers, it is questionable whether officials seeking objective appraisals should turn to the same organizations that lobby them for particular outcomes.

4. Often the data are weak, old, or uneven, and the criteria for evaluating them all but nonexistent.[28] Agencies lack basic facts about their own programs or are slow about making the facts available. Large-scale measures of the condition of higher education are notoriously unhelpful for policy purposes. Educators themselves cannot agree on the significance of a given indicator or on the proper way to calculate it. Without any agreement even on such basic questions as institutional accounting, it is little wonder that national survey data on college and university finances are inadequate and that students of the subject cannot settle on uniform techniques or criteria for analyzing such information as there is.

Numerous government organizations share the task of data gathering. The National Center for Education Statistics,[29] a unit within HEW, compiles much information relating to institutions, but to find out about student characteristics one must consult the Census Bureau. Federal outlays to colleges and universities are tallied by the National Science Foundation, but to get figures on student aid expenditures one must go to the several agencies running the programs. And there, particularly for such large programs as basic grants, veterans' benefits, and social security, the kinds of information needed are often not available. The Social Security

28. See Christoffel and Rice, *Federal Policy Issues and Data Needs*, and Thomas R. Wolanin, "Congress, Information and Policymaking for Postsecondary Education," in *Federalism at the Crossroads*, pp. 81–93.

29. This, the principal executive branch agency for collecting and analyzing education data, is very small in comparison to other federal statistical units. In fiscal 1976 it spent $10.5 million, whereas the Bureau of the Census spent $41 million; the Bureau of Labor Statistics, $54.2 million; and the National Center for Health Statistics, $25 million. *Special Analyses, Budget of the United States Government, Fiscal Year 1978*, p. 157.

Administration, for example, has surveyed the characteristics of its student aid beneficiaries only once in the twelve years of the program's existence. The Veterans Administration knows what states it mails checks to but not where the recipients are actually enrolled. Often the analyst or policymaker must turn to nonfederal sources—the higher education associations, study commissions, and private tallies—that gather their own information from surveys and samplings, sometimes in forms that are not readily matched with government categories.

The absence of reliable information and the attendant shortage of credible analysis cause difficulties for researchers, government officials, and the higher education industry alike. With the experts unable to agree on what the objective situation is, officials with no time or inclination to study it for themselves must resort to subjective judgments—or they may dismiss the problem altogether.

The Background of Reform

For almost half a century study groups and commissions have found the government's handling of education policy in urgent need of change. The judgment of President Hoover's National Advisory Committee on Education in 1931 is still relevant in the late 1970s:

The Federal Government has no inclusive and consistent public policy as to what it should or should not do in the field of education. Whatever particular policies it seems to be pursuing are often inconsistent with each other, sometimes in conflict. They suggest a haphazard development, wherein policies of far-reaching effect have been set up as mere incidents of some special attempt to induce an immediate and particular efficiency.[30]

Roosevelt's Advisory Committee on Education echoed this theme five years later: "These various activities [of the federal government] are not well coordinated from an educational point of view."[31] Truman's Commission on Higher Education was "unanimous in the view that the status of education in the Government must be raised," and offered three fresh organizational models to choose from.[32] Eisenhower's Committee

30. National Advisory Committee on Education, *Federal Relations to Education*, pt. 1, *Committee Findings and Recommendations* (1931), p. 8.

31. President's Advisory Committee on Education, *Report of the Committee* (1938), p. 188.

32. President's Commission on Higher Education, *Higher Education for American Democracy*, vol. 3, *Organizing Higher Education* (1947), p. 42.

on Education Beyond the High School judged that the "interests of both the Federal Government and the educational institutions require a much higher degree of continuing interagency coordination in Federal activities which have an impact on post-high school education than exists among the large number of Federal agencies involved at the present time."[33]

Johnson's Task Force on Government Reorganization observed that "the Government has never had a comprehensive policy for the advancement of education" and recommended structural reforms to facilitate the development of such a policy.[34] Nixon's "transition task force" on education in 1968–69 maintained that "the chief problems today in regard to the Federal Government's performance in education are the inadequacy of its mechanisms for policy formulation and for intra-Governmental coordination. The Federal effort has, indeed, in recent years been characterized by a multiplicity of uncoordinated, and sometimes conflicting, initiatives from many different departments and agencies of the Executive Branch and from the Congress."[35] In 1970 the Carnegie Commission on Higher Education pronounced it "doubtful that the requisite quality of program and policy review can be achieved through the present fragmented organization or through sporadic task-force recommendations on the appropriate federal role in support of education."[36]

As a rule, official commissions and study groups abhor disorder and prize coordination.[37] The issue-specific character of federal education programs might therefore be expected to prompt exactly the sorts of conclusions that it has. Yet the proferred solutions have not been heeded. George Zook's melancholy prediction of 1945 has come to pass: if corrective action is not taken, "we may some day wake up to find at the end of our generation, as the result of patchwork and piecemeal legislation, a distorted and disjointed national policy in education which represents neither the considered judgment of educational leaders nor the needs of our society."[38]

33. The President's Committee on Education Beyond the High School, *Second Report to the President* (1957), p. 107.

34. Quoted in Miles, *Cabinet Department of Education*, p. 42.

35. *Congressional Record*, March 12, 1969, p. 6104.

36. *Quality and Equality: Revised Recommendations* (McGraw-Hill, 1970), p. 29.

37. For a discussion of the "orthodoxy" of executive branch reorganization schemes, see the introduction to Seidman, *Politics, Position, and Power*.

38. George F. Zook, "The Role of the Federal Government in Education," *The Inglis Lecture, 1945* (Harvard University Press, 1945), pp. 1–2.

The Ambivalence of Higher Education Leaders

One reason for the enduring disarray is that many of the "educational leaders" to whom Zook referred, particularly at the college and university level, have found that their federal interests are far from homogeneous and that governmental fragmentation can sometimes be useful. Teeming programs and limited jurisdictions permit a flexibility that responds to the diversity of the academic enterprise and that may also temper the threat of federal domination. Therefore, over the years many higher education leaders have preferred to live with veiled, decentralized, and sometimes redundant government interventions rather than to risk the consequences of orderly policy and consolidated authority. James Perkins described this ambivalence in a 1973 address to the American Council on Education:

The higher education establishment cannot decide whether a federal position and policy with respect to higher education are developments devoutly to be wished or stoutly to be resisted. Thus far federal support and decision making have been scattered. . . . There have been times when this has been described as a happy state of affairs. . . . On the other hand, the absence of a top-flight Cabinet officer for education, or even higher education, has sometimes been lamented as the source of much uncontrolled evil. . . . The higher education establishment appears to regard freedom and autonomy with a Hamiltonian cast when federal action is desired and in the Jeffersonian style when federal action is feared. This ambivalence of attitude about the proper federal role in higher education has not been resolved.[39]

As early as the mid-1950s the rapid growth of federal higher education activity—then largely in research and development—under multiple agency jurisdictions had convinced universities benefiting from it that plural funding sources allowed them pliancy in securing their various ends. Any thoroughgoing consolidation of the government's research efforts, such as the newly created National Science Foundation might bring about, would cause difficulties. In 1954 a committee of the American Council on Education hailed the establishment of the NSF but cautioned that "the government not concentrate its general-purpose research funds in any single government agency, since such concentration might result in creating a powerful bureaucracy, which could exert too much control of education and which might lose the great advantages in research management of diversity in method and objectives. No single

39. James A. Perkins, "Coordinating Federal, State, and Institutional Decisions," in John F. Hughes, ed., *Education and the State* (American Council on Education, 1975), pp. 189–90.

government agency, however ably managed, could have all the 'right' policies and methods."[40]

Harvard University's 1961 study of its federal relations was more blunt: "From the point of view of the universities, it may be better to live with the difficulties of the present disorganized system than to increase the risk of political interference with university independence by putting all our eggs in one basket."[41]

This general theme—that decentralization is a good thing, that universities obtain more money with fewer encumbrances if they can "shop" among varied sources of funds—has persisted in the minds of many academics. As recently as 1972, Kenneth H. Ashworth, vice chancellor of the University of Texas, warned that "under a centralized agency we might find that the total of the appropriations for the whole, as centralized, is less than the total of the appropriations for the parts at present."[42] The same attitude has shaped some of the actions of higher education lobbyists weighing the merits of proposed structural changes. Thus in 1976, when Senator Adlai Stevenson's committee-reform plan for the Senate contained a proposal to transfer jurisdiction over the National Science Foundation out of the Human Resources panel and into a reconstituted Commerce Committee, charged, among other things, with oversight of scientific research, several university associations protested, in effect setting their interest in the NSF as a funding agency ahead of a "rational" approach to comprehensive policymaking in the field of science.

Other higher education spokesmen have thought differently. Some recognized that to settle for piecemeal project support handed out by a number of government agencies, and for policies forged in numerous congressional committees, was tacitly to accept the view that Washington had no responsibility for the well-being of higher education as a whole. A pattern of government activity that impressed one university with its beneficent pluralism could strike another campus as willfully uncaring. In 1962 Homer Babbidge wryly commented on the "economic royalists" of higher education who "thrive on the deficiencies of federal

40. Committee on Institutional Research Policy, *Sponsored Research Policy of Colleges and Universities* (American Council on Education, 1954), pp. 19–20. For another sound analysis from this period, reaching much the same conclusion, see Charles V. Kidd, *American Universities and Federal Research* (Harvard University Press, 1959), especially p. 213.

41. "Harvard and the Federal Government," A Report to the Faculty and Governing Boards, September 1961, reprinted in Lewis B. Mayhew, ed., *Higher Education in the Revolutionary Decades* (McCutchan, 1967), p. 212.

42. *Scholars and Statesmen* (Jossey-Bass, 1972), p. 133.

programs" and use academic freedom as a front for their own avarice, opposing a coordinated federal policy under which the have-nots of higher education might fare better. "Is there no place in all this," Babbidge pleaded, "for the development of policies for higher education that have their foundations in more than the welter of particular interests within higher education?"[43]

In the late 1960s, with the "new depression" hard upon them, more academic spokesmen began to declare themselves ready for greater coordination in federal higher education policy. In 1968 the Carnegie Commission proposed the "establishment of a Council of Advisers on Higher Education attached to the White House," and months later the American Council on Education brought itself to endorse "the concept that the creation of a coordinating council, assigned responsibility for all facets of higher education, is desirable." Both recommendations were linked to pleas for more money from Washington: the Carnegie group sought an increase in federal support from one-fifth to one-third of total institutional expenditures; the ACE appealed for "general institutional support." Apparently, both groups had judged that piecemeal policymaking was unlikely to yield the specific policy changes they wanted.[44]

The Push for a Department of Education

Seldom acknowledged by interest groups recommending structural changes—or by public administration technicians seeking greater efficiency, better coordination, and more streamlined management—is an axiom of governmental reorganization that elected officials ignore at their peril: in Congressman John Brademas's words, "Reorganization is a fundamentally political act, not political in the partisan sense (although it may be) but political in that every organization—and every reorganization—means a distribution—or redistribution—of power and influence over the substance of policy."[45]

43. Homer D. Babbidge, Jr., "Scientist Affluent, Humanist Militant: Faction in Higher Education," *The Graduate Journal*, vol. 5 (1962, Supplement), pp. 157, 160.

44. Carnegie Commission on Higher Education, *Quality and Equality: New Levels of Federal Responsibility for Higher Education* (McGraw-Hill, 1968), p. 51; American Council on Education, *Federal Programs for Higher Education: Needed Next Steps* (ACE, 1969), p. 20.

45. "Federal Reorganization and Its Likely Impact on State and Local Government," *Congressional Record* (daily edition), September 19, 1977, p. H-9653. See also Herbert Kaufman, "Reflections on Administrative Reorganization," in Joseph A. Pechman, ed., *Setting National Priorities: The 1978 Budget* (Brookings Institution, 1977), pp. 391–418.

Nowhere is the sagacity of Brademas's observation clearer than in the long-lived crusade by many educators and some politicians for creation of a separate, cabinet-level department of education in the federal government. The idea has flickered and sparked ever since the U.S. Office of Education was created in 1867.[46]

Since the early 1900s, bills to establish such a department have regularly been filed in the House and Senate. But despite the efforts of their sponsors and the occasional enthusiasm of the National Education Association, not until the fall of 1977 did any congressional committee hold hearings on the proposal.

In 1931 President Hoover's advisory committee argued that the appointment of a department secretary at the cabinet level would establish "an official spokesman for education, competent and influentially situated in the Government." The committee also believed that the new department would reduce the threat of federal control over education by limiting the number of agencies involved with it and by having programs coordinated by someone presumably attuned to academic sensibilities. It would also inject efficiency and order into government's variegated attempts to harness education to national needs.[47]

Then, as now, the hard question was where to draw the line between programs that addressed education as a purpose in itself and those that used it as a means to other ends. The advisory committee, recognizing that many government activities bearing on education were firmly bound to other federal pursuits, insisted that any reorganization "leave those federal educational activities which are instrumental or incidental to the proper administration of some other primary function of the Federal Government under jurisdiction of the Department which is responsible for that primary function."[48] Seemingly ignored was the possibility that the education department might thereby end up with *no* functions!

In 1939 President Roosevelt moved the Office of Education from the Interior Department into the new Federal Security Agency but changed nothing else, and during the Truman administration Herbert Hoover himself had the opportunity of taking a new look at the structure of the executive branch for dealing with education. In a major study prepared for the Hoover Commission Task Force on Public Welfare, Hollis Allen

46. For a brief chronicle of the history of the department of education proposal, see Miles, *Cabinet Department of Education*, especially chap. 3.

47. National Advisory Committee on Education, *Federal Relations to Education*, pt. 1, p. 94.

48. Ibid., p. 96.

concluded that evidence and logic both dictated the creation of a separate and independent education agency, outside the cabinet, with a National Board of Education setting its policy direction and having much to say about the selection of the commissioner who would run it.[49] But the Hoover Commission itself took a different approach, foreshadowing in its recommendations the creation a few years later of the Department of Health, Education, and Welfare, which engulfed the old Office of Education but transferred to it few additional powers or duties. Declaring that most education programs should continue to "be administered by the agencies whose functions the particular programs serve to promote," the commission echoed Allen's main reservation about his own plan: the clash between a desire to upgrade, rationalize, and give strong leadership to the federal education agency, and the perception that there were other interests at stake.[50]

As the years passed, the number of federal education programs mounted, appropriations soared, and more agencies entered the field, but the basic organizing principles of the Hoover Commission endured. The Office of Education gradually took on more responsibilities, but it remained a subdivision of HEW, and other education programs continued to be housed in their parent governmental units.[51]

Ideas abounded, however, for structural changes meant to elevate the status of higher education within the government and—the inescapable corollary—to slip general support for colleges and universities onto Washington's ever-lengthening list of explicit pursuits. In 1960, for example, John A. Perkins, president of the University of Delaware and former HEW undersecretary, and Daniel W. Wood outlined plans for a federal educational foundation, modeled on Britain's University Grants Committee, with an autonomous board of trustees and with broad discretion over a periodic "lump sum appropriation."[52] In 1964 President Johnson's task force on government organization, chaired by Don K.

49. Hollis P. Allen, *The Federal Government and Education* (McGraw-Hill, 1950), especially chap. 14.

50. Commission on the Organization of the Executive Branch of the Government, *Social Security and Education* (GPO, 1949), p. 32.

51. Homer Babbidge observed in 1962 that the "dissatisfaction and impatience" of many higher education leaders with the organization and operations of the Office of Education reinforced their willingness to see many programs housed in other agencies and abetted the "balkanization" of educational responsibility within the government. "Scientist Affluent, Humanist Militant," p. 161.

52. "Issues in Federal Aid to Higher Education," in Douglas M. Knight, ed., *The Federal Government and Higher Education* (Prentice-Hall, 1960), pp. 140–75.

Price of Harvard, recommended that a department of education be created, couching its rationale in these words:

The advancement of education and of the basic research programs that are carried on primarily in educational institutions is the keystone of our future progress. The Federal Government has become a major supporter of these purposes, but without having a comprehensive organization that could help the President develop a policy for them. . . . Because the schools have been afraid of Federal domination, the Government has never had a comprehensive policy for the advancement of education and research. But it is unrealistic to think we can protect the freedom of education by pretending to ignore it. . . . We therefore recommend the creation of a Department of Education. . . . We do not believe that it should be the only channel by which aid is given to educational and research institutions. Every major agency will need to have its own programs of research and education, and many will need to support basic research. But a Department is warranted in order to help deal with the fundamental policies of aid to State and private institutions and to the general advancement of knowledge as the basis of national progress.[53]

President Johnson ignored—indeed he suppressed—this recommendation, but others openly voiced similar views. Congresswoman Edith Green, then chairman of the House Special Subcommittee on Education, pursued her own quest for a department of education. She argued for the merger of the Office of Education with the National Science Foundation, for the creation within the executive branch of a strong interagency council on education, for the establishment of a national advisory committee on education at the White House level, and for congressional reorganization (to include a joint committee on education). But even her own subcommittee declined to support her plea for a cabinet-level department of education and manpower training.[54]

Still more programs sprouted up in the late 1960s, new agencies appeared, old ones grew, and the purposes of federal support broadened, but no comprehensive policy or structure emerged. Interim steps were taken: an enhanced role for the President's science adviser, initiation of the Budget Bureau's "special analysis" of education spending, the creation of FICE, and the addition of Douglass Cater to the White House staff.[55] Yet proliferation outpaced coordination.

53. Report of the President's Task Force on Government Organization, quoted in Miles, *Cabinet Department of Education*, pp. 42–44.

54. *Study of the United States Office of Education*, H. Doc. 193, 90:1 (GPO, 1967). See also Edith Green, "The Federal Role in Education" *The Burton Lecture, 1963* (Harvard University Press, 1963).

55. Cater was a senior aide to President Johnson given responsibility for education and health policy, and played a large role in the development of presidential education initiatives. Many educators recall with evident nostalgia the days when they "had someone they could talk to" who in turn had the ear of the chief executive.

The Nixon administration paid momentary attention to the structural side of higher education policy. In late 1969 White House aide Daniel P. Moynihan privately urged the President to seek creation of a department of higher education and research in order to concentrate the government's higher education activities in a single unit. Although that particular idea evoked little enthusiasm elsewhere in the administration, Nixon's eventual proposal of a "National Foundation for Higher Education" echoed Moynihan's reasoning (as well as a Carnegie Commission recommendation and the earlier Perkins-Wood idea), specifying that one of the foundation's three principal purposes was "to provide an organization concerned, on the highest level, with the development of national policy in higher education."[56]

In the early 1970s the National Education Association—which takes credit for having persuaded "President Andrew Johnson and Congress in 1867 to establish a national education agency"[57]—spearheaded an intensive drive to secure a department of education. Joined by other organizations of elementary and secondary educators, the NEA prevailed upon Senator Abraham Ribicoff and Congressman Carl Perkins to file bills to that effect in the Ninety-second Congress.[58] By then, however, the administration had embraced the idea of consolidating education within a vast department of human resources, and most of Congress' energy for attending to structural matters was consumed in prolonged consideration of the Nixon proposals. Neither house even held hearings on the Ribicoff-Perkins bills, and by 1974 the proposal had slipped well down on the NEA's list of legislative priorities, there to remain until Jimmy Carter's candidacy revived interest.

Yet a modest step had been taken. The 1972 creation of an Education Division within HEW represented, at least in the eyes of the Senate Labor and Public Welfare Committee, "notice that consideration of a Department of Education is now in order."[59] Four years later the com-

56. "Special Message to the Congress on Higher Education, March 19, 1970," *Public Papers of the Presidents: Richard Nixon, 1970* (GPO, 1971), pp. 282–83.

57. Statement of John Prior, President, National Education Association, before the Senate Governmental Affairs Committee (October 13, 1977; processed).

58. Ribicoff remains the only former HEW secretary publicly to advocate the fracturing of HEW into more manageable units. Introducing his department of education bill in 1971, he reminded his Senate colleagues that he had offered similar proposals in 1965 and 1967. (*Congressional Record*, April 5, 1971, p. 9543.) As chairman of the Senate Governmental Affairs Committee and chief sponsor of the department of education bill which that committee reported out in mid-1978, he is a powerful ally for this proposal.

59. *Education Amendments of 1971*, S. Rept. 92-346, 92:1 (GPO, 1971), p. 82.

mittee declined to follow that rhetorical lead, but, paralleling a recommendation of the American Council on Education, it proposed to the Senate in 1976 that the Education Division be elevated within HEW so that its head would hold the rank of under secretary and would have statutory responsibility for the programs conducted within his domain. The full Senate concurred, but the House of Representatives did not, and the latter prevailed in conference. Education stayed put.

Just as the idea of a separate department of education seemed to be languishing, Jimmy Carter revived it. While campaigning for the presidency in 1976, he repeatedly voiced his support for the proposal. Shortly after he had reiterated this pledge at the annual meeting of the National Education Association in July 1976, that organization—with its millions of members and increasingly active political involvement—gave him the first presidential endorsement of its history.[60]

During the first year of the Carter presidency, there were signs that his administration was far from unanimous about the wisdom and practicality of creating such a department. HEW Secretary Joseph A. Califano, Jr., in particular, offered alternatives for raising the status and improving the management of education without lifting it entirely out of his department. But by late 1977 it was clear that the President intended to honor his commitment and that only the shape and content of the education department remained to be decided.

In his January 1978 State of the Union message, Carter publicly signaled his intentions, and in a message to Congress in late February he outlined his reasons in language that department advocates of the past half-century would have found familiar, even to the assurances that state and local primacy would endure:

> I have instructed the Office of Management and Budget and the Department of Health, Education, and Welfare to work with Congress on legislation needed to establish a Department of Education which will:
> —let us focus on Federal educational policy at the highest levels of our government;
> —permit closer coordination of Federal education programs and other related activities;

60. For an earlier statement of Carter's commitment, see "If I Am Elected," *Change*, vol. 8 (February 1976), p. 11. See also *New York Times*, December 8, 1976; Noel Epstein, "Creating a Separate Education Department a Sensitive Issue," *Washington Post*, December 31, 1976; and Rochelle L. Stanfield, "Three 'R's' of the Education Debate: Reauthorizin', Reorganizin', Reckonin'," *National Journal*, December 4, 1976, pp. 1745–49.

—reduce Federal regulations and reporting requirements and cut duplication;

—assist school districts, teachers, and parents to make better use of local resources and ingenuity.

A separate Cabinet-level department will enable the Federal government to be a true partner with State, local and private education institutions in sustaining and improving the quality of our education system.[61]

Appraising Some Alternative Reforms

With the President of the United States, for the first time ever, in favor of a separate education department, and with a majority of the United States Senate cosponsoring a bill to create such a department, probably some sort of education department will be established within the next few years. Still, it is important to ask whether this is a prudent move, particularly as it may affect the government's ability to make *higher* education policy. Other approaches might work as well or better. This section examines several possibilities: changes in Congress, a new interagency council, and a national academy of education, as well as alterations in the executive branch.

Although it is tempting to seek structural solutions to substantive problems, it is difficult and risky. First, structural and jurisdictional arrangements that leave responsibility for higher education scattered throughout the government may be admirably suited to handle other federal missions in orderly and efficient ways. Regrouping them around higher education could weaken the government's ability to deal properly with these other tasks. Why, it may be asked, should veterans' education benefits be stripped from the Veterans Administration and its committees and recast as a higher education program? Why should the Environmental Protection Agency's grants and contracts to universities be viewed differently from those to other research organizations? Why should funds to operate West Point be regarded as higher education outlays rather than as an integral part of the Army's personnel effort? So long as government actions bearing on higher education are conceived and conducted as integral parts of distinctive federal missions, moves to appraise and manage them according to their impact on colleges and universities will be disruptive.

Second, because the structures through which Washington deals with

61. *Congressional Record* (daily edition), February 28, 1978, p. S2512.

higher education encompass federal activities affecting elementary and secondary education, any changes in those structures will inevitably touch schools as well as colleges. The priorities of precollegiate education do not often coincide with those of postsecondary education, particularly when a finite amount of money must be shared among them, and there is no reason to expect that an organizational change tailored to one group's needs would be well fitted to the other's.

Third, a tension always exists between arrangements that serve the needs of interest groups and those that serve the needs of the President and the Congress, let alone the needs of the "public interest." Government officials must weigh competing values and concerns, and that task is not eased by organizing the government around one set of values to the exclusion of all others.

Still, some organizing concepts must be selected. The federal government would be paralyzed if the design of its major structural components did not subordinate certain interests to others. In examining the wisdom of the present selection and appraising possible changes in it, I start with several assumptions that ought to be made explicit, and favor a set of goals that also need to be spelled out.

Assumptions and Goals

The present internal organization of HEW for making and executing education policy is seriously flawed. The division of responsibility between the assistant secretary for education and the commissioner of education, the low rank and limited purview of the Office of Education officials nominally in charge of higher education programs, and the absence of any department-wide focus for a set of interrelated issues that are formally lodged in different units—all argue for change.

It is futile to think of aggregating all federal education activities, particularly the far-flung federal programs affecting higher education, into a single administrative unit. Even Rufus Miles, an ardent champion of a separate cabinet department, concedes that "the notion of using the education rubric as a justification for the creation of a single department or agency within which to group all federal programs that disburse funds to educational systems and institutions . . . is not grounded in good theory and would be infeasible in practice."[62] Thus limits must be imposed on the number and range of education-related activities that can

62. *Cabinet Department of Education*, p. 73.

reasonably be grouped together. Because this means some pertinent activities will be left in agencies organized around other missions, problems of policy and program coordination will persist.

There is no "right" answer to the question of which other federal missions enjoy a symbiotic relation with higher education and are prudently housed with it. Some argue persuasively that education should not be separated from employment training and manpower development. Others argue—just as persuasively—that a seamless conceptual and programmatic web binds higher education to scientific research. Still others, also convincing, contend that the obvious unifying idea is "human services," which would imply a continued amalgamation of health, welfare, child development, and similar activities with education programs.

Even if no single plan can be truly comprehensive, it is still possible to list a set of reasonable objectives.

—Within the executive branch, some official, or a carefully articulated group of officials, should be in a position to look at federal higher education policy as a whole; that is, on the one hand, to become familiar with the needs and problems of higher education and, on the other, to comprehend the full range of government activities that affect it, wherever they may be found on the organization chart.

—Those entrusted with this responsibility should also hold high enough positions that (a) distinguished men and women can readily be recruited for the posts, (b) they have a plausible claim to take part in executive branch policy deliberations bearing on higher education, and (c) they can expect their own views to receive a respectful hearing by agency heads, the President, and the cognizant congressional committees.

—There should be a coordinating mechanism within the executive branch for systematically reviewing issues of higher education policy, program management, and regulatory behavior that cut across program and agency boundaries but do not require presidential attention. Such a mechanism could also serve to review issues and sharpen choices that may eventually require White House decisions.

—Actual administrative responsibility for federal programs and other activities affecting higher education should continue to be assigned to government units according to their primary missions. Insofar as a program can be characterized as having the advancement of education, the strengthening of educational institutions, or the welfare of students as its principal rationale, it should be housed in the main federal education agency. But where a program arises out of another discrete federal objective and supports another mission, it should be assigned to the relevant agency, although subject to the policy coordination mechanisms noted above.

—Executive branch agencies should ordinarily be large and comprehensive, rather than small and particularized. The rapid growth of the federal government argues for curbing the number of organizational units answerable directly to the President and for giving responsibility for trade-offs and policy coordination to subordinate officials whenever possible.

—Though Congress should (and will) continue to organize itself around primary federal missions, it, too, should have a capacity for considering issues of higher education policy that cross jurisdictional lines and for evaluating programs and decisions according to their effect on higher education. On Capitol Hill, as in the executive branch, policy-level officials should have analytic support staffs able to provide them with the necessary data and technical expertise.

—An independent analytic agency should also exist, outside the regular governmental chains of command, to provide objective information about the condition of higher education, to conduct impartial appraisals of federal policies and programs, and to monitor the overall relation between the federal government and higher education. This organization should not be controlled by elected officials, but neither should it be part of the academy's own efforts to secure favorable treatment in Washington.

Reform of the Executive Branch

The literature contains many designs for a department of education and other structural changes intended to strengthen the federal executive's grasp of education policy issues. A full-dress review of these models would fill many pages. But a sketch of four general approaches will serve at least to mark the boundaries of the debate. Two demand the creation of a separate department of education and two give alternative methods of reform; each starts from quite different ideas about education and the proper organization of the government.

"MINI" DEPARTMENT OF EDUCATION. The present Education Division would be taken out of HEW and given separate cabinet status. As the departmental alternative least disruptive to other agencies and interest groups, this one is the simplest and politically the most feasible. A few programs and bureaus might be wrenched from other agencies and affixed to the new department, but most of the government activities that affect schools and colleges but that are not now housed in the Education Division would stay where they are.

This is the general approach taken by the Carter administration in its proposed education department. As explained by OMB Director James T. McIntyre, Jr., in testimony before the Senate Committee on Governmental Affairs on April 14, 1978, two-thirds of the new agency (measured in terms of budget authority) would consist of the old HEW Education Division. Of the remainder, much the largest part would be the school lunch programs previously housed in the Agriculture Department. In addition, the education department would run the schools previously administered by the Defense Department (for dependents of military personnel stationed overseas) and the Bureau of Indian Affairs. The head start program would also leave HEW to join the new agency.

It may be noted that all these substantial additions to the Education Division are concerned with elementary and secondary (and preschool) education. The Carter proposal was reasonably comprehensive with respect to precollegiate education, except for the employment training programs funded by the Labor Department. From the standpoint of higher education, however, the programs suggested for inclusion within the education department are small and of little consequence: a portion of the NSF science education program, a student loan program run by the Justice Department, the college housing program located in HUD, the graduate school affiliated with the Agriculture Department, and the responsibility for financial support of Howard University. Of greater significance than any of these programmatic additions is the decision to shift to the education department those portions of the HEW Office for Civil Rights charged with affirmative action and civil rights compliance in schools and colleges.[63]

The administration avoided controversy and political difficulty by declining to move to the new agency any of the major higher education programs not already located in the Education Division—veterans' education benefits, social security student benefits, health, manpower—or any of the major research units such as the National Science Foundation

63. Statement of James T. McIntyre, Jr., Director, Office of Management and Budget, before the Senate Governmental Affairs Committee (April 14, 1978; processed); see also *Higher Education Daily*, April 17, 1978, p. 1.

and the National Institutes of Health. Nor did it propose inclusion of the arts and humanities endowments, although it "reserved for future consideration" the "option of transferring these programs."[64]

It is significant that most of the higher education associations, although generally supportive of the objectives and principles that undergird proposals to create a separate department, have carefully refrained from endorsing the proposal itself. "These principles," Charles B. Saunders, Jr., reminded the Senate Committee on Governmental Affairs in March 1978, on behalf of nine of the principal Washington associations, "could be accommodated by several organizational options," including changes within the existing Department of HEW.[65] In part such hedging reflects the academy's historic ambivalence toward putting too many of its eggs in one basket. But in part it mirrors the genuine problems that creation of a separate department implies for higher education. The new agency would be modest in size, as cabinet departments go, and its narrow constituency base would confer little advantage in the competition for the President's attention and the OMB's budget priorities. Its secretary would still have jurisdiction over a mere fraction of the federal programs and monies for colleges and universities. The task of interagency policy coordination would grow no easier; in some respects it would get more difficult, since social security, NIH, and various other postsecondary activities of HEW would stay where they are. Cutting off the education lobby from other influential interests with which it is now allied, however awkwardly, could rob it of strength. Higher education would probably fare no worse than it does today, but it would not fare much better, either.[66]

If the President had not committed himself to an education department, the prospect of a "mini" department such as he has proposed would be cheerless from his perspective. It runs contrary to the recent trend of centralizing related federal activities in large cabinet agencies, such as

64. Statement of McIntyre.

65. Statement of Charles B. Saunders, Jr., before the Senate Governmental Affairs Committee (March 21, 1978; processed).

66. For skeptical appraisals of the department idea, see Albert Shanker, "Where We Stand," *New York Times*, July 11, 1976; and Christopher T. Cross, "Do We Really Need a Department of Education?" in *Chronicle of Higher Education*, January 17, 1977, p. 36. "Pro and con" discussions are presented in John Ryor, "The Case for a Federal Department of Education," and Gerald E. Sroufe, "The Case against a Federal Department of Education," both in *Phi Delta Kappan*, vol. 58 (April 1977), pp. 594–600. For related comment, see Chester E. Finn, Jr., "The Super-Superintendent Fallacy," in the same issue, pp. 601–02.

Housing and Urban Development, Transportation, and Energy. By doing away with the buffer that the HEW structure provides, by giving
education a seat at the cabinet table, and by ensuring the escalation of
more budget choices and policy disputes to the presidential level, the
burdens on the White House will mount. Moreover, as noted above,
although the Carter proposal comes close to making a "clean sweep" of
federal activities for elementary and secondary education, it accomp-
lishes nothing of consequence for higher education. It could actually
worsen the government's capacity to approach higher education policy
in a rational, purposeful, and holistic manner. The main argument for it
is that it will curry favor with schoolteachers and other educators by
giving their activities the symbolic status some of them desire.[67] On balance, and notwithstanding the earnest and public-minded views of some
proponents, such a reorganization must be seen as designed more to have
a political appeal than to facilitate the development of sensible policy
and the orderly management of government activity. And from the
standpoint of higher education, even its political appeal is marginal at
best.

"MAXI" DEPARTMENT OF EDUCATION. Alternatively, HEW's Education
Division could be merged with other government programs and agencies to form a large cabinet-level unit organized around a broad conception of education. One version would take employment training out of
the Labor Department and vest it in a department of education and manpower. Another, echoing Moynihan's suggestion to Nixon, would en-
velop the National Science Foundation and related activities in a department of education and research. Still another, considered (but ultimately
rejected) by the Carnegie Council on Policy Studies in Higher Education, would regroup much of the executive branch into a huge agency
devoted to the trinity of health, education, and science, pulling such
disparate entities as ERDA, NASA, the NSF, the Smithsonian, the arts
and humanities endowments and most of HEW's health units into the
new department, along with the Education Division.[68] As ambitious as
the human resources department proposed by President Nixon, it differs

67. Not all, to be sure. Shanker, who is president of the American Federation of
Teachers—the NEA's principal union rival—has been an outspoken critic of the idea
of a department of education. See "Where We Stand."

68. A preliminary version of this Carnegie Council study was circulated in 1976.
It is echoed, though in more modest form, in the idea for a department of health,
education, and science favored by the council in its final report: *Federal Reorganization*, pp. 5–8.

in that it would include most of the federal science agencies but would leave labor, welfare, and veterans elsewhere.

The evident problem with a "maxi" department of education is that it would disrupt as much as it consolidates, and the grander its conception the more disruptive it would be. Every move toward enlarging the jurisdiction of an education department would complicate other federal missions and provoke other constituencies. Manpower programs, for example, are entangled with economic and employment policy issues at least as much as they are with vocational and occupational education. Research activities do not readily separate from the missions of the agencies that conduct them, and drawing entire scientific agencies into the education orbit would remove them from other important policy areas like national defense and health care. It is difficult to believe, for example, that energy research should be regarded as an "education program" and located with student aid and humanities activities rather than be firmly attached to the new Energy Department, whose concerns most people regard as even more pressing than those of higher education.[69]

None of these activities can easily be transferred to a new agency organized around education, nor will their established clienteles cheer the prospect of submerging their accustomed federal relations in such an agency, even if Congress were willing to sort out the massive confusion over committee jurisdictions that would result. Yet from education's perspective—at least from higher education's—a great many submersions of this sort must occur, or little will be gained. If large domains of federal policy affecting colleges and universities stay separate, the familiar dilemmas will linger. Though the prospect of designating education as a fundamental organizing principle is naturally alluring to educators—and a large department, if created, would surely ease the task of making education policy—not many others would view it as a sensible way to structure the federal government.

69. Certain other federal programs bearing on higher education are today run by free-standing agencies such as the National Science Foundation, the National Foundation on the Arts and the Humanities, and the Smithsonian Institution. Though each has its own distinctive constituencies and its own rationale for continued independence within the executive branch, merging them into an education department would not require removing them from other mission-oriented agencies. Following this logic, one could design a new unit that would be larger than the "mini" department but smaller than the "maxi" one.

SPECIALISTS IN THE WHITE HOUSE. Agency missions and configurations could be left much as they are now if the Executive Office of the President became the main locus for education policymaking and coordination. Whether the chosen vehicle is a cabinet committee, a permanent council of education advisers, or a single presidential aide, the two apparent attractions of this idea are, first, the proximity to the Oval Office that it gives to education and, second, elevation of interdepartmental disputes and initiatives above the level of officials with strong institutional interests in their outcomes.

The proper way to appraise this idea is not from the perspective of educators but from the standpoint of the presidency. No interest group can be blamed for wanting a "friend at court" or for thinking that its dreams will come closer to reality if someone with the President's ear is sensitive to its desires. The rapid growth of the White House staff and other executive office units in recent years, and the tendency to escalate more and more decisions to the presidential level, can only reinforce this perception.

Any President so disposed could assign a staffer to attend regularly to higher education policy issues that cut across program and agency lines; in their different ways, Johnson, Nixon, and Ford all did so upon occasion.[70] But resolving problems of executive branch policy coordination by installing specialists, or interest group representatives, on the President's staff is generally a misguided solution.[71] Though it is reasonable to ask a White House aide to look into a specific problem, or to chair an ad hoc task force designing an administration position on a particular issue, it is quite another matter to organize the presidency so as to force knotty issues to resolution at that level on a sustained basis. Distasteful as the realization may be to educators, higher education is one of those intricate policy domains with limited federal leverage and scant political visibility that seem destined to receive erratic and spotty attention in the White House. Its very intricacy compounds the problem, for it flows across standing jurisdictional and functional assignments even within the White

70. Although less evident in the Carter administration, recent presidents have also tended to appoint university professors and other "higher educators" to influential positions within the White House staff, creating the potential for—and sometimes the reality of—a subtle higher education lobby within yards of the Oval Office, even when no explicit assignment of portfolio is made.

71. See Stephen Hess, *Organizing the Presidency* (Brookings Institution, 1976), especially chaps. 8 and 9.

House staff and seldom repays the effort needed to unscramble it, except when a touchy issue arises or a legislative deadline looms.[72] The President needs the flexibility to organize his staff according to his own style and needs, and the ability to shift assignments as the kaleidoscope of "presidential issues" turns. He needs versatile generalists loyal to him, not representatives of interest groups wanting him to pay them greater heed. This does not mean that nobody in the White House should carry the education portfolio, simply that to expect the President's staff to compensate for structural deficiencies elsewhere in the executive branch is to expect too much.

EDUCATION SUBDEPARTMENT. The drawbacks inherent in the creation of any sort of education department, and the need for augmenting it with other mechanisms if higher education policy issues are to get systematic attention in Washington, suggest that a different approach ought to be considered. One possibility, as undramatic as it is obvious, is to revamp the internal structure of HEW and supplement it with some extra-departmental machinery designed to handle issues that cross agency boundaries.

The simplest way to begin is by elevating the entire Education Division to subdepartmental status, either by copying the "Pentagon model" and creating a trio of semidistinct departments within the larger one, or by establishing an HEW under secretary for education with operating responsibility for all the explicitly educational programs and activities of the department.[73] The American Council on Education proposed such a a scheme in 1975, and the Senate approved a similar one in 1976, retaining the historic designation of "commissioner" for the position here described as under secretary but according it the added rank and pay. That scheme disappeared in the Senate-House conference, but the Carnegie Council revived the idea in 1977 with its proposal to create within HEW an under secretary (or secretary) of education, research, and advanced studies. One key feature shared by all these versions is the insistence that the new under secretary—or whatever the position is titled —would absorb the duties and responsibilities of both the assistant secre-

72. For an elaboration of this point, see Finn, *Education and the Presidency*.

73. In some agencies, the second echelon position is titled deputy secretary, and the under secretaries occupy a third tier. If it were thought desirable to give the secretary of a reconstituted Department of HEW an all-around deputy, then the head of the education (and health, and welfare) division within the department would logically still be an under secretary.

tary for education and the commissioner of education. "Whatever else happens," the Carnegie Council sensibly insists, "this unnecessary and unclear duality of supervisors should be eradicated."[74]

With education raised to subdepartmental status within HEW and headed by an under secretary, higher education would deserve the equivalent of an assistant secretary. Indeed, the elevation of primary responsibility for higher education to that level should be a major element of any structural reform, whether separate department or subdepartment. Though the title has no magical properties, it would confer subcabinet status of the sort that generally commands access to the top policy councils of the executive branch and a respectful hearing before congressional committees, especially when the holder of the title also has line responsibility for programs costing billions of dollars each year. The Executive Level IV payroll slot normally assigned to an assistant secretary yields a salary that should attract able individuals to a tour of duty in Washington.

It is thus noteworthy that the major department of education bills filed in the Ninety-fifth Congress—including the one for which Senator Ribicoff acquired fifty-four cosponsors—did not charge *any* senior departmental official with responsibility for higher education. The Carter administration did, however, suggest to the Senate Governmental Affairs Committee that the new agency should have an "assistant secretary for postsecondary education," although it shed little light on a host of critical second-order issues.[75] Those include the relation between student aid and other postsecondary programs, the locus of responsibility for higher education policy development and program analysis, the links (if any) between program administration and regulatory activities such as civil rights enforcement, and the assignment of data collection and evaluation in the field of higher education.

74. Carnegie Council, *Federal Reorganization*, pp. 3–4. For the 1975 ACE plan, see *Higher Education Legislation, 1975*, Hearings before the Senate Labor and Public Welfare Committee, 94:1 (GPO, 1975), pt. 1, pp. 523–24 and 556–57. For the version adopted by the Senate, see *Education Amendments of 1976*, S. Rept. 94-882, 94:2 (GPO, 1976), pp. 104–06.

75. Statement of James T. McIntyre, Jr., before the Senate Governmental Affairs Committee (May 17, 1978; processed). See also S. 991 (the Ribicoff bill), 95:1, and "Comparison of Bills to Create a Separate Department of Education," Senate Governmental Affairs Committee, 95:1. (n.d.; processed). It may be noted that the revised bill that the committee reported out in mid-1978 did follow the administrations suggestion in this regard.

The Interagency Council

Because neither the internal reconstruction of HEW nor the creation of a "mini" department of education can address the interagency issues that beset higher education policy, it would be necessary to establish another mechanism to serve that purpose. The Federal Interagency Committee on Education should be abolished (or at least stripped of any responsibility for postsecondary issues) and replaced by a new multidepartmental council on higher education policy.[76] Whereas FICE was a creation of the executive branch, the new panel should have legislative sanction as well as presidential support.

This idea could be elaborated in either of two ways, depending primarily on how the President wanted executive branch policy to be made.

If he wished to continue in the direction of recent years, treating cabinet and subcabinet officials as "parties at interest" in major policy decisions and assigning his own staff advisers to provide disinterested analysis and make recommendations, then the interagency council on higher education should be given independent standing and staffing outside HEW or the education department—in effect be made a specialized extension of the White House domestic policy process—and should be chaired by a senior presidential aide.[77]

If the President adopted a different approach, however, if, for example, he sought what Stephen Hess terms a "more collegial presidency,"[78] if he curbed the tendency to escalate issues to the Executive Office, trimmed the White House staff, conferred more authority on

76. This general approach could be extended. The Carnegie Council on Policy Studies in Higher Education, for example, suggests creation of *three* policy-coordinating bodies to handle various education matters that cross agency lines. (*Federal Reorganization*, pp. 4–5.) The Carter administration, however, advocates retaining and strengthening FICE rather than creating a separate group for higher education. Unfortunately, there is no way that a single interagency committee can oversee all of education; improved policy development and coordination at the postsecondary level will be unlikely.

77. This could be the science adviser, the chief domestic policy adviser, or another person deemed knowledgeable about the subject but ultimately "loyal" to the President.

78. For a description of this approach, see Hess, *Organizing the Presidency*, especially chaps. 8–11.

his appointees within the agencies, entrusted them with the analysis of complex problems and the shaping of administration policy, and made them his envoys—rather than his message carriers—to the Congress, then it would make sense to regard the higher education council as an arm of the secretary of HEW or of the secretary of education.[79] It should be chaired by the secretary, and its staff should be directed by the assistant secretary for higher education, who would assume that function concurrently with his or her responsibility for administering a number of programs.

Whichever approach the President chose, the higher education policy council should be given a triple mandate:

1. It would advise the President on the shape and direction of federal higher education policy, supplanting the White House "working groups" and other ad hoc task forces that have fulfilled that function in recent years.[80]

2. It would coordinate the administration of complex government activities bearing on higher education that cut across agency lines and would try to solve problems that do not require presidential attention.

3. It would serve as a high-level forum where academic leaders could gain a hearing; it would informally adjudicate their grievances and examine their requests. In this capacity the council would bear some resemblance to a "regulatory commission" for higher education, weighing evidence, seeking to ensure fairness and due process, and—if Congress granted it the authority—curbing the harmful effects of duplicative regulation by multiple agencies.[81]

It follows that an effective interagency council on higher education policy would consist of senior officials who either run their departments or enjoy the confidence of those who do. Its participants should include

79. Most recent presidents have begun their administrations with the assertion that cabinet members and agency heads would play dominant roles and that the White House staff would be reined in. President Carter did likewise. While it is too early for a full assessment of his performance in this area, there is some evidence that he has relied more heavily on some cabinet members than on the White House domestic policy staff. Predictably, there is also evidence that he is not entirely pleased with the results and is therefore moving to enlarge and strengthen his staff.

80. See Finn, *Education and the Presidency*.

81. Such as interagency council, coupled with a consolidated higher education unit within HEW or in a new education department, could thus ease some of the regulatory burdens described in chapter 6.

agency heads or senior deputies from all the principal departments and units that are involved with higher education.[82]

Along with a serious commitment to its work by senior executive branch officials, an interagency council would require a talented secretariat. Its staff should evolve into the principal repository of executive branch knowledge and expertise on higher education policy issues and should therefore be constructed as a permanent professional unit in the tradition of the Bureau of Economic Analysis and the Bureau of Labor Statistics. As noted above, it could either be lodged within the principal education agency or be made independent. Although the second course would lead to some duplication of effort, it would remove the policy staff from direct responsibility to officials apt to have a strong interest in the council's decisions and recommendations.

Would the council make a difference? The record of interagency committees in Washington, particularly in domestic affairs, hardly fosters optimism. As a general rule, they have an influence only when the President wants them to, and are useful only if he finds them to be. They also have some built-in limitations, notably their lack of power to compel agency heads to subordinate their own policy convictions to other considerations. An interagency committee can bring conflicts to the surface far more easily than it can resolve them. It may be, for example, that four-year sectarian colleges would benefit from a greater infusion of federal funds for social science curriculum development, or from looser controls on veterans' education benefits, but that does not mean that an interagency council on higher education policy would succeed in persuading the Science Foundation or the Veterans Administration to change its ways.

The council could, however, identify such issues and present them to the President, along with its appraisal of the effects of present policies

82. In addition to HEW's education subdepartment (or new department of education), obvious units would be the National Science Foundation, the departments of the Treasury, Labor, Energy, Defense, and Agriculture, the National Endowment for the Humanities, the Veterans Administration, and some independent research agencies like NASA. The Office of Management and Budget and constituent parts of HEW located outside the Education Division—notably the National Institutes of Health and the Social Security Administration—should have seats at the table as well. Pertinent regulatory units, such as the Office for Civil Rights, the Equal Employment Opportunity Commission, and the Civil Rights Commission, might also take part. Although they are not executive branch agencies, the Library of Congress, the General Accounting Office, and the Congressional Budget Office could also be invited to send representatives.

on colleges and universities and the pros and cons of possible policy changes. It might also be able to limit the redundancy of various reporting requirements and encourage the coordination of certain administrative practices. Though it would be wrong to expect dramatic gains in the coherence, rationality, or benevolence of federal higher education policy, nothing would be lost by the experiment.[83]

Changes on Capitol Hill

Strengthening the ability of the executive branch to handle crosscutting issues of higher education policy may be valuable in itself, but some of that value will be lost if Congress persists in dealing with the subject piecemeal. As with the executive branch, however, the more obvious organizational reforms on Capitol Hill would lead to irksome consequences. The creation of standing Senate and House committees on education, for example, is much like forming a department of education: the longer its reach, the more jurisdictions it invades and the more noneducational endeavors it confuses; but less ambitious conceptions add to the proliferation of congressional units without easing the problem of policy coordination. Many government activities of great importance to the academy would elude a committee on education. It is doubtful, for example, that it is either wise or feasible to extricate tax and social security issues that bear on higher education from the domain of the Ways and Means and Finance committees.

Both houses of Congress have recently scrutinized their own committee structures; the initial reform plans came to seemingly opposite conclusions about education. The "Bolling committee" urged the House to split its Education and Labor Committee in half, creating a separate standing committee on education.[84] The "Stevenson committee" proposed that the Senate enlarge Labor and Public Welfare into a broadgauged Committee on Human Resources.[85] But the House, encouraged

83. A trial period would be advisable. If the interagency council failed to demonstrate its value within five years, it should be terminated rather than be allowed to linger on.

84. *Committee Reform Amendments of 1974*, H. Rept. 93-916, 93:2 (GPO, 1974), p. 373.

85. For a summary of these proposals by the Temporary Select Committee to Study the Senate Committee System, see *Congressional Quarterly Weekly Report*, November 27, 1976, pp. 3237–40. For background, see *Senate Committee System*, Hearings before the Temporary Select Committee to Study the Senate Committee System, 94:2 (GPO, 1976), and *The Senate Committee System*, First Staff Report to the Temporary Select Committee, 94:2 (GPO, 1976).

by higher education spokesmen, chose to keep Education and Labor intact, while the Senate created a stripped-down version of the Human Resources Committee.[86] Thus, with respect to education, both chambers have ended up approximately where they were before, with program jurisdictions scattered and with the principal education units also responsible for many other concerns.

Congress has occasionally found it worthwhile to create a joint committee of the House and Senate able to address itself to policy issues and priority dilemmas that cross jurisdictional lines. Practically never does a joint committee have the power to report legislation.[87] Usually it is either a panel, like the Joint Economic Committee, which conducts hearings and commissions studies, or, like the Joint Committee on Internal Revenue Taxation, little more than a holding company for staff experts who serve both houses.[88]

Education would certainly benefit from creation of a joint committee able to hold hearings, solicit expert advice, review the programs of various agencies, and examine the applicable policies developed by standing committees with primary legislative responsibility. Such a committee, which would presumably include members of the House and Senate interested in and knowledgeable about higher education, would also provide a Capitol Hill forum where educators could gain a hearing.

Congress, however, has been reluctant to burden itself with many committees of this sort. Apart from the inherent difficulty of bringing senators and representatives together in the same setting, most members have trouble enough keeping up with the work of their substantive panels and little energy to spare for bodies that may think deeply but that report no legislation. Thus it is necessary to consider alternatives, such as developing further the notion of "special oversight authority" like that given the House Education and Labor Committee in 1974 when it was empowered to review the education-related work of other committees. If similar powers were granted the Senate Human Resources

86. As finally reported by the Rules Committee and adopted by the Senate, for example, the proposal retained a separate Veterans' Affairs Committee, which the Stevenson proposal would have merged into Human Resources. For a summary of the committee provisions as adopted, see *Congressional Quarterly Weekly Report*, January 29, 1977, pp. 161–64.

87. One that did, the Joint Committee on Atomic Energy, lost that ability at the beginning of the Ninety-fifth Congress, retaining just study and advisory functions.

88. A third type of joint committee supervises congressional housekeeping matters.

Committee, and if the pertinent subcommittees of both the House and Senate units were adroit in exercising them and adequately staffed to do so, comprehensive issues of higher education policy could come under scrutiny. No new units would need to be created.

At the very least, all the committees concerned with education should have access to a staff unit of sufficient size and caliber to comprehend the totality of higher education policy.[89] The Library of Congress, the Congressional Budget Office, the Office of Technology Assessment, and the General Accounting Office all have the potential for providing such analyses to the legislators. Indeed, all of them have recently strengthened their capabilities and their performance in the field of higher education policy, and it is likely that this trend will continue.

The work of the Congressional Budget Office is particularly promising. Although higher education is one policy domain that is poorly served by the "functional categories" in which Congress has chosen to examine the federal budget for purposes of large expenditure trade-offs, the CBO staff has begun to transcend those limitations and produce secondary analyses that divide the federal enterprise along other lines. Such efforts can help the lawmaker interested in, say, the combined effect of student aid and scientific research on colleges and universities.[90]

A National Academy of Education?

If education were elevated within HEW, a new interagency council formed, and steps taken to strengthen Congress' grasp of the subject, a key piece would still be missing. Education also needs a quasi-governmental organization in Washington to supply objective appraisals of its condition, to gauge the impact of myriad federal policies, to unravel the analytic mysteries that plague government officials trying to grapple with the subject, and to relieve education spokesmen of the need to feign disinterestedness.

Each executive branch agency, congressional committee, and college association will presumably want its own machinery for policy analysis.

89. This statement takes for granted that Congress will continue its general tendency to duplicate many of the analytical functions of the executive branch.

90. A fine prototype of such analysis is the Congressional Budget Office background paper on *Social Security Benefits for Students* (CBO, 1977), in which a program within the jurisdiction of the Ways and Means and Finance committees is examined as if it were a higher education program. Similar pioneering work has been done in the area of college tuition tax credits.

But it would also be desirable to have an impartial arbiter with the capacity to undertake studies and analyses that would not be readily dismissed because of the presumed biases of their authors.

The National Academy of Sciences and its affiliated National Research Council offer a serviceable analogue in the field of science.[91] Since the Civil War this body of distinguished scientists has functioned as a high-level broker between diverse federal agencies and the nation's scientific community. It surveys federal policies and programs, conducts useful studies of knotty issues, and serves internationally as the semiofficial voice of American science. Although its congressional charter commands the academy to undertake such studies when requested, and although the sponsoring agencies pay for them, it is not an agency itself, beholden to administration policies and constraints. Neither is it a "lobby" with a detailed policy agenda of its own. It is a mediator, a monitoring body, an interpreter, and a source of expertise, performing useful services in two directions and fairly well regarded by both its audiences.

In 1970 a White House task force led by James Hester, then president of New York University, urged the creation of a similar organization for higher education. The proposed national academy of higher education would be composed of "educators and citizens of the highest standing who can be expected to reflect not simply the needs of special segments of higher education, but the needs of the entire nation and all the institutions that serve those needs. The Academy should study all matters regarding higher education of major concern to the American people and to our colleges and universities."[92]

The Hester group's proposal still makes sense, although it may not be necessary to charter a new organization in order to achieve the same purposes. There is already in existence a small National Academy of Education, with interests spanning all levels of education. It was founded in 1965 and now consists of one hundred distinguished scholars with a tiny staff based at Stanford University.[93] It has shown an increased willingness to undertake "policy studies" on behalf of federal

91. The National Academy of Public Administration provides another example of the species.

92. *Priorities in Higher Education,* Report of the President's Task Force on Higher Education (GPO, 1970), pp. 17–18.

93. At this writing, the NAE, under the leadership of Stephen K. Bailey, former vice president of the American Council on Education, is relocating its principal offices in Washington, D.C.

agencies, sometimes in conjunction with the National Academy of Sciences, and could be asked to do more.[94] Because it receives no sustaining funds from the federal government, the academy can function in this capacity only when it is given a grant or contract to do so. Presumably the same would be true of any new entity designed along similar lines, but a long-term contract—such as one to prepare an annual report on the condition of higher education for the interagency council—could serve to stabilize the organization and regularize its work.

Some will scoff, certain that the last thing the nation needs is another outfit studying higher education. Privately funded organizations, such as the Carnegie Council on Policy Studies in Higher Education, already do creditable work of this sort. The National Center for Education Statistics gathers data. The National Institute of Education has a mandate to inquire into all aspects of the educational enterprise. Other federal agencies pay private organizations for policy analyses in their areas of concern. An active national academy of education would probably reduce the need for some of these efforts or bring them within its own orbit. Needless proliferation is not the intent, but neither is the task likely to get done with rigor and credibility so long as executive branch agencies, private interest groups, and congressional units are left to appraise their own needs and accomplishments and to vie with one another for title to the "definitive" study. Indeed, one explanation for the current efflorescence of studies is the fact that no present group has the prestige, the talent, the presumption of objectivity, and the permanence to discourage others from covering the same ground.

Conclusion

In sum, organizational reforms are desirable if the federal government is to strengthen its ability to shape higher education policy. The structural framework is already in place and ready to be built on. It is therefore unnecessary to think of "starting from scratch," such as by creating a "mini" department of education at the cabinet level. That idea has plenty of symbolic and political appeal, but from the standpoint of higher education policy it will be wasted effort unless its internal design is attentive to the distinctive requirements of that subject and unless it is also accompanied by extradepartmental changes, such as an effective

94. See, for example, the report *Fundamental Research and the Process of Education* (National Academy of Sciences, 1977).

government-wide council on higher education policy. Even then, it will accomplish nothing that could not also be done within the structural context of HEW. Short of rebuilding most of the federal government around the concept of higher education, however, no organizational reform will solve the underlying problem: many federal activities of profound importance to higher education are directed, in the first instance, to other government objectives and cannot be run from the perspective of higher education without disrupting those other missions. Hence the most that should be expected is a series of improvements in the general ability of government policymakers to recognize the effect of their actions on higher education and occasionally to make that effect more salutary than it would otherwise have been.

Chapter Eight

Looking Ahead

FEDERAL POLICY toward higher education is remarkably like the university itself, characterized by Cohen and March as an "organized anarchy"; "it does not know what it is doing. Its goals are either vague or in dispute. Its technology is familiar but not understood. Its major participants wander in and out."[1]

This does not mean that federal policy is incomprehensible, unstable, or mindless, merely that it is complex. Insofar as it has unifying ideas, they center not on the inner visions that animate the academic enterprise but on the *uses* society makes of higher education. Still, those ideas have proved to be a serviceable and flexible basis for federal policy in a sensitive domain where government can do harm as well as good if it tries to do too much. Federal leverage is a mixed blessing, particularly for institutions that prize their independence; and the more purposeful and orderly it becomes, the more risks it presents.

From the standpoint of university presidents and others primarily interested in campus welfare, the problem with a utilitarian approach to federal higher education policy is its lack of attention to institutional well-being. Many of them would like Washington to assume more responsibility for ensuring the economic vitality and sovereignty of colleges and universities, and would like such considerations to play a central role in the formulation of pertinent laws, regulations, and appropriations. In addition, they would like the federal government to begin providing unrestricted funds to support the institutions in their ordinary activities.

It is natural for college and university leaders to want their concerns to rank higher among national policy objectives. But insofar as that means stipulating that the welfare of higher education institutions is a direct federal responsibility, they are likely to remain frustrated for a

1. Michael D. Cohen and James G. March, *Leadership and Ambiguity* (McGraw-Hill, 1974), p. 3.

number of reasons: governmental inertia, some political resistance, factional disputes within the higher education community, vigorous competition for available resources from such formidable rivals as the proponents of national health insurance, a widening sense that Washington's foremost interest in higher education lies with students rather than with institutions, and a conviction that the states should continue to bear the main responsibility for colleges and universities.

In any case, the health of those institutions that happen to exist in 1978 should not be equated with the well-being of higher education as a whole. The preservationist approach is tempting; it is usually easier in public policy deliberations to argue for freezing the status quo than to define, and win converts to, any formula for changing it. Yet there is no reason to assume that the three thousand colleges and universities in existence today are the ones the nation will need ten or twenty years hence, and there is ample reason to resist policy formulations meant to keep them as they are. At the same time, there is reason for caution in urging federal officials to design the kind of higher education system that the society will need in the years ahead, to pick and choose among existing institutions, to succor some and ignore others.

Nevertheless, as I have suggested throughout this book, the federal government *does* have a responsibility to consider the effects of its actions on the overall welfare of higher education. This does not mean it has an obligation to guarantee the health of individual colleges or of the postsecondary enterprise as a whole. I assume that federal policies affecting higher education will continue to be driven primarily by national missions to which colleges and universities are ancillary. But in carrying out these missions, Washington should be alert to a host of second-order consequences and should seek to ensure that they are beneficent, or at least neutral, in their effect on higher education.

In its student aid programs, Washington should devote the energies and resources necessary to recast a confusing set of disparate programs into a unified assistance structure in which a prospective college student can readily learn what aid he is entitled to, and in which his choice of college is not unduly influenced by peculiarities in the federal programs. In fact, the most appropriate action the federal government could take to strengthen the higher education system is to remove some of the distortions from the student marketplace and allow colleges to compete for students on a fairer basis.

As for financial support to the institutions themselves, Washington should—as it will—refrain from unrestricted aid. As it continues to pump billions of dollars each year through various "categorical" programs, however, the federal government would be well advised to continue placing heavy emphasis on merit and on the ability of individual colleges and universities to carry out federal missions effectively. In particular, it should resist the efforts by some factions within the academic community to convert research monies into maintenance funds, even as it takes pains to ensure that a significant part of such monies is available to support basic, rather than applied, research. This recommendation is unabashedly aimed at the well-being of the fifty or one hundred major research universities. For in the field of higher education, if there is any one responsibility—apart from aid to needy students—that history has bequeathed to the federal government, it is to preserve the high quality of the research and graduate training associated with those campuses. Fortunately, that responsibility is entangled with the federal mission of supporting scientific research, and the two will succeed (or falter) together so long as the policies that link them are unbroken.

The issue of government regulation is at least as complicated as the issue of financing. In the main, the regulatory intrusions that university leaders find obnoxious are inevitable outgrowths of federal funding practices and of the increased responsibility for "social regulation" that has been entrusted to the government. Still, higher education has begun to display greater ability to win limited exemptions or variances in regulatory matters that closely affect its sovereignty. Although some restraint and restructuring on the federal side would ease the situation, here the principal challenge of the next decade is for the academic community to devise better ways of regulating itself, even as it strengthens its defense of academic freedom.

At present, the federal government lacks any reliable mechanism or structure for making "higher education policy" or for appraising the effects of diverse programs and actions on higher education as a whole. Some changes in the policymaking structure will be needed before any government official can even be expected to understand the composite effect of federal programs and actions on higher education, let alone to do anything about that effect. Unfortunately, the most obvious and politically appealing structural changes, notably the creation of a cabinet-level department of education, in and of themselves portend no improvement in Washington's capacity to make wise policies for higher education. To bring about real improvement would require a series of changes in both organization and organizing principles that extend across the executive branch, to Capitol Hill, and out into the world of research, data gathering, and policy analysis. Even then, the fact that colleges and universities remain the means toward a number of primary federal ends, rather than ends in themselves, suggests that other considerations will continue to dominate policy decisions that have significant impacts on higher education.

Moreover, those impacts will remain uneven. Whether the issue is the allocation of student aid monies, the distribution of research grants, the limitations of a particular categorical program, the role of tax-assisted philanthropy, or the fiscal and spiritual exactions of compliance with a social regulation, no two colleges reap quite the same harvest in the fields of federal policy. Part of the reason lies in the idiosyncratic nature of programs that were never meant to treat all schools alike. Part of it lies in the distinctive characteristics of individual colleges and students that lead to different outcomes even when a government provision would seem uniform and evenhanded.

The United States would not be better off if those peaks and valleys were somehow leveled and every program rendered homogeneous in its effect. One of the glories of the American higher education system is its rich variety; the corollary challenge to federal policy is to tailor programs that respond to and perhaps enhance that variety. Insofar as this challenge is successfully met today, much of the reason lies in the very multiplicity and ill-coordination of federal programs that bear on higher education. With greater "method to the madness," some of the flexibility, responsiveness, and diversity would be sacrificed.

Still, the record of recent years suggests that these programs and the policies underlying them will undergo more careful scrutiny by higher education's Washington-based representatives, increasingly sophisticated in their ability to predict consequences and more determined to advance their own interests. On the whole, this is a desirable development, the more so if Congress and the executive branch match it with an improved capability for anticipating the consequences of their own actions.

Such modest reforms will nevertheless exact a price. "It is an all too American belief," David Riesman observes, "that all reforms are compatible."[2] Sometimes the cost can be measured in dollars; a heightened

2. "Small Steps to a Larger Vision," in *The Third Century: Twenty-six Prominent Americans Speculate on the Educational Future* (Change Magazine Press, 1977), p. 28.

concern for higher education's well-being, or for the quality of any group of colleges, students, or programs, will leave less money for other federal objectives. Sometimes, however, the costs are subtler: programs whose design and execution are complicated by new considerations previously deemed irrelevant; other government missions made harder to conduct; slower and more cumbersome procedures; more projects stopped or altered because the postsecondary equivalent of an "environmental impact statement" reveals problems in the original conception. But a vigorous higher education system is important enough to the society that the federal government should pay some of these added costs and endure the attendant nuisance.

Such costs will naturally be least among the government activities most readily classified as "higher education programs." The majority of the conflicts found there are spawned by differing interests *within* the higher education community. Most important among these programs are the need-based student assistance schemes administered by the Office of Education. GI bills may come and go, regulatory enthusiasms wax and wane, and research priorities change with the times, but the commitment to reduce financial barriers encountered by a person seeking a college education seems likely to endure in the evolving American welfare state. This may be sound social policy; it is certainly a reasonable basis for much of federal higher education policy, a way for Washington to channel funds into the "demand side" of the marketplace on behalf of needy students and there to let institutions compete for such students and for the resources they bring with them.

The next decade will not be an easy time for American higher education. Competition among campuses, the frail health of some of them, the uncertain course of postsecondary policy in the fifty states, and the mounting effect—mostly for good but sometimes for ill—of government actions on colleges and universities will make it hard for the academy to remain strong, vital, and sovereign. From its perspective, as well as from Washington's, the expansionary challenges of the fifties and sixties were easier and more enjoyable to meet. The ten years ahead will be characterized by many situations of a kind that public officials find singularly vexing: the judicious parceling out of limited resources among anxious, jealous, and fiercely competitive elements of an enterprise that is growing in some places, static in others, and dwindling in still others.

Higher education should not be expected to resist the temptation to lay many of its concerns at the federal doorstep. But that does not mean all of them should be invited in. While to speak of a "higher education community," as I have done from time to time in the preceding pages, may imply more unity than is really there, government officials should act as if such a community existed and insist that it set clear priorities, discipline its own members, and pay as close attention to their efficiency, productivity, and social behavior as it does to the government actions that affect them.

Rather than wait for cost controls to "be forced on higher education willy-nilly by public officials," Alan Pifer suggests, "it will behoove higher educational institutions themselves to undertake some substantial experiments in major cost cutting right now, with a view to finding out how this may be done with the least damage to quality."[3] Hans Jenny gave similar advice, in stronger words: "If the academy is as astute in analyzing its own future as it professes to be when it addresses itself to its customary disciplines, the realization may dawn upon it that in a world of diminishing resources it could by example teach others how not to grow, how not to render its services at inflationary costs, and how to become less gigantic as gracefully as possible."[4]

The federal government today supplies about $14 billion annually in direct and indirect assistance to higher education. Although not all this money is well spent, the federal taxpayer and the public as a whole are surprisingly well served by the social return on this investment. Still, with little or no growth in the number of people directly served, and with a consequent decrease in the proportion of the population actively partaking of higher education, there is good reason for the academy to heed the advice of friendly counselors like Pifer and Jenny. This does not contradict the earlier suggestion that higher education is important enough to warrant some leniency in the application of cost-benefit standards for federal programs and policies. Rather, if lawmakers and their constituents see colleges and universities as efficient, socially aware, and orderly enterprises, they will be more apt to tolerate the requisite flexibility in federal policies.

Self-control, flexibility, patience, and circumspection—these do not seem to be a very exciting set of prescriptions by which to guide the future relation between higher education and the federal government. The main reason is that the patient is not very ill. The academy is basically

3. "A Clash of Tangled Forces," in ibid., p. 63.
4. Hans H. Jenny, *Higher Education and the Economy*, ERIC/Higher Education Research Report no. 2 (American Association for Higher Education, 1976), p. 49.

healthy. The current array of federal policies and programs, while messy, is surprisingly responsive to the varied needs of the enterprise. Some difficulties lie ahead, to be sure, and the federal government will probably have a greater influence on higher education than it has had in the past. But it would be a mistake to prescribe too much. Neither the government nor the higher education industry is accustomed to doing what its diagnosticians think best, particularly when the recommendations are too elaborate. What is remarkable is how well that combination of stubbornness and inner direction has worked for both. Well enough, in the event, that there is little reason to fear for the future.

Index

Ability-to-pay criterion, 57, 65, 97, 101, 163; uniform methodology for, 161
Academic freedom, 13–14, 150–51, 154, 161, 167, 174, 219, 221
Academic Freedom Act of *1977*, 174n
Accredidation, 25n, 156, 157–71; by education commissioner, 160; by private panels, 158–59; 163–64; as self-policing, 159, 162–64, 170
ACE. *See* American Council on Education
ACT. *See* American College Testing Program
Administrative cost of campus, 5, 45, 77, 99n, 116–17, 121–22, 129, 134, 146n, 147, 173, 211n
Admissions: by recruitment, 35, 43; regulation of, 143, 144, 152–53; selectivity in, 33–35, 152; without defining possible aid, 83n
AEC. *See* Atomic Energy Commission
Affirmative action, 143, 148, 156n
Agricultural Extension Service, 5, 106
Agriculture, Department of, 212n; institutional grants and, 109, 183; school lunch programs, 203. *See also* specific bureaus
Aid to education. *See* Institutional grants; Outlays, federal; Student aid
Alfred P. Sloan Foundation, 173n
Allen, Hollis P., 194–95, 197
American Association of Community and Junior Colleges, 165–66, 169
American Association of Land-Grant Colleges and State Universities, 86n
American Association of State Colleges and Universities, 86n–87n, 105, 133
American College Testing Program (ACT), 161, 162, 163
American Council on Education (ACE), 21–22, 25n, 27n, 28, 30n, 38, 64, 72n, 88n–89n, 121, 123, 134n, 177n, 188, 191; Committee on Institutional Research

Policy, 192n; education department and, 193, 198, 208, 209n; Special Committee on Campus Tensions, 25n; tuition proposals of *1973* and, 131–32
Amherst College, 151n
Andersen, Charles J., 38, 166n
Andringa, Robert C., 186n
Applications, enrollment, 24–25; campus selectivity and, 33–35; influenced by available aid, 14, 57, 63, 64, 67n, 70, 72–73, 74–75, 90, 101; quality of, 34; tuitions and, 43n, 51, 57–58, 59, 63, 70, 72–73, 74–75, 87. *See also* Enrollments
Appropriations. *See* Outlays, federal; Outlays, state
Ashworth, Kenneth H., 192
Association of American Colleges, 24, 131n, 133
Association of American Universities, 24, 188
Astin, Alexander W., 25n, 28n, 34, 58n
Atelsek, Frank J., 70n, 76n, 77n, 80n
Atomic Energy Commission (AEC), 60, 117

Babbidge, Homer D., Jr., 7, 61n, 122, 123n, 161, 169, 192–93, 195n
Baby boom of *1940s*, 22, 28–29
Bailey, Stephen F., 216n
Bankruptcy of campuses, 37, 39, 41–42. *See also* Fiscal health of campuses
Basic Educational Opportunity Grants (BEOG), 65–66, 67–70, 75, 81, 84, 162; advantage of, 69; fully funded, 103n; half-cost limit of, 87, 96; incentives of, 70; trade-off between campus-based aid and, 82, 87–88; two-tiered scheme for, 96–98, 101–02
Bauman, Robert E., 166–67
Bayer, Alan E., 25n
Bell, Terrell H., 162
Bender, Louis W., 148n, 172